THE OLIVE PICKER

THE
Olive Picker

PURSUING HUMAN POTENTIAL

Peter M. Kalellis

Paulist Press
New York / Mahwah, NJ

Cover image: "The Olive Picker." Photo by Panos Marinatos—a gift from the island of Lesvos, Greece. Used with permission.
Cover and book design by Lynn Else

Library of Congress Control Number: 202193705

ISBN 978-0-8091-5585-9 (paperback)
ISBN 978-1-58768-987-1 (e-book)

Published by Paulist Press, Inc.
997 Macarthur Boulevard
Mahwah, New Jersey 07430
www.paulistpress.com

Printed and bound in the
United States of America

*I am profoundly grateful especially to my precious wife, Pat,
who patiently endured my silent moments when
I needed time to reflect and record.*

*Heartfelt thanks to anyone who reads about this adventure
and can visualize herself or himself as co-travelers—friends
and relatives, my two sons, my two daughters, my five
grandchildren, and my two great-grandchildren.*

Disclaimer

The Olive Picker is an autobiography—a recounting of my life's events, episodes, and experiences. Writing it has been similar to a true and much-needed confession, possibly to a priest, a father confessor, or to some spiritual and trusted person.

Fully aware that memory tends to be selective, I chose a number of events and episodes that offered me instruction and gave shape and form to my life. The process proved to be an encyclopedia of psychological, spiritual, and supportive messages, offering readers a unique opportunity to understand *who I am* and, in turn, to allow them to ponder *who they really are* and to pursue their own *true human potential*.

With due respect and sensitivity, I have used the real names of close relatives, intimate friends, and other important persons who had a real impact in my life. It is my hope that I have maintained everyone's reputation and not hurt anyone's feelings. If so, it was certainly not my intention in writing this personal story.

Contents

CONTENTS

Contents

CONTENTS

Prologue

My story spans more than ninety years. It was made possible by the encouragement of my loving daughters Katina, and Mersene, and my dear friend, Andy McCabe, who traveled with me all the way to Lesvos, a Greek island, to see the place where this journey began. And Paul McMahon who took my original manuscript, gave it skillful and professional form and shape and made it attractive for publication.

All encounters and experiences are true events. For purposes of narrative, the time and clarity, on a few occasions, have been moderately changed. For example, an event that unfolded in April of one year may be presented in August of another year. Likewise, a disturbing episode with some church personality has been smoothed with sensitivity and respect.

While this book is about one man's journey, it is written in hope that people who read it will find something of special benefit in their own life's journey. The hope is that each reader rediscovers his or her true self and pursues reconciliation with people who some time ago might have hurt their feelings. Every human being who has walked and is still walking on this planet will realize that good and bad things, joyful and sad events, triumphs and defeats are inevitable parts of our earthly journey, all in all resulting in a bittersweet melody called life. Friend, be kind to yourself and enjoy your life's journey. I wish to thank you for reading my personal journey and I also thank all the readers of my previous psycho-spiritual books, and I do welcome with appreciation and gratitude all my new readers.

Acknowledgments

Writing this book has been a rewarding experience, not only because it has helped me to reflect on the invaluable gifts of life, but also because the process of writing involves a community of people who have supported me on this adventurous journey.

I am most grateful for the ongoing support of Fr. Mark-David Janus, the president of Paulist Press and his editorial members of production and marketing teams: in particular, Donna Crilly, Melene Kubat, Trace Murphy in the editorial department; Diane Flynn and Kimberly Bernard in production; Lynn Else in design; and Bob Byrns and Gloria Capik in marketing. I am also thankful to my editor, Paul McMahon, who always provides valuable input into the editing process. All these people help to make the book a reality and get it into the hands of the reader.

Finally, I am most grateful for the gift of faith in a God who gives me hope and is constantly strengthening my soul throughout my life to continue my spiritual writing that helps readers to experience God's presence in their life.

Part I
PLANTING

1

PICKING UP OLIVES

On a cold February day in 1939, at 13 years of age, I suddenly became aware of the freedom that comes with adulthood and earning one's living. The exact time of day was 11 a.m. when I climbed to the top of a huge olive tree in my father's olive grove, where I hung uncomfortably on a shaky branch, filling my bamboo basket with plump, quality olives. It was a Thursday, and this was the eighth basket I had filled to the top. By Saturday, if the weather held, I was hoping to fill at least seven more baskets with choice olives that I would then cure, jar, and sell. With the money earned, I would buy the shiny red bicycle displayed in a shop window in Mytilene, the capital city of the Greek island of Lesvos. I had been eyeing that bike for a whole year. My plans and wish to own the red British bike, however, were unexpectedly stifled. My father gave money to a trusted friend and asked him to buy me a good bike. A week before Christmas, his friend showed up, one evening, carrying a brand new blue German bicycle. My instant reaction was hostile. I hated that blue bike. It was not the red bike that I had set my heart on, and I could not even thank my father nor his friend.

These two defining moments—picking olives and not getting the red bike—took place eighty years ago. I should not think about them now, but what I have noticed about the past is that it always claws its way to the surface, and becomes the present.

Early Monday morning, September 14, 1996, my cousin Dimitri called from Athens, Greece. Through the phone, anxiety resonated in his voice as he asked me to visit as soon as possible. Pressing the receiver of the phone against my ear, I had the feeling it wasn't just Dimitri calling, but everything and everyone I had known growing up in Greece as well. A kaleidoscope of faces swirled before my eyes—my sister Kiki, my brother Jimmy, and other relatives, Eleni, the attractive girl I had promised to marry but didn't, and a number of other childhood friends.

"It's important that you come to Greece as soon as you can because it may be the last time that you and I can see each other." Dimitri's serious tone both shook and scared me.

"Dimitri, I need to think about this. It's a long and difficult trip," I said, as an avalanche of frightening thoughts invaded my mind—was he hiding something? Perhaps, a terminal illness? Or some other dramatic family episode? It is a familiar tradition throughout many centuries that the Greek mind thrives on drama.

In a state of euphoria, I got in my car to go to work, but instead of turning left onto Euclid Avenue, the daily usual route to my office, I found myself absentmindedly heading toward the Garden State Parkway. Within 45 minutes I began smelling the salty air of the ocean. More and more thoughts, triggered by the unexpected invitation, tumbled through my mind, invading my consciousness.

I parked the car and, lost in thoughts of my childhood home, took off my shoes and walked on the wet sand, leaving deep footprints behind me. The late afternoon sun sparkled on the foamy waves of the New Jersey shore where small boats sailed, propelled by the cool breeze. On the distant horizon a huge ship cut, undaunted, through the ocean. Again, Dimitri's voice echoed in my head: *Come to Greece as soon as you can because it may be the last time that you and I can see each other.*

I took a few deep breaths, and as the cool salty breeze entered my lungs, it calmed my spirit. All I needed was a comfortable recliner to doze off. I visualized my good-natured, chubby younger cousin, Dimitri, who had probably already started cooking gourmet meals for my arrival in Athens. I smiled. Of course, I have missed him and his generous hospitality. Sitting cross-legged on the sand, again I noticed that huge ship moving slowly across the horizon. To my eyes, it looked like the Edison, the ocean liner that had taken my father and me to Greece way back in September 1929.

The sunset, still far from approaching, gave a reddish-orange glow to the clouds on the west horizon. Eventually, the ocean liner disappeared. But my thoughts about the life I'd left behind in June 1946 lingered. How fast my past surfaced in my mind. And how this past had carved my current life like a sculptor, giving it shape and form. It became my present once again.

2

LESVOS

My mother died unexpectedly at the age of twenty-six on February 7, 1929. And no one told me. On June 3 that same year, I was three years old. My mother was not at our home to celebrate my birthday. "Your Mommy is a little sick, and she needs to be in the hospital for a while." That's what I was told repeatedly by my father and my godmother, in whose house in West Philadelphia we stayed for several months.

On September 8 that same year, I accompanied my father to Greece on the Edison, a spectacular ocean liner that crossed the Atlantic over fifteen cold and turbulent days. My father's intention, unbeknownst to me, was to find another Greek wife, who could also be a mother to me. I was too young to articulate my thoughts, challenge my father, and say, "Dad, there must be millions of women in America. Can't you find one to marry? Why do we have to travel all the way to Greece?"

Without explanation, my father had uprooted me from my familiar surroundings in Philadelphia, Pennsylvania, where I was born and where—as far as I knew—my mother was still living. He transplanted me to his native town of Moria on the Greek island, Lesvos, which he referred to as the "Diamond of the Aegean." For me, Moria represented a compulsory exile, where I had to adjust to relatives, loving and caring people, all of whom were unknown to me. They spoke a language that was unknown to my three-year-old ears. How we got from Athens, the harbor of Piraeus, where the Edison landed, to Moria, I have no recollection.

Under an enormous almond tree near a small whitewashed house, three older women dressed in black sat on a multicolored sofa facing my father, who had stretched out on a straw recliner across from them. Minutes later, I found out that one of the women was my mother's mother—my grandmother—and her two sisters, who lived on the same block. They listened eagerly to what my father had to say. I sat on a short leather stool at my father's feet and leaned my head against his knees as he dramatically described the turbulence in crossing the Atlantic Ocean, and how well the ship's personnel took care of us. Though I couldn't understand a word they said, I could see the sadness in the women's eyes. My father touched my shoulder and appeared to be praising me, saying, "Takis is a good boy."

Two young girls from the neighborhood came in that little house and sat on a brown-carpeted floor near me. Curiously, they kept reaching out to touch me. Their hands were soft and warm. I didn't mind them touching me, but seeing no smile on my face, they pulled back.

After handshakes, hugs, and kisses, I saw my father corner the tallest of the three women and say, "Kleonike, I want to have a few words with you." Her wrinkled cheeks were framed in a black mantle, a sign of mourning. She turned and looked at me, and I felt magnetized by her powerful gaze. Dark bluish eyes, bosomy, and elegant, she stood defiantly in front of my father and eyed him with evident pain. I could hardly imagine the questions she would have had about how Mersene, her daughter and my mother had died, nor the pain her motherly heart experienced, knowing that she would have to live out the rest of her life, not seeing her daughter.

What had my father whispered to her? I discovered much later that he'd said, "Kleonike, I want a mother for your grandson and my son," lest taunting tongues criticize him for wanting to remarry a mere six months after my mother's death.

The tall woman reached out unassumingly and gently took me in her arms. Instantly, I felt her warmth. I wanted her to hold me for a long time. "I'm your *Yiayia*," she said affectionately and quickly allowed a tear to roll down her cheek, before she had to wipe it with her mantle.

My father rushed to explain, "*Yiayia* in Greek means grandmother."

I looked at him sadly and said, "I want my Mommy. When is she coming and why did she stay back?"

"Taki (my name was Takis then, but I was mostly called Taki), I've told you before, and I'm telling you again. Your mother is in a hospital in America. She is at the Jefferson Hospital; that's where you were born. When she gets well, she will come to us." His voice was firm, hoping to comfort me with words he knew to be a lie.

3

GALATIA

It was hard to believe that my mother was still in America and that someday she would come to join us. But there were a few moments before going to bed when somehow it seemed possible. *Maybe my mother is still at the hospital, and when she gets well she will come to me*, I thought and began to remember my life with her, holding me, smiling, feeding me, telling me stories, tickling me, and amusing me with songs. She responded to my every need. How could she have disappeared? Was she ever coming back to be with me?

Every day when I woke up, I asked the same question, "Dad, is Mommy coming back to us today?"

"Not today," my father would say, shaking his head, "but she will come back. Just stop worrying."

When I saw mothers holding and caring for their children or playing with them, my heart would beat faster. The grief of my mother's absence, which I tried to repress as children often do by focusing on playthings, then resurged in its pure essence. I remember running to my room and crying, "Mommy, where are you? Are you ever going to come to me? In this place I have nobody to love me." Even today I still wonder what happens to children who lose a parent, especially their mother. Can anything ever fill the gap left in a child's heart by a mother's death?

Gradually, I stopped asking whether Mommy was coming today, but inside, I kept hurting badly. Early one morning, I could not control the tears that turned into sobbing. Yiayia must have sensed that something was wrong. She dashed upstairs to my room and pulled me into her arms. She wiped my tears with her mantle, kissed me on the cheek and said, "*Poulaki* (an endearment Greek mothers use that means 'little bird'), why are you crying? Let's go downstairs. A big surprise is waiting for you."

"A surprise?" I screamed joyfully. *It must be Mommy! She's come from America*, I thought. I stopped sobbing, instantly excited in anticipation of seeing my mother again. Yiayia could not walk down the steps fast enough. But when I reached the first floor, my excitement evaporated as quickly as it had begun. All I saw was a young girl sitting on a straw chair holding a rolled-up sweater in her arms. Gingerly, the girl stood up. "My name is Galatia," she said, unrolling the sweater. She pulled out two tiny kittens. "I want you to have these," she said, placing them gently in my arms. At the sight of those pearly blue eyes and pink noses, I smiled. My sobbing sighs ceased.

"Pushy cats," I murmured delightedly. "Pushy cats," I said again, holding them close to my heart. In that moment, something magical happened. The kittens were so soft and had beautiful white fur with symmetrical brown spots on their faces and bodies. They exuded such love as they snuggled in my arms, purring. For at least a few brief moments, I no longer wanted or needed anything or anybody else. I had my kittens; they had become my whole world, and I theirs. That precious moment marked the beginning of my lifelong love of cats, which continues to be an irreplaceable source of joy.

My eyes fell upon the unexpected guest, who was responsible for this joyful present. Galatia, a girl of about nine years old, was wearing a light brown dress woven of sheep's wool and brown leather sandals. Dark chestnut-colored hair shaped her face as it fell around her shoulders. When she smiled, her cheeks took on the rosy hue of two small, perfect pomegranates. Instinctively, I knew this was a girl that I could love.

With an affectionate smile, she said, "Taki, I am your cousin, and I'm happy that you are here. You and I can have fun together. I can take you to nice places if you like. The sea is near our village; only ten minutes away. We can go there anytime, and if you like swimming, I can help you."

"Thanks Galatia," I said, and placing the kittens momentarily on the leather stool, I threw my arms tightly around her waist and said, "I love you." She kissed the top of my head, then dropped down on her knees and gave me the most loving hug and a warm kiss on each cheek. Aging, yet ageless, in her mid-nineties, Galatia continues to be my most loving cousin and best friend.

4

THE TRUTH

What if my mother was still in America? In moments of isolation or loneliness that question kept knocking at the door of my heart. One night, I had a dream of my mother holding me tight in her arms, combing my hair, and dressing me. She tried to teach me a Greek song: *How fast the years of youth go by, and they never come back.* I had no idea what that song meant, but for her it might have had a meaning. I remember when she used to lull me each night with a different song until I fell asleep. Her voice and words still echo in my ears:

> *Come, dear sleep, take my precious son to your*
> *beautiful garden and fill his arms with fragrant*
> *flowers, his heart with lasting joy, and bring him*
> *back home to me as a big and happy boy.*

Now it was Yiayia who poured her affections gracefully on me at bedtime. I would nestle my head between her mountainous breasts and visualize my mother, still hoping that she might return someday. No one had yet told me the truth about my mother. Although the idea of death was beyond my comprehension—an abstract idea too far removed from my three-year-old experience—if someone had tried to explain to me that she had died, I probably would have stopped asking when she was coming home. I may also have adjusted to the reality that I was one of those children that had no mother.

Every Sunday, my father took me to church. Each time, I was fascinated with the experience—the icons of saints, the burning candles, and the melody of the Byzantine chant sung by two adult male singers and the priest who looked like a prophet. When we returned to Yiayia's home, I would put a big scarf around my shoulders and pretend to be like that priest, and try to chant like him: *Kyrie eleison—soson Imas Ie Theou* ("Lord, have mercy—save us, O Son of God").

After church one particular Sunday, instead of taking the familiar path to Yiayia's house, my father took me through a different neighborhood with stone-paved narrow alleyways. A number of people glanced curiously our way, strangers wondering who we were and whispering words I could not understand. Finally, we arrived at a huge freshly painted, dark green door, where my father grabbed my hand. He knocked gently, combed his hair first with his fingers, then pulled a comb from his back pocket and ran it through his hair. Somehow lost and confused, I wondered where that door would take us.

After a few seconds, the door opened and a huge woman appeared, dressed in shades of pink, including a cherry-colored apron. "Good morning and welcome," she said hesitantly, blushing. "Please come in. I've been waiting for you."

She reached out to caress my face. Her fingers smelled of garlic and it made me sneeze—a couple times. "God bless you!" she shouted in a jarringly loud voice. "I have been waiting for you," she repeated.

My heart began to beat faster. Curiously, I looked up at this unknown woman. Her dark brown shiny hair was pulled back and tied in a bun with a blue, velvet ribbon. *Waiting for me? But she doesn't even know me!* I looked suspiciously at my father's face, then turned back to keep an eye on that strange woman.

My father leaned forward and kissed her. *He must have met her before*, I thought. Abruptly, I grabbed my father by the legs, shook him up and growled, "Let's go to my Yiayia's house!"

"Taki, this is your mother. She came from America three days ago. You have not seen her for a long time, and you have probably forgotten what she looked like."

"That's not my Mommy," I hissed through my teeth, holding back my tears.

Smiling nervously, the strange woman bent over me. "Of course I'm your mommy," she said, feigning a motherly concern and trying to take me in her arms.

"Don't you remember me? I'm well now and I'm back, and I'll be with you forever. Let me hold you in my arms, the way I used to. Let me tell you how much I've missed you." While the words seemed warm, I could feel they were not matched by that woman's tone, which was cold and rehearsed.

"You are not my Mommy, and I don't want you to touch me," I said emphatically. I caught a grimace of disappointment in her face. Clinging to my father, I stared at her. I knew she was not my mother. She didn't look, feel, or smell like my mother.

"I want my kittens. Let's go back to Yiayia's house now," I whimpered and wedged my face between my father's knees.

"Taki, we'll be just fine here." Then he said something I could never have predicted, "This will be our new home now."

"No, I won't be fine," I sobbed. Noticing the sadness in his face, I wanted to hug and shake him up and accuse him of lying and trying to trick me. What words could I have said to convey how painful it was not to have my real mother? Could he hear me or understand how I felt? I wanted my father to be like a good friend and listen, but he had distanced himself from me and stood by this woman, holding her hand. From his behavior I came to the conclusion that most fathers do not listen to their children, especially to their sons. Even when I became older, I found that my father still would not listen to what I had to say.

A week later, I was able to walk out of that big house and, with mild hesitation and not a soul around, I roamed the stone paved street to explore the neighborhood. An elderly woman approached me. Scared for a second, I pulled back, thinking she might be a witch. She was dressed in black, head covered with a wool woven shawl allowing her small wrinkled face to show.

"What a good-looking boy you are," she said, "but Katerina, the woman in that house is not your mother, she's your father's second wife, and she will be your stepmother." And with a pretend smile she added, "She's a good woman, but boy, she's tough!" Her face took on an ugly look that frightened me, so I ran back into the house, back to my room, and began to cry. Someone had finally told me the truth.

I laid in bed with tears still in my eyes and kept looking at the ceiling that seemed as far away as the sky. For a moment, I thought I was at Yiayia's home but soon became aware that I was no longer there. I felt lost in my stepmother's house; no longer loved or secure. I wanted to search for that lost child, but how could I find him? Since I lost my sense of direction on my way here, for sure, I would lose my way if I tried to return to Yiayia's home. In this strange environment, my heart kept pulsing faster and I felt cold and confused. Will I ever find my way back home to my Yiayia's place?

5

MY FAKE MOTHER

My father and I never returned to my grandmother's home. We took up residence in my stepmother Katerina's house, a huge emotional change for me after living with my grandmother for a few loving months. For some unknown and inexplicable reason, I was not allowed to visit my grandmother nor was she allowed to visit me. So Yiayia, like my mother, had disappeared from my life, along with the kittens and Galatia.

I literally felt split in two. In my grandmother's home, I had felt like a small bird in a warm nest where life was permeated with care and affection. In my stepmother's house, however, I felt like a useless piece of furniture to be moved around, here or there, according to my stepmother's disposition. I had to capitulate to my father's wishes, live in this new place with his new wife, and try not to think about what I had lost. Like a flower deprived of sunlight and water, I began to wither and felt physically too weak and sad to even go out and play with other kids.

With the role of mother artificially imposed on her, my stepmother probably resented my presence, which understandably interfered with her newlywed life. In her effort to make her husband happy, she made it her mission to convince him that she could be a real mother to me. At first, she behaved lovingly and made efforts to please me. But can anyone satisfy a young boy who has lost the primary love, his mother? And is it fair to ask someone to try? She provided meals, clothes, shelter—evidence of her caring for my physical needs.

"Taki, my son," she would often say, "you have forgotten me because I had to stay in the hospital for such a long time, but being there, I really missed you so much." These words were served up at bedtime several nights in a row, but the only response she got from me was silence, a deep sigh, and a sad face. In my frequent thoughts, after all the time I'd spent hoping that my real mother would return, I was also hoping that this new, fake mother would disappear for good from my life.

I felt so lonely and completely unable to express what I was feeling. I was in tremendous emotional pain and shocked by the lies that people told me, but no words came out. My tongue failed to adequately convey the incredible impact that this strange environment had upon me. Being trapped inside me, my feelings of grief and loss felt all the worse. Emotionally detached, my stepmother towered over my bed at nighttime, staring speechlessly at me. She heard only my sighs, not aware that my soul cried in the darkness, until I finally realized that I no longer had a mother, who would truly love me and whom I could love in return.

6

PAPAVASILE

Sometime between the ages of 5 and 6, my situation changed. My stepmother sent me seven long blocks away from her house to stay with her sister, Olga, who had two sons who were about my age. I didn't understand why she sent me there—it was a complete mystery—but I welcomed the idea of being away from my father's wife for a few weeks of fun with Olga's sons.

Olga and her boys liked me a lot and wanted me to stay with them forever. Unlike her sister, Olga was a happy woman who accepted me like a son. She enjoyed playing games with us and making us laugh with funny jokes and stories. Sometimes, she would make pancakes and hot chocolate late at night, and then she would roll a huge mattress out on the floor so all three of us boys could go to sleep. She tucked us in and kissed each one of us, then turned off the lights. Good night!

When I returned home, my stepmother was holding a tiny baby. The mystery was solved. The baby was a little girl named Kiki, "Taki, come and see. Now you have a sister." I took a quick look at that tiny creature, pretending to smile in order to hide my instant jealousy, and ran to my room to hide. With Kiki's arrival, the whole climate of our house changed. For days, relatives and friends—people I had never met before—

came to see the newborn, turning the experience into a celebration and making my stepmother the happiest woman.

Eighteen months later, I returned from another few weeks at Olga's house, and again my stepmother was holding another new baby, this time a good-looking baby boy named Jimmy. Now, my stepmother's attention was totally focused on her two children. To her guests she said, "This older boy is my husband's son. He's an orphan."

Around June that same year, my father and stepmother left Kiki and Jimmy with a neighbor and took me to their friend's wedding at St. Basil's Church. During the ceremony, the priest, a tall, bearded man, lit a white candle and with a smile handed it to me to hold. He indicated that I should stand next to the bridal pair. Nervously excited about my role in a wedding, I seemed to grow several inches taller in an instant, feeling manly and proud. But my moment of joyful exuberance was cruelly interrupted by a woman's guttural voice. "This boy is an orphan; he cannot hold a candle at a wedding," she said as she snatched the candle away from my hands, leaving me in shock.

The priest shook his head, placing a compassionate hand on my shoulder, and whispered, "Another silly superstition." I had no idea what the word *superstition* meant, but discovered later that the villagers believed that bad luck would follow a wedding *if the candle for the bridal pair was being held by an orphan.* The word, *orphan*, as used by the villagers, denoted a child who had lost one parent. It seemed as if being orphaned were a contagious and incurable disease. I backed away and hid in a corner of the church. Eyes brimming with tears, I kept looking at the icons of saints that decorated the church; my gaze gravitated to a specific icon: Mary, the mother of Jesus. She looked, I thought, so sad and beautiful, affectionately holding her son Jesus at her breast.

When the wedding ceremony was over, the priest approached me quietly. His bearded face had a serious look, intense but not lacking fatherly care. He asked me if I was okay. Papavasile was a loving and compassionate priest. He said, "I see sadness in your face, and I'm sorry for what that woman did to you today. The villagers thrive on superstitions." He pointed at the icon and said, "Mary, the mother of Jesus, is the only one who understands and comforts us. She is your mother and my mother, and the mother of all humanity. She protects us, visits the sick and those in pain, and cares for and loves the motherle...," but he didn't finish the words, *motherless children.* Obviously, he knew the truth about my mother's death.

Everybody needs a mother who looks like Mary in the icon, I thought. It was soothing and made me feel very special that I could be the Virgin Mary's son. It was at that hour that I adopted the church as my symbolic "mother," whom I later sought to serve first as an altar boy and eventually as a choir member singing in the Byzantine chant. The melodic church ritual, poetic language, artistic iconography, and the priest's chanting fascinated me. I was able to imitate the tone and variations of this priest's voice. Now, the mold for my future life was cast. *Someday*, I vowed to myself, *I will be a priest like Papavasile.*

7

SCHOOL DAYS

Three large windows illuminated the first-grade classroom and somehow made the pictures of heroes on the opposite wall look alive. I sat at a desk in the second row next to George Tsakiris, a chubby boy with wavy blond hair and blue eyes. My neighbors and peers had finally stopped calling me an orphan. They called me *Americanaki*, "the little American," a title that I cherished for many years.

Eulalia, the teacher, was a plump woman about thirty years old with permanent dark brown hair. She wore a perfume we could smell when she was still a mile from our school. When she finally arrived, she held a thin stick from an olive tree in her right hand. Periodically, she would pound that stick on her desk, making a thundering noise that demanded the attention of a sea of frightened students. She was a strict teacher, who never let the slightest mischief in her class go unpunished.

Ironically, Eulalia means "sweet spoken." By the second week of school, this supposedly sweet-spoken teacher demonstrated her disciplinary skills when she observed Tsakiris munching on fried potato peels while she read us a story. Six times she whacked each of his hands with her stick, leaving red welts on his oily palms. My poor friend bit his lip in defiant silence, and I shrank in my seat, heart pounding, afraid that I might be her next target. That scene terrified us all and stayed with me throughout my first grade. That first year of school was one of intimidation and fear of being a victim of her wrath. Most of us had no choice but to obey Eulalia's every command.

The following year, as second graders, we had Theodora ("God's gift"), who was a very different woman, as our teacher. She was a tall brunette with wavy hair and thin eyebrows over her dark brown eyes. It was true what my stepmother said of Theodora: "That lady has renounced married life and dedicated herself to teaching God's children." Each day, Theodora started our class with a prayer and a reading of a verse from the Bible. Besides being a general classroom teacher, she also taught theater. She loved her students and was particularly patient with those who had learning disabilities. I liked her very much, but I also had a hunch that she liked me. *If I were older, I would marry her*, I thought. In class, I was attentive to her every word and felt a strong attachment to her. I was beside myself with joy when she assigned me the major role in a school play. I fell incurably in love with her and dreamed repeatedly that she and I were the same age and were playmates.

The play was based on a historic event that took place in 1821, when, after four hundred years of oppression, the Greek nation was liberated from the yoke of the Ottoman Turks. The plot described how the Turks captured a Greek hero, Athanasios Diakos, and subjected him to horrible tortures. They tried to force him to deny his faith in Christ and to worship Allah. Diakos refused to accept the Muslim faith, and as the Turks applied more painful torments, he screamed at them, "You blind fools. Can't you see that Christ is standing by my side? He is the One who gives me courage and strength that sustain me." As a result, the Turks burned him alive slowly, on a skewer.

The part of Athanasios Diakos was assigned to me, and Theodora coached me. I felt like the luckiest guy in her class.

Within the four weeks of intense rehearsals, I internalized the martyr's agonizing death. I could feel his pain. Suffering appealed to me. At home, I was diligent in rehearsing my lines and wearing a soldier's uniform, I looked in the mirror. Then I no longer saw myself; I saw the brave and mighty warrior, Athanasios Diakos.

The day we presented the play, Theodora hugged me and kissed my forehead as the audience applauded. She grabbed my hand and lifted it high as though I were an Olympic champion. I must have done justice to the play, for the audience gave me a standing ovation. On that memorable day, I felt like I grew five inches taller and was the most important person in the world.

Theodora gave me plenty of attention. Later, as I grew older, I learned that she was terribly in love with my uncle, Anthony, my stepmother's older brother. A deep-dyed romantic, she was the one who told me that I had beautiful brown eyes. Many years later, on seeing my first published book, she wrote me a letter:

> *When you were only fourteen, you came to see me, proud that you had started your second year in high school. You stood near my desk that morning, and the light from the window fell across your head and features illuminating the expression on your face. Then a thought came to me of the great future that was ahead of your life.*
>
> *The best of all wishes, your former teacher,*
> *Theodora*

As I read her letter, vivid images of the play paraded across my mind. Instantly, I went back to those innocent days of youth when I had so much admired Athanasios Diakos's faith and martyrdom. He was my hero, and I wished that someday I, too, would go down in history as he had, defending my faith. I was just a young boy with fantasies of grandiosity and power. No longer could I fear death and humiliation, if I gave up my life for my country.

"I think Theodora must have brainwashed you," my friend George said.

"You must be jealous," I said.

"Jealous of what? That you want to be a hero? You must be losing your mind."

"I'm not losing my mind. I'd be lucky to be like Athanasios Diakos."

"Barbequed on a stick, and you call that lucky? We can admire heroes and be strong, but we don't need to become heroes in order to be men. Mythical heroes, war heroes, sports heroes are meant to inspire us to find the potential within ourselves."

George brought me back to earth. And as the culture of the island seeped into my psyche, his words reverberated in my mind. I wanted to be a boy scout, but I feared that my stepmother and my father would not approve. I needed to find the right time and the right words to tell them what I want.

8

AN AMERICAN YOUTH IN EXILE

In 1938, I was twelve years old, finally old enough to join a Cub Scout program. But my stepmother said, "There is no time for cubs. Take that idea out of your head." My father agreed with her. Seething with frustration, I held back my tears, but in bed that night I wept inconsolably. How much I wanted to belong to a Cub Scout program, go camping, have fun, and be one of those lucky boys!

One day after school and still early in the afternoon, I overheard my stepmother speaking softly to our neighbor, Maria: "I'm forty-two years old, my hair has begun to turn gray, and I have no life with my husband. I have become a house-keeper and mother of my two children and my husband's son." Hearing my stepmother's complaints, it was evident that she thought of me as an intruder to her married life. The resentment she felt toward me went deeper. I believed that, despite their marriage, she felt like little more than a maid and that my father had hired her to take care of me.

For a while, I put away my desire to be a scout, compelled to conform to my parents' wishes. School and play with my friends kept me out of the house. Summers were sweet but short; winters were long and gloomy. At home, with my siblings asleep, dinners were quiet, and I did not say much or eat much. My stepmother would break the silence to talk about her children, and my father would respond in a laconic manner: "Oh! Great! Nice.... Really...? That's very funny." Then he would withdraw to the couch and read the newspaper. As for me, I repressed any strong feelings I had. Like an exiled stranger, I did not think it mattered to them what I thought or felt. What I did outside the house did matter to them, however. Their concern seemed to be always about maintaining the family's good name, its good reputation, as if we were royalty.

My parents' bedroom was adjacent to mine, and at night I could hear my stepmother whispering, "He's a troubled child, I don't know how to deal with him anymore." She did not reveal how she was dealing with me in my father's absence, using a stick on my back and threatening me: "If you tell this to your father, I will kill you." I believed her. She had killed two big cats that had crossed our front yard. If she could do that to poor animals, I was afraid she could kill me in one of her angry outbursts.

9

THE HARMONICA

One night, I had a dream. In the front line of a parade, George and I were dressed in khaki uniforms and marching like soldiers. A number of scouts followed us. Puffed up with pride, he played the bugle, and I accompanied him with my drum. Exuberant in spirit, we passed by the town hall as hundreds of spectators applauded. But suddenly a young girl's screaming interrupted the applause. As I turned to see who it was, I saw a girl with long hair, dressed in sky blue marked with white stripes, like the Greek flag. I recognized her instantly as she shouted over and over again, "Hurrah for our heroes!" Her voice woke me up, and I realized that girl was Eleni, the prettiest girl in our class.

Out of a dozen or so good-looking girls in the fifth grade, it was Eleni that I loved and wished that she would love me in return. I don't think she knew my feelings then. Greece in those days was nothing like the present-day United States. There was no such thing as holding hands, dating, or going steady. Parents usually decided who their children would marry. I wanted Eleni for myself, and I didn't want any of the other boys getting too friendly with her. I thought of her often, and periodically I would secretly slip a note into her school bag, telling her how pretty she was and that I loved her, hoping she would read it. But I never got a response.

THE OLIVE PICKER

On Easter Sunday that year, her father had a massive heart attack and died. Eleni went into deep mourning. She wore black and seldom smiled. I attended her father's funeral and offered my condolences. An image of sadness, she looked at me with tearful eyes. I wanted to take her in my arms, wipe away those tears, and tell her that I totally understood her loss and shared her pain of being fatherless, because I already knew what it meant not to have a mother. I discussed the matter with my friend, George, who knew how I loved Eleni, and he encouraged me to write her a sympathetic letter. I wrote,

Eleni,

No words can be of comfort to you and your family, during these critical and painful hours. I can only imagine how you must feel over the sudden loss of your father. Please accept my heartfelt sympathies, and know that I think of you and your family. I will also pray that our Lord will embrace you with his healing power and love and bring you comfort and hope.

Respectfully,
Takis

Grief-stricken Eleni replied in two days:

Dear Taki,

Your friendship has been a great comfort to me. In reading your letter, my mother said, "Takis is such a fine young boy."

Thank you.
Eleni

10

BREAKING THE CHAINS OF CONTROL

On June 21, 1938, a cloud of grief darkened the spirit in Moria. Luke, a young boy who went swimming in the nearby Aegean Sea was swept out by a huge wave and drowned. Sad and scared, most parents of the village forbade their children to go swimming without supervision. But many of the kids of my age paid little attention to parental restrictions and spent their summer days secretly splashing about. The Aegean Sea was only a couple of miles away from the village of Moria, so the temptation to go swimming was very strong, especially in the hot summer weather.

One day, in defiance of parental restrictions, George and I decided to join some other daring friends and go swimming. Our friend, Patroklos, did not want to swim, he preferred to stay home and write poetry. As perspiration trickled down our spines, we couldn't wait to jump into the Aegean Sea for an hour of paradise. Crazed with forbidden fun, diving and splashing each other, we did not emerge from the sea for a long time.

When I returned home two hours later, my stepmother took one look at my face, looked at my eyes, obviously red from the sea salt, then reached out and touched my neck with her index finger. With a suspicious look on her face, she brought her index fingertip to her mouth and licked it. "Salty! Salty! Salty!" she barked angrily, realizing where I had been. My heart began to pound seeing her face turn red and her eyes enflamed. "Salty!" she screamed again, picking up her stick from behind the door. "I know where you've been, you prodigal son," she said and began hitting me mercilessly across the shoulders, yelling, "I told you not to go near the sea, but you did not listen. If you get sick, I'll let you rot in bed!"

Frightened by her anger and seeing how their mother kept hitting me, Kiki and Jimmy, my stepsiblings, burst into tears, screaming, "Mommy, stop it! Mommy, stop it!"

"You two shut up," she bellowed at them and continued hitting me until I was sprawled on the ground. Unable to escape, the blood rose to my head, and my temples pulsed painfully. Slowly, I managed to stand up and with all my strength swung a fierce blow at her chest, yanking off the gold necklace she wore around her neck. Shocked at my rage, she grasped her breast with both hands and cursed the day she had accepted me into her life. As she pulled away from me, I heard her whispering, "I wish that she—meaning my mother—had taken you with her when she died."

This unfortunate episode marked a turning point in my relationship with my stepmother. She never touched me again. Now, in my mind and vocabulary she became *Katerina*. Lacking significant emotional and personal involvement with her, I finally broke away from her dominance. She, in turn, shut the door of her heart in my face. She withdrew her care so rigidly that I felt she would never think of me again. In later years, even in my adult life, early memories of life with my stepmother would make me wonder how I ended up with so many negative feelings about myself. At what point did things go haywire?

That night I went to bed sick. Early the next day, Katerina invited Anthony, the local doctor over. He happened to be her brother's friend, and rushed to inform him that I probably caught a cold when I went swimming. As he examined me, he noticed the black and blue bruises on my back. He shook his head as he was leaving our house, unable to define what caused the bruises, "This young boy should recover soon after some tender care. Leave him alone and let him rest," the doctor said.

Could Katerina ever understand that I just wanted to be a boy like other boys? I wanted to be a normal, strong boy, but I felt that her control prevented me from growing, being manly, and having fun. Whenever she disapproved, I felt like a naughty little child. My fear was that she would take away my manhood, and I hated her. I no longer cared if she had stopped loving me. I didn't need her love.

That evening, when my father came home, he asked why I was in bed so early. Assuming motherly concern, Katerina spoke like a woman with a broken heart: "Although I told him not to go swimming, he disobeyed me and went, so I punished him. But he attacked me and even yanked my gold necklace from my neck and broke it. I'm still in shock, and I'm worried that he has caught a serious cold. The doctor who examined him this morning saw some dark spots on his back and said, "This young boy seems to have a cold. He should stay in bed."

My father believed his new wife's story to be the gospel truth. Only God and I knew that her story was a keen manipulation to fool my father into thinking that she was truly concerned about my health. "I don't want you to worry too much," he said. "He will have to abide by the rules of our family. If he doesn't conform and misbehaves, I will send him to the orphanage in Mytilene. Just let me handle him."

The next morning, my father towered over my bed, ready to *handle* me, whatever that meant. How else could he please his wife? I generally thought of my father as a strong and successful man, but that morning I saw him become frightened in the face of his wife's anger.

I once told my uncle, Thanos, who was my real mother's brother, how Katerina used her stick to punish me, and he said, "Hell has no fury like a woman who is even slightly disgruntled." It certainly seemed true. "I'm sorry that you have to live with her," said Uncle Thanos. He was good to me. Like a loving father, he used to comb my hair and make sure that my shoes were shined. He also made sure to give me a fresh cup of rice pudding that he had just made in his dairy store.

My father cleared his throat and said, "I want you to listen and to listen very carefully." I nodded my head in silent agreement.

"Mama loves you, and you should obey her. If you did whatever she told you to do, there would be no problem." Then the tone of his voice changed, and his face took on the grimace of a fatherly authority. "You had no business going swimming; you're still too young, and look, you got sick. Your mother had a right to be angry. And I heard that you attacked her. Well, young man, should you dare to touch Mama again, then you will find out from me what real punishment can be."

"Mama is not my mother," I wanted to scream at my father, but I knew he would not listen. I could have said, "If she were my mother, she would not have used that hard stick against my back." But it was easier to repress my feelings than to defend myself in vain.

11

THE TASTE OF LIBERTY

Growing up among the gigantic olive trees that bordered the little town of Moria kept me from being idle. Reaching through the branches for the olives strengthened my arms, and sorting the harvest by hand made my fingernails firm. Gradually, I became an expert at stretching my limbs to reach the olives and sorting the results of my efforts. Standing next to my father, the proud olive grove owner, I would watch as the warm oil from the freshly pressed olives was poured and stored in steel barrels. With a sense of pride, he would say to me, "Someday, this oil will pay for your education, so you don't have to work as hard. You could be a doctor, have your own office, and live a comfortable life."

Even in my early years, my father had big plans for me. A proud American citizen, the idea that his son might make a career of olive picking and olive oil producing was intolerable to him. I don't know how he got the idea that I might become a doctor. His wish haunted me each time a thorn got between my fingernails as I picked up the olives that lay spread all over the arid ground. Obviously, he had regrets that he had brought me back to Greece and that his wife did not want to go to America.

Periodically, he would admit to me how much he missed America, his secret love. "Every morning, the moment I wake up," he would say, "I see the American flag in front of my eyes, waving, caressing my face, and I visualize the tall buildings, broad streets, and busy people rushing to work." Eventually, he persuaded his wife that it would be financially beneficial to the family for him to return to America, possibly for one or two years, work hard, and send money back to her to support the family.

"That's where the money and opportunities are, and that's where I want to be," he said, imagining the United States as the Promised Land.

In September 1939, before the harvest of the olives had begun, my father bade us farewell and returned to the country of his dreams. With his absence, I became even lonelier. By this time, I was used to the fact that I had no real mother, but now, missing my father, I felt that fate had cheated me out of him as well. Other kids my age had two parents who cared for them.

Katerina, to serve her own needs, tried to make me feel important by calling me "the man of the house." I liked the title, but I did not believe what she said. Out of rebellion against her and her increased expectations, I spent less time at home and more time at the marketplace with my friends, observing the adult population. Of course, it felt good to feel important and be admired. I wanted to excel and be accepted by my peers. Being at liberty to entertain myself, I went behind Katerina's back and spent more time in Alexis's tavern, where I learned to drink wine and eat octopus with some of my peers, mainly George Tsakiris and Patroklos Pantsaris.

Even now, I can visualize Alexis—a short, sharp looking, jovial man, the personification of mischief—carrying a sizzling octopus on a ceramic platter and proudly pouring glasses of wine that he had made himself. One afternoon, after I had a second glass of wine, I got up and danced *Zeibekiko*—a Greek dance much favored by the young adults. It was at moments like those that I wished Eleni could see me, drinking wine and dancing. That's the taste of my teen years on the Greek island.

One morning on my way to school, there was a great deal of commotion in our neighborhood. Loud women's voices were coming from Vasiliko's front yard. She lived two doors down and across from our house. I ran over to see what was going on. Five disheveled and disturbed women were gathered in a circle around a light brown goat lying on the ground, groaning in pain and stretching its hind legs. "It's a breech birth... Oh, it's a breech birth! Oh, the poor animal is not going to survive."

I had no idea what a breech birth was nor what they were hollering about, so I crawled between them and knelt over the poor goat. Softly, I began rubbing her swollen belly. "She's not dying," I said loudly, as I noticed a tiny baby's leg popping out between the goat's hind legs. A month before, I happened to have seen an older man helping a ewe, who had a hard time giving birth. I had watched him curiously and I saw exactly what he did. When I saw the poor goat agonizing, I said to myself, I could do exactly what that older man did with the ewe.

"Taki, don't touch the poor animal!" Vasiliko, a skinny middle-aged woman in a tattered dress screamed. "I had this goat for three years; she gave me gallons of milk for my three children."

Ignoring Vasiliko's scream, I wanted to help the poor goat. Her baby seemed to be coming out one foot first. Biting my lips and holding my breath, I reached for the other baby's leg with my two fingers and thumb and slowly brought it out. Once the two front legs were out, I reached in the birth canal for the tiny head. Mysteriously, the rest of the baby goat slid out, covered in membrane, blood, and mucus. There was a soft cry of maa...maa...maa... from the brand new baby, as its mother caringly with her tongue began to clean her offspring. Meanwhile, the women around me began to applaud and repeat, "Taki is a midwife! Taki is a midwife!" That was a title I preferred my classmates not to hear.

When I returned from school that day, my stepmother said with a smile, "I welcome Moria's new midwife!" I did not trust her smile, until she said, "Vasiliko told me the whole story of how you saved her goat. Well, I suppose you are ready now to join the Boy Scouts," I could hardly believe what she just said. It seemed that she was giving me the okay.

There are times, even today, that I can close my eyes, take deep breaths, and recall the bold, fecund aroma of the Aegean Sea, exquisite and sensual, the fragrance of Greece, old and new, in a lasting orgasm of springtime. The openness of the traditional Greek character, the zest for life that was always evident at social events. Parties were always flavored with humor, laughter, serious conversations, satire, singing, and dancing. The Greek spirit stems from their ancestors' philosophy: *Eat, drink, and be merry, for tomorrow we die.* Tomorrow was never an issue. In the noble simplicity of my compatriots, I sensed a silent greatness. My deep yearning was to be one of them someday, and my thoughts had become wishes: *Why does adulthood take such a long time to arrive?*

12

MISCHIEF AND WISDOM

Like a mosaic, my life was gradually taking form, shape, and color—a mixture of Alexis, the free-spirited rascal, and Papavasile, the spiritual giant—a vital interplay between reality and idealism. My school time demanded that I be a good, virtuous, and wise student. Church provided time for prayer and inspiration. Fragments of Papavasile's sermons slowly began to penetrate my teenage mind. Often, he would emphasize that God's gift, the power to survive, within each human being is unfathomable.

"The potential for healing damaged emotions is great if we do not hinder it with negative thoughts." His admonitions were emblazoned in my brain: "Do not waste precious time. Avoid idle talk...show respect for your elders...be grateful for what you have, and don't whine about what you don't have... be open-hearted, loving, patient, and generous...be aware of your thoughts; they precipitate feelings, and feelings result in behavior...if you want to be happy, learn to smile...walk with straight shoulders, and look at life fearlessly in the face. Do not surrender to waves of random worries...keep Christ in your heart and cherish his loving presence in your life."

Growing up and feeling unloved by Katerina was not an ideal mother-son relationship. But in later years, during my father's absence, I gradually came to realize that Katerina did care about me, otherwise I would have died in early childhood. She did not have to love me, but she chose to show me reasonable care. My part was to live by her rules. All humans have to learn to live by rules to survive, and if I wanted to be loved by her, I had to be lovable. Papavasile, my mentor, agreed with my new approach to life with Katerina.

Having to choose between placating Katerina and leveling her power, I chose to cooperate with her wishes, and being disciplined in this way made me emotionally stronger. I learned to play with Kiki and Jimmy, and became like their elder brother. I grew to love them dearly. As I became more involved with them, I stopped resenting their presence. Seeing us happy together, Katerina's attitude toward me changed, and she started treating me like a son of her own flesh and blood. In turn, she began evoking different feelings in me. I no longer thought of or referred to her as Katerina. I saw her as a mother and began to call her Ma.

It took me a long time to realize that Ma was basically a good, loving, and moral person. From her I learned many of my humane principles: Be kind to other people; be concerned about the misfortune of others—the poor, the disabled, and the elderly; be honest; be truthful; be generous to the less fortunate. When you are kind to others, you receive kindness back. These traits were instilled in me during my teen years, and in trying to imitate Ma, I've tried to be mindful of the needs of others all of my adult life.

The gradual realization of the good deeds Ma did and how she did them were significant. She never made a display of the good that she did. For example, at one end of our village, a poverty-stricken elderly widow named Amalia lived alone in an old shack. Just before family dinnertime, with a tender smile, Ma would say to me, "Take this dish of food to Amalia while it's still warm. There is no need to tell anybody on the way where you're going. This is our secret."

There was something magical in her voice that gave me joy as I followed her instructions. She reached out to help the poor without expecting anything in return. She needed no praise, nor did she boast of her good works. Her reward came from the knowledge that a hungry woman ate the food she had prepared. The joy she gave to Amalia became her own joy. Her frequent and surreptitious generosity has left a lifelong mark on me.

Saturdays were appropriated for charity. Our home was a mini-center for the hungry and homeless. To any hungry or poor person who knocked at our door, Ma would give a thick slice of homemade bread, a handful of olives, a piece of cheese, or a little bottle of virgin olive oil. No one left Ma's presence empty-handed. Her generosity came from a special place, from a compassionate heart where her soul lived. "We listen to our heart's voice when we help others," she said. "We all have something to give; it may not be a grand gift, but no matter how small, what we share suffices when it comes from our heart." Seeing Ma's compassion for the less fortunate, I began to admire her silent efforts to extend a helping hand wherever there was a need. I no longer had hostile feelings against her. Reconciliation made me a better person.

13

MASCULINITY

In September 1940, during World War II, my father returned to our family after being in America for less than two years. He was glad to be back in Lesvos and proud that he had crossed the Atlantic Ocean undaunted on an American ship. Soon after his return, he began again to exercise a father's authority over me. Constantly on my back, he would ask endless questions: "Where were you last night until 11 o'clock? I'd like to know with who you're hanging out with these days. How is school these days? I haven't seen you opening a book."

I detested such questions and answered vaguely. "Don't worry about me...I did okay when you were away...I'm doing just fine now." When my father was at home, he did not impress me as a role model of masculinity. He sat in his special chair like a patriarch, criticizing and pontificating. To me, he was a source of irritation, and I perceived him as weak. When I did not do as he demanded, he would lose control, his face becoming fiery red, and then he would strike me with his belt and call me "incapable and worthless." His punishments caused many emotional scars, but I thank God they were not fatal.

Troublesome as life had been initially with my stepmother, it was preferable to the third degree my father put me through. I was fifteen years old and, upon his return from

America, I lost the freedom I had enjoyed while he was away. At this point, my relationship with Ma was more favorable than that with my father, resulting in a display of subtle hostility and anger toward him. I wonder if he felt displaced or jealous because of the attention I gave to his wife. Or maybe he realized I was growing up and he could no longer control me.

There was a part of me that always wanted to break away from my family. Regardless of whatever good my father and Ma could offer, there remained a young, adolescent urge in my heart to cut loose. I wanted to break out and discover forbidden things for myself, and I did not want authoritarian voices telling me what I must do. It was a natural feeling, wanting to find my own answers, solve my own problems, and discover my own truth of who I really was.

My father's voice echoed in my ears, "This is how to behave. This is how to relate. This is how to do this and not do that. Our home is the school for you."

But in defiant silence, I thought, *To hell with all that! I want to live my own life without parental voices. I don't want to have answers before I've even raised any questions. I don't want to be given all the right ways before I have learned on my own about wrongdoing.*

This was my time for self-discovery and self-acceptance. Granted, my father knew much about life because he had lived longer than I had, so his concern was natural and good. But at the same time, everything in me was saying, "It's my life, not yours. Let me go free." And I also knew that my feelings were natural and good. I really wished my father would recognize how natural it was for me to want to cut loose and do something other than what he considered to be decent or appropriate.

The apparent impossibility of resolving the broken link with my father promoted my friendship with Alexis, who became my mentor. My father tried to stop me from going to Alexis's tavern. "It's bad for the reputation of our family," he said. "You are too young to be frequenting taverns. Places like that are for lazy characters and losers. You are wasting your time there." Home had become an arena where issues could not be worked out, so I found comfort where I could.

When the school day ended, George, Patroklos, and I, along with some other good friends spent the afternoons playing soccer. And then, as a group, we would proceed to our hideout in the backyard of Alexis's tavern. Alexis offered us something vital: the picture of competent masculinity. There was nothing he could not do. Besides telling us heroic stories of his younger years and giving us a glass of wine, he was a father and mentor to us. He was the image of what I thought an older man should be—overly driven and experienced, smart and successful, accomplished and sensitive, qualities that I subtly admired. My generation of boys who grew up without caring fathers or male mentors to emulate were left to guess what men should be like. We relied on cultural icons—larger-than-life images—as our role models of masculinity.

If I were ever going to reconcile with my father and earn his love, I would have to do my part, but I wasn't sure what that was. I started paying him silent homage. I spent long hours in our olive groves and, like an adult, learned how to harvest the ripe olives, to prune trees, and to chop wood for our fireplace. One cold late afternoon, I came home carrying a heavy load of firewood on my shoulders and perspiring profusely. It was the first time I ever saw my father smile with approval at something I'd done.

"That's pretty heavy!" He said. "How did you manage to carry all this? Let me help you unload." Noticing my increased involvement, he nodded favorably to his wife and whispered, "He's growing up, finally."

One Sunday morning, after church services, my father handed me a card, which he said he had meant to give me but had misplaced. Read it! It's from the President of the United

States, Calvin Coolidge. It's dated 1926, the year you were born. I read the card slowly:

> *Nothing in the world can take the place of persistence. Talent will not; nothing is more common than unsuccessful people with talent. Genius will not; unrewarded genius is almost a proverb. Education will not; the world is full of educated derelicts. Persistence and determination alone are omnipotent. The slogan "Press on" has solved and always will solve the problems of the human race.*

I was impressed that my father knew the name of America's president in 1926. But his message in my card was difficult to understand. As I read the card again and again, I chose to memorize some power words that I thought applicable. The words I chose were: "Press on" and "persistence and determination." I made them both my life's purpose and a sign to move forward with my life.

14

THE INVASION

Weeks later, shortly after my father's return from America, I was riding my bike to school, free-spirited and happy, along the six-kilometer stretch on a paved road from Moria to the capital city, Mytilene. When the old castle of the capital came into view, I saw a strange sight. I blinked my eyes in shock. The sky-blue Greek flag that had waved over the castle every day as far back as I could remember had been replaced by a swastika. A *swastika!* Breathless, I skidded to a halt. *Oh, my God, what my father and what Moria's population feared mostly has happened*, I thought. *The Nazis have invaded our island!*

At school that day, the one-armed teacher, Mr. Lianos, who had just come back from the war in Albania, fighting against the Italian Fascists, raised his left arm high and addressed the entire high school student body with a thunderous yet sad voice, "Our Island, my dear young people, succumbed to the enemy last night. Like the rest of Europe, Greece is under Hitler's yoke. But we need to be of courage and patience!" He shouted. "I lost my right arm fighting against the army of Mussolini, who decided to invade Greece. Now once again, I'm ready to fight against the Nazis with my left arm. I want you to remember, the Nazis may conquer our land, but they can never conquer our Greek spirit."

Thunderous and long applause interrupted our brave teacher's voice, as the students spontaneously began to sing with courage:

Invaded but never defeated,
Our Greece's afraid of no one.
Enduring the pain of slavery,
Again we will earn glorious victory.

That fateful day, I hurriedly rode the six kilometers home from school to find my father cowering in a corner of our kitchen. Beside him, my stepmother sat in tears as two Nazis ransacked our home. Conrad Muller, a tall, slim Nazi with a grin, reached for my bike and grabbed it from my hands.

"Leave my bike alone, you lizard-face monster!" I screamed, scared and in tears. "Please don't take my bike, please." My tears must have evoked courage in my father's heart. Bravely, he stood up in front of the Nazi invader and said, "Officer, two of your comrades have taken our bed and chairs, our dining table, and other precious items from this house. I beg you not to take away my son's bike. Every day he needs it to go to school, which is six kilometers away." My father's tone was firm but not offensive. A Greek man, a Nazi accomplice, interpreted my father's words.

The Nazi invader replied with a sarcastic giggle, "He's young; he can walk to school. It's good for him," he said indifferent to my tears and my father's plea. With an arrogant look on his face, he rode away with my bike. It wouldn't have mattered at all to him that I had gathered many baskets of quality olives, cured them, and sold them for two long years to earn enough money to buy that bike.

The havoc that occurred in the ensuing days is hard to describe. Armed Nazi soldiers harassed the innocent population, entering houses at will and gathering precious artifacts, beds and blankets, plates and silverware, tables and chairs. They piled everything they had confiscated into their jeeps and brought it to our high school, which they had converted into their barracks. In utter despair, the people of Lesvos panicked.

Soon after their arrival, the invaders posted yellow plywood signs in large black Gothic script, indicating directions and names of each town and names of the streets. Enraged that I no longer had a bike and feeling a need for revenge, a tempting idea surfaced in my mind.

Already a 6 p.m. curfew had been declared by the Nazis. Circulation by civilians after that time was forbidden. One evening, before it got dark, I went and met George and Patroklos in the hope of sharing a plan.

"Taki, your eyes are red. Is anything wrong?" Patroklos asked.

"Plenty wrong," I replied. "The Nazis ransacked our house and took many things. Worst of all, a tall Nazi officer confiscated my bike."

George knew what that treasured bike meant to me. "The bastards," he said angrily and tied his fists.

After a silent moment, sadness etched on their faces, they both reached out and gave me a heartfelt hug. "I'm sorry," they said. As they pulled back, they looked at me curiously.

"Are you thinking what I'm thinking?" I asked.

"My friend," George answered, "I see mischief in your eyes. Whatever you're planning to do smells of danger. These monsters carry guns. Let's be careful."

"It's time to get even with the enemy," I said.

"I want to join you, but I'm scared," George said.

"Guys, let's not do anything stupid." Patroklos squeezed my hand.

So one moonless night, the three of us defied the curfew and crept through the narrow village alleys, destroying all the yellow plywood signs that we could see. Scared to death, each of us took a different direction. I brought a large one home, planning to make it into a table, since the Nazis took our dining table away.

When my father saw me carrying that big yellow plywood sign with the Gothic letters emblazoned with the word "Moria," his face froze in fear.

"Are you crazy? The Nazis will burn us alive if they find out you insulted them like that."

"I don't care," I said. "They took my bike. Should I keep sitting on my hands?"

"You committed sabotage. Do you know what that means?"

"It means I no longer have a bike to go to school, and I hate the Nazis," I said. "I want to see them dead. My friends and I have made plans. Somehow, we are going to fight them our way."

"I can understand how you feel," my father said with his right hand on my shoulder. "I went back to America to improve the financial situation for our family. But because of the war, I came back sooner just to be with you. Our times are dangerous, and you are a growing young man. The occupying forces do not play games. They could draft you and send you to Germany to work in their factories manufacturing weapons, or they could send you to a concentration camp. So just be very careful. I ask you not to do anything so foolish again, do you hear?"

He put both his arms on my shoulders, he shook me gently and looking at my eyes painfully, he said, "Now help me get rid of this sign." Silently, he cut the plywood into small pieces, and I put each piece one by one into our fireplace. I watched the flames with vengeance in my heart, and as each piece burned, I visualized the burning of a Nazi soldier.

I couldn't sleep that night. I was angry with my father for breaking up and burning the plywood sign that I had brought home and thereby ruining my plans to make a table out of it. Each time I closed my eyes, hoping to fall asleep, I saw scenes from that cruel encounter with the Nazi lieutenant—the flick of his cigarette lighter as he burned the little American flag which I had attached to the handlebars of my bike. The enemy, with his sneering face, rode my bike down the street as my eyes brimmed with tears watching him.

At dawn the following day, I was awakened by the distant goose steps of Nazi soldiers. I stood at the top window of the house and watched the German battalion, SS soldiers, some eight hundred, flowing through our small town. Armored jeeps and military trucks, loaded horses with weapons, and motorcycles clattered in the narrow streets, leaving behind a heavy odor of sulfur and perspiration as each phalanx passed by. After a thunderous parade through the marketplace, the soldiers were dismissed and two by two they entered homes and took whatever they needed—furniture, beds, sheets and blankets, and kitchen utensils.

I pulled away from the window in despair and sat on the edge of my bed, feeling numb. The thought of Nazi occupation, especially of my little town, was intolerable to me. In my second year of high school, Mr. Lainos, our history teacher, taught us about the four-hundred years occupation of Greece by the Ottoman Turks, from 1453 to 1828. What if that should happen again? My spine tingled with fear and helplessness. When I went back to the window, heavy drops of rain began to fall like tears, drenching the trees and flowers. I opened the window slightly, and the cool air mixed with a sweet smelling fragrance as it crept into my room. I lay down on my bed, buried my head in a big pillow and attempted to go back to sleep.

The Invasion

That morning, thick fog blocked the sky, an unusual sight during springtime in Lesvos. The sun seemed to have retired behind the gray folds of clouds. Olive trees dripped dew on the grass and on the faces of the few students making their way to school. Most of the students were barefooted wearing faded blue pants and white blouses. Under one arm they carried books and with their other hand, they held paper bags filled with cured olives for lunch. Food had already become scarce because the army of occupation had confiscated most of our supplies. The familiar fun and laughter was absent from the young, and their parents, on their way to work, showed no optimism that this day would be better than the last. The reality of the Nazi invasion had sunk in, and the occupied islanders began to think that their yesterdays were better than their todays.

A week later, crossing the market place on my way to school on a Monday morning, I saw a Nazi soldier standing at the door of a big house of which he had already taken possession. He was flapping his leather gloves against his palms and whistling. I avoided looking at him and, lowering my cap, I increased my pace to pass him.

"Hey you, come here." Hearing that harsh voice, I turned to see who was being spoken to, and I saw a wiggling index finger pointing at me, directing me to come closer. In broken, accented Greek, the Nazi soldier said, "*Yiati den les kalimera?*" (Why don't you say good morning?) And he began to slap me across the face with his gloves repeating, "*Yiati den les kalimera?*" My nose began to bleed. Blood trickled over my lips. Holding back my tears, I spat blood on the ground, and under my breath I swore, *I shall look for revenge until my last breath.* By the second week of May, the occupation of Moria was an unexpected reality. Young and old, the besieged inhabitants appeared lifeless and sad. Even the sea breeze that wafted from the Aegean Sea every morning and late evening had taken its relief elsewhere.

So began one of the darkest periods in all of Greek history. From the Yugoslavian border, Nazi tanks had moved through the Greek towns with invincible power. Fighting airplanes furrowed the ever blue sky of Greece, vomiting fire and showering death upon the innocent below. The scourge of Hitler's war reached the entire Greek nation, even the little island of Lesvos.

15

PENELOPE'S FATE

The well that provided drinking and cooking water for Moria lay on the west side of the town, a five-minute walk east of the Roman aqueduct. Twice a week, Penelope went early in the morning and filled two ceramic pitchers for her family.

Today, she walked faster than usual, thinking about making stuffed tomatoes and eggplants for dinner. She felt excited that she could make an especially luscious dinner to surprise Patroklos, her brother, and her mother, but her thoughts were suddenly interrupted. A jeep stopped behind her. She smelled the car's diesel fumes and instinctively increased her pace, not daring to look back.

She was nearly at the well when two Nazi soldiers grabbed her by her arms. They took the ceramic pitchers out of her hands and mumbled something in broken Greek that Penelope didn't understand. The sound was scary enough to provoke a cold shiver down her spine. She had done nothing wrong. She had never spoken one word against the occupying forces. Something was not right. In an ineffectual attempt at self-protection, she buttoned the upper button of her blouse and tried to hold her blue skirt over her knees.

In the hands of Nazis, one learned quickly to avoid challenges and to cooperate. Penelope's limbs and mind went numb as the soldiers herded her into the jeep. For a moment all she felt was blank terror as both soldiers climbed back into the jeep. Her chestnut-brown hair waved in the air as the jeep whisked her away. When she managed to sneak a look, she saw a pair of shiny boots, an impeccable uniform, and an expressionless face shaded by what seemed an officer's cap.

In less than ten minutes they arrived at the elegant villa of the wealthy olive oil merchant, Theodore Zerbinis. Guards opened the gate, and the jeep continued to the very end of the long drive, finally stopping in front of the marble stairway that led to the main building of the villa. From the corner of her eye, Penelope saw a tall Nazi officer with "ARKO" pinned to his collar in shiny brass letters approaching. Scared, and in short breaths, she could sense her heartbeat increasing.

As they climbed the steps, one by one, Penelope shrank from the officer's breath in trepidation. The stiff-necked ARKO Nazi officer gave orders to his subordinates who, after opening the door, saluted and left.

Her whole body shivering uncontrollably, Penelope felt cold and disoriented. Why was she brought into this room? As she observed the strange movements of the Nazi officer, her scared glance perused the room. In the center hung a brilliant chandelier, representing centuries of wealth. Walnut chairs were placed at even intervals against the walls. To her left was a chestnut-brown grandfather clock, and at the other end of the room was a fireplace, topped by an enormous austere portrait of Hitler. In front of the fireplace was a huge leather sofa. Heavy draperies on the windows allowed very little light to enter. The only sounds she heard were the boot steps of the officer, Conrad Strauss, and his repeated finger snapping.

Eyeing Penelope's youthful body, Strauss crumpled a newspaper and put it under the firewood. It wasn't long before the dry olive wood ignited and began exuding a sweet fragrance. Looking at Strauss defiantly, she thought he looked like a ferocious hungry alligator ready to devour his prey. He poured some liquor in two glasses and brought one of the glasses to Penelope's lips. She shook her head. "No!" she said with determination, shaking her index finger angrily. Fear and contempt made her nauseous.

"You don't have to drink," he said. "Come and sit by the fire." He finished his cognac, left the glasses on the table, and escorted her to the sofa by the fireplace.

"I want to go home," she said. "My mother and family will be waiting for me."

"*Jawohl,*" he replied and pointed to the sofa.

She decided to cooperate. Hoping he would let her go, she sat on the right corner of the sofa and Strauss on the left. His eyes reflected the flames, and he spoke words that rhymed in German. Occasionally, he got up to poke the fire, and each time he returned to the sofa, he sat closer to her.

"Please, let me go," she implored, her eyes swimming in tears. She felt trapped, like a helpless insect caught in a web who sees the cunning spider in every detail—the sharp angularity of the awkward legs, the white cross on its body, and the brutal mouth—so too, Penelope, with appalling clarity, saw him above her, ready to bear down and drain the sap of her life. She began to smell his breath and the scent of his perspiration. He took off his jacket, and grunting with sudden desire, his edging nearer to her was interrupted by a strong knock at his door. He stood up instantly, put back on his jacket and opened the door.

What Conrad Strauss saw was the shock of his life. In front of him stood a bearded man with a tall hat and wearing a black cassock. He was Moria's priest, Papavasile, who stood courageously in front of the invader Nazi officer, holding and pressing a huge silver cross against his breast. He spoke a language that left Strauss in wonder. Along with four church members, I stood behind our priest for support, determined not to leave Zerbinis Villa without Penelope.

Bobby, a young Greek former classmate of mine and now a Nazi accomplice, was summoned to interpret the priest's claim: *Penelope is a sixteen-year-old and kindhearted daughter, and the people of Moria seek her immediate release. She was snatched away for no reason, causing terrible pain to her family and shame to our town that has been grieving silently over the invasion.*

Hearing Bobby interpreting, Papavasile kept looking at Straus's eyes pleadingly.

"*Jawohl! Jawohl!*" he replied, shaking his head, and looking at the interpreter said, "*Tell the priest and his friends that this young girl soon will be sent to her family with an escort for her safety. Bringing her here, it was a misunderstanding by two young solders. A terrible mistake, he shook his head to disguise his supposed regret.*"

Conrad Strauss, defeated by a priest, feeling tired and disappointed, ascended the stairway to his bedroom upstairs. On his way, he winked at a subordinate and said, "She's all yours, comrade, get rid of her."

"Please, please, don't touch me," Penelope cried at the approaching soldier.

As Penelope cowered in the corner of the sofa, and the comrade reached his hand to her, she pulled back in fear and knocked a ceramic vase off a little table. The vase broke, tulips and golden daisies scattered across the floor. The comrade squatted and gathered the flowers and the broken pieces of pottery. She noticed gentleness in his eyes. But could she trust him? This soldier was not the ferocious ugly enemy that had his eyes on her. Yet her heart continued to pound in fear. She clutched the cross that hung around her neck, determined to die rather than submit to humiliation. She wanted to get up and run, but her knees felt sore and weak. The soldier took the flowers to the kitchen and came back with a warm wet washcloth.

Penelope, seeing his smile as bait, pulled back, tearing the chain and cross from around her neck. "Please, don't come near me." She kissed the cross and gave it to him with imploring eyes. "Please, take this, but don't touch me, let me go out of here."

Lifting his brows in silent sympathy, he said, "I won't hurt you. Don't be afraid." He handed her the washcloth and put the cross in his pocket without even glancing at it.

She burst into hysterical sobs and pressed the cloth against her face. It was warm and soothing. Coming out of the lethargy that had possessed her, she wiped her face thoroughly.

"Please, let me go," she pleaded, her lips parted in desperate anxiety, hoping to spark some element of humanity in this man before her.

He saw her terror and, behind those impenetrable eyes, the captive's yearning for freedom. The echo of his superior's words, "She's all yours, and get rid of her," disgusted him. He was not about to comply with Strauss's whims.

"I'll help you get out of here," said the soldier.

Penelope pressed her hand against her breast and bowed. "Thank you," she said eyeing his face with hope. *If he really means what he says*, she thought, *I shall be eternally grateful.*

The soldier led her out, walking a few steps ahead. At the gate of the villa, he spoke to the guard, who saluted and opened the gate. Silently, they walked together for a short distance. Then the soldier took a roll of brand-new marks from his pocket and handed it to her. "Take this; buy something for your family."

Penelope looked to see if anyone was watching. The gate was no longer within view. The horror she felt in that accursed place was behind her; she was free. The comrade was a guardian angel, but Penelope's heart, troubled with anger, momentarily blinded her. *Where will I go? What will I say?* She wondered. She bowed in gratitude once more to her escort, then threw the marks on the ground and ran off without looking back.

16

FEAR AND RAGE

It was Ascension Day, forty days after Easter, when I met Papavasile on my way to school in Mytilene. I was pleased to walk with him because I wanted to tell him about the incident with the Nazi soldier and find out if he had heard anything further about Patroklos's sister, Penelope. As we walked silently for a few moments, we were distracted by Stratis, a barefooted seventh grader, who was also one of his altar boys. He was carrying a big bottle of milk for his mother, who was in the hospital. Just then, a Nazi soldier on a bicycle whizzed past us. Instantly, my anger rose. "Papavasile," I said, "That's my bicycle that a Nazi officer snatched from my hands," but before I could finish telling him how the Nazis had invaded our house, the soldier was approaching Stratis. Slowing down he lifted his boot and kicked him into a ditch.

In pain, Stratis screamed, "*Voithea!*" (Help, please!)

In his flowing black cassock, Papavasile and I stormed after the Nazi. I was out of breath as I heard Papavasile scream, "You accursed son of the devil, why did you do such a terrible thing to an innocent boy?"

The Nazi sped off laughing raucously, leaving the boy in the ditch crying painfully. Blood gushed out of a deep cut in Stratis's shin, caused by the broken milk bottle. At the sight of the blood, I tore a long piece from the bottom of my shirt and gave it to Papavasile, who carefully wrapped it around the boy's wound.

"Papavasile, I haven't done anything wrong," Stratis sobbed, wiping his tears with his sleeve.

"I know," the priest said. He handed me his leather briefcase, then carefully lifted Stratis into his arms and began the long walk, carrying him to the nearest hospital. "Teach them justice and compassion, Lord Jesus," he whispered.

Nearing the city of Mytilene, Papavasile saw the red and black swastika waving at the top of the castle. Sensing young Stratis's pain, he sighed deeply and said, "How long, my God, will these vultures suck the blood of our souls?" His legs were tired and his eyes welled with tears as he paused to rest by the sea, but the undulation of the waves reminded him of the unpredictable outcome of this Nazi invasion of his town.

In 1948, seven years later, I was attending the Greek Orthodox Seminary in Brookline, Massachusetts. One Sunday afternoon, I went to see a soccer game in Boston. As a seminarian, I was expected to wear a black suit, a white shirt, and a black tie regardless of where I went. That day, as I sat to watch the soccer game, a young man, tall and robust, dressed casually approached me, and with a slight accent he said, "Are you by any chance Takis Kalellis?"

"Yes, I am," I said surprised. "And who are you?" I asked.

"Stratis Mavrikios, the one kicked in a ditch by a Nazi, don't you remember? I was on my way to see my mother who was in the hospital."

"Dear Lord," I said, "I did not recognize you...you have grown to be so tall, strong and a handsome man."

"But I recognized you the moment I saw you," Stratis said,

"And seven years later or more, at last I found you to say thank you, dear Taki."

Now, as an adult, he was wearing long pants. Gently, he bended forward and lifted the pants of his right leg. There was a big scar in his shin.

"You tore a piece of your shirt and gave it to Papavasile, our priest, to tie my wound. I was in severe pain and the priest carried me to the hospital."

It was the deep scar in Stratis's shin that brought back the memory of Papavasile, Stratis, and myself to the Nazi occupation of Greece and humans' cruel inhumanity to humans.

I could not help wonder how in the world, among hundreds of viewers at the soccer game, Stratis found me. Instead of watching the game, we sat close together and we talked for the rest of the afternoon. I was delighted to hear that Stratis came to America with a scholarship to study at Boston University's pre-medical school. I felt truly blessed to see his excitement over being a student in a school for future doctors.

Papavasile's presence was universally heartwarming. His thick, salt-and-pepper mustache blending with the prematurely gray beard that nearly covered his lips somehow bore witness to his deep compassion. Every wound and grievance of his priestly life had signed its name on his face, offering proof of his thirty-three years of dedicated service in God's vineyard.

Early in the afternoon upon his return to Moria that same day, Papavasile stopped at Alexis's tavern. He wanted to know if Alexis had any recent information about Penelope's disappearance.

"The presumed kidnap," Alexis said, "has incited deeper fear and rage in Moria's citizens. Speculation was rampant. Some of Penelope's neighbors said that a Nazi soldier must have found her attractive, and might even marry her, while others said that she was probably shipped to Germany. After filling two small glasses with wine, he said, "Papavasile, please take a sip of my new wine and relax for a few moments."

Thinking of Penelope and her family, Papavasile felt a burning sensation in his stomach that prevented him from drinking wine. As he sat with Alexis, he tried to figure out what he could possibly say to my friend, Patroklos, and to his mother. The Nazi officer, through his interpreter had said, Penelope would be escorted to her home for safety. But Papavasile was still agonizing about the Nazi officer's promise.

17

BOILED DANDELIONS
FOR DINNER

On my return from school later that afternoon, I carried a big paper bag full of dandelions that I had picked in the nearby fields. It was around five o'clock in the afternoon, and the marketplace was quiet as I slowly walked up the hill of St. Basil. Soothed by the smell of the olive trees, I noticed that most of Moria's men were still in their olive groves, pruning their trees. Some of the older folks had gravitated to the coffee shops, which had nothing but mountain tea to offer. Well, tonight's meal would consist of nothing but unappetizing boiled dandelions drowned in olive oil, I thought.

In front of Alexis's tavern, I saw Alexis and Papavasile sitting on two straw chairs, worried and whispering—probably about the recent events in our town taking place under the Nazi occupation. I rested my bag on one of Alexis's stools, greeted the two men and sat down near Alexis. I noticed a frown on the priest's face and wondered what else had happened to cause him such pain.

"Taki," Papavasile called me affectionately by my Greek

name, "before curfew tonight, could you come to St. Basil's Church and sing at the service?"

"A service?" I asked, surprised. I was sure that tomorrow was not a holy day.

"A supplication service for Penelope, your friend's sister."

"Have you heard anything more?"

"Not a word," he sighed, tugging at his long gray beard.

Seeing the priest's agony and feeling a wave of sadness, I said, "I'll be at St. Basil's before the curfew."

"Bring your friends," he said.

I lifted my bag and, looking at Alexis, quipped, "Boiled dandelions. Care to join us for dinner?"

"I'll bring the wine," he said with a sardonic smile.

I lingered a few minutes, still cherishing the calming presence of these two patriots. The priest quietly continued telling Alexis what he had heard on his hidden radio, "The Voice of America said that thousands of Greeks are homeless. The Nazis have burned dozens of small villages. The country at large is ruined and in disorder. The harbors, ships, railroads, bridges, and telephone lines are destroyed."

"The vultures will destroy us," Alexis said, as the priest prepared to leave. "Papavasile, what's frightening to me is that they have already drafted young men between 17 and 25. They'll send them all to Germany for compulsory work in the munitions factories."

"Let's hope not," the priest said, thinking of Moria's teen-age youth, children that a few years ago he had baptized.

I said goodbye and began looking for Patroklos, whom I had not seen for a while. Even Alexis, who seemed to be at the center of recent events that were shaping our destiny, was unable to provide news of my friend other than that his father was still in prison for stealing a baby goat to feed his family.

After I stopped at our home to deliver the dandelions, I hurried to meet George at his father's former bakery, where not even a morsel of bread was available anymore. "Friend, let's go to St. Basil's at five o'clock. Papavasile wants us to sing at a service for Penelope."

Hoping to get more information about Patroklos and his kidnapped sister, George and I went to visit Margo, Patroklos's mother, who lived in a small house below the hill of St. Demetrios Church.

Margo received us gracefully, dressed in black, still sunk in sadness from the imprisonment of her husband. She looked elegant, rosy cheeks, and sparkling but teary red eyes, all framed in a black shawl. Any ray of happiness at seeing us was tinged with an even deeper grief over the disappearance of her youngest daughter. She had the kind of face her two daughters could love and her son worshipped.

"You boys, I know you're my son's friends," she said looking straight in our eyes. "I know you love my son, and I know he loves you. But I haven't seen him since yesterday."

"You mean you don't know where he could be?" We asked, concerned.

"Yesterday morning at daybreak, he brought me a basket of wild chicory—said he'd gathered it the previous evening, and it would be good for me. And then he left, looking despondent. The kidnapping of his sister will kill him," she said.

"And I won't be able to stand seeing him doing something crazy and getting himself killed," George said.

I felt very bad about Penelope's situation: she was a sweet seventeen-year-old girl, eager to run errands for my stepmother and other neighbors to make a little money for her family. Now she was in the hands of some enemy, and the local gossip was ugly.

18

A BROTHER'S LOVE

Patroklos had found comfort in the fields. He made himself a slingshot and went hunting, hitting anything in motion, particularly lizards. Each time he traumatized a lizard, he would perform a ritual of torture, and then he would dissect the unfortunate creature, envisioning one of the two cruel soldiers who had kidnapped his sister. Finally, he would crush its remains with a big stone. And for a little while, his nagging rage would subside.

When Patroklos first learned of his sister's abduction, he had followed his impulse to run the four kilometers to Kara Tepe Camp, where the Nazis initially established their base, to seek help from a soldier, a supposed friend, whose shoes he had polished a couple times for a slice of bread. The soldier claimed he had neither seen nor heard of the incident, but he volunteered to drive Patroklos to Mytilene and inquire at the official German headquarters.

When Patroklos pulled his sister's picture out of his wallet, two arrogant SS soldiers in Mytilene merely glanced at the photo in apathy and laughed. Patroklos and his soldier friend returned to Kara Tepe sorely disappointed. His friend insisted that Patroklos should come into his quarters. The smells from the kitchen signaled supper, and he filled an aluminum porringer with soup and gave it to Patroklos. Food is food, and his mother needed it; as for his own stomach, Patroklos felt no hunger, for anger darkened his mind. He took the soup and ran home.

It was dark and late, and when he arrived home, he found his aging mother crouched on the hearth in front of the fireplace, her head touching her knees with her hands supporting it. Grief-stricken, she could hardly talk and had no news to share. She offered her faith, saying, "I went to St. George's chapel and lit a couple candles, one for our Penelope's safety and the other for your peace of mind. I pray for our ill-fated family every day."

Patroklos poured some soup into a bowl and offered it to his mother. Neither God nor demon can help us, he thought. His capacity to turn inward, to build an invisible wall of defense around himself, was astonishing—a mystery to his mother and a challenge to his friends. He felt compelled to roam in the field collecting chicory or to run through the woods killing lizards. He avoided contact with people lest they question him about his sister, Penelope. His pride kept him even away from his friends. Although we were always available to be with him, each time George and I met him, we avoided asking questions about his sister.

"Your friends were here earlier. They wanted to see you," his mother said.

"What about?" His abrupt tone cut sharply into her heart.

Margo, sensitive to her son's pain, yet not knowing what to say for comfort, shrugged her shoulders and whispered, "They care, my son."

As the fire slowly died, Patroklos went to his bed in the loft. Penelope's cot was there too, empty and hidden behind a curtain. He felt her absence sorely. His mother put the rest of the soup in a cupboard; she, too, had no appetite. He kicked off his shoes and buried himself under the covers.

He tossed and turned in despair, and when slumber finally conquered, a haunting nightmare disrupted his sleep. He sat up in fear. He had seen himself in chains before the Nazi authorities. In front of him stood his father, dressed in a Nazi uniform. "Where is my sister?" Patroklos asked. His father laughed and answered in German, a language he had grown to loathe. Still, it was only a dream. Shaken and cold, he shivered and drew the covers over his head.

19

MOST HOLY MOTHER!

George and I shook hands firmly, and looking straight in each other's eyes said in the same tone of voice, "What kind of friends are we to our friend, Patroklos?" It was not too long ago, that I recalled Papavasile saying what Christ had said about a true friend, "Greater love has no one than this, that a man lay down his life for his friends, and that is what Christ did."

"Well, my friend, you and I are not Christ, but we can think and imitate his example," George said shaking his head, "and we love our friend, and it's time for us to start right now in search of his sister."

George and I disguised ourselves in ragged clothes, looking like shepherds and hiding behind tree trunks and rocks. Each one of us held a shepherd staff in our hands, we acted like we were looking for a lost sheep. Later that evening in the twilight, we spotted a human being moving quickly among the trees and wild shrubs. We both fell flat on the ground and began to crawl like young kids. "That's a young woman," George whispered.

"I can swear, she looks young, I bet that's Penelope," I said, "but let's crawl and follow her silently to see where she's heading. We don't want to scare her."

THE OLIVE PICKER

There was not a soul around, just endless clusters of rocks, shrubs, and olive trees. We saw this young person running scared and barefoot through the olive groves and vineyards, screaming in a frenzy, "*Panagia mou*, Most Holy Mother!" It was Penelope. The sound of her voice faded to a shattered echo.

After she escaped from Zerbinis Villa and the Nazis, Penelope wandered like a gazelle, hiding in mountain caverns each time she needed rest. Hopefully, George and I followed her at some distance. We saw her approaching a familiar old fountain. The water trickled clean in a curved stone tub where peasants watered their animals. She plunged her face into the water and drank, probably trying to fill her empty stomach.

Certainly, images of the Nazi officer's hands grabbing her arms and his evil demands haunted her. Perhaps to wash out the ugly memory, she scooped water into both palms and kept watching it dripping like tears from her fingertips.

"*Panton prostatevis agathi.*" (You protect all of us, Good Mother, who come to you in faith.) The singing voices of distant women wafted through the thick woods. "In danger, sorrow and affliction, sinful and suffering, we come to you, Mother of the Most High, let your grace embrace us and protect us." As we listened to that sacred song, George and I each began to make the sign of the cross, and even from a distance, we saw Penelope crossing herself and walking briskly toward the sound that promised safety.

One hundred and fourteen carved stone steps, protected by a steal gate, led to a plateau where the pristine, whitewashed chapel of St. Mary stood like a seagull gazing at the sea below. Assuming that Penelope was heading toward St. Mary's Convent, George and I, hiding behind, followed her to see if she would reach the gate of the Convent. If she did, we were eager to hurry back to Moria to tell our friend, Patroklos, not to worry and that his sister was safe at St. Mary's Convent.

As the setting sun brightened the chapel, Penelope collapsed on the ground, her arms reaching through the rails of the steel gate. Momentarily, she lost consciousness.

A matins service had just ended, and we glanced at the nuns, who were emerging two by two from the chapel, when suddenly one of them spotted a body sprawled on the ground in front of the gate and ran to see what had happened. As she unbarred the gate, two other nuns came to help. They struggled to lift Penelope's limp body. Cuts and scratches on her legs were covered with dirt.

George and I identified ourselves as being friends of her family and that we had been searching for Penelope since her abduction. The two nuns invited us inside the convent to wash and drink some hot herbal tea. "Sister Anthusa may have some questions to ask you," one of the nuns said.

In a hushed infirmary on the first floor of the convent, Sister Anthusa, who was also a professional nurse, washed away the dried dirt, examined Penelope's bruises, and covered her with a warm, white, woolen blanket. Seeing possible fever in her face, she moistened a cloth with vinegar and put it on her burning forehead.

When Penelope regained consciousness, Sister Anthusa said, "Good daughter, who did this to you?"

"The enemy," Penelope whispered, tears blurring her vision.

"But why?"

"I don't know," she wept. Still dazed, she noticed a crucifix on the wall. Sister Anthusa followed Penelope's eyes with concern. "You're safe here," she said.

"I know." Penelope sighed, and smiling slightly, her mind drifted again. Her enormous dark-brown eyes twitched still with fear as the horrible episode in the hands of the Nazis replayed itself in her semi-sleep. When she finally emerged from her daze, Zerbinis's mythical palace faded away like a bad dream.

Crossing herself repeatedly while looking at the crucifix on the wall, she realized that she had survived a terrible nightmare. Sister Anthusa reached out to hold her hand, and as she caressed her forehead, she said in a soft, compassionate voice, "Our sinless and innocent Lord Jesus suffered humiliation, mocking, scourging, and death on the cross, but came back into a new life."

When we finished drinking our tea and were preparing to leave the Convent, we heard Sister Anthusa affectionately speaking to Penelope. "In some sense, you suffered like our Lord Jesus. You may be wounded, but the meaning of life is just beginning for you. This is the day the Lord has made for you; be at peace. He has felt your pain and humiliation, but he has enveloped you in his caring and healing love."

With her eyes on the cross on the wall, Penelope felt a twinge of relief and whispered, "Lord Jesus, thank you for your caring love and protection. Show me the path that I should be taking each hour of the day that leads me to you."

Months later, Patroklos happily informed Papavasile and Alexis that his sister decided to become a nun. He said that his mother is very happy that Penelope, now a novice, found the convent to be a warm and loving environment. In a year from today, she will be ordained as a nun and shall be called Sister Monica.

20

THE DANGER WITHIN

I was 18 years old when the Nazis finally began to retreat from Greece. Liberation finally arrived for the young and old of Lesvos, and Moria's people were preparing to celebrate. In the early morning of September 10, 1944, a solemn parade was about to take place. The priest gave me a big silver cross to carry, he gave George a banner depicting the Resurrection of Christ, a symbol of liberty, and he gave Patroklos the Greek flag. As our friend waved the Greek flag, young and old proudly began to sing:

> Greece will never die.
> We have suffered the Nazi cruelty.
> Now our time has come
> To celebrate our liberty.

Altar boys dressed in white robes carried luminaries, and two men with baritone voices chanted the doxology. Dressed in colorful vestments, Papavasile led the procession with a radiant face. Behind him a large crowd of exuberant townsfolk followed, dressed in their Sunday-best clothes. The procession stopped at the center of the town. When silence prevailed, Papavasile began to intone a prayer, "O Christ, our God, who at all times, in heaven and on earth, you are worshipped and glorified," but he was interrupted. The people turned and looked upward in shock at the source of the disruption.

Two men stood on the balcony of Moria's town hall and called for attention. The first was Seraphim, a teacher to whom the people of Moria had entrusted the education of their children for many years. The other was Anthony, a communist who had never worked a day in his life, although he was reputed to be an intellectual. The crowd looked toward the two men on the balcony, with mouths open in wonder followed by scattered applause.

Next to a small Greek flag, a red flag as large as a blanket was raised. It was embroidered with the hammer and sickle, symbols of Soviet Russia. Anthony, the tall, middle-aged "patriot" enthusiastically clapped his hands and demanded everyone's attention. Seraphim was ready with an obviously rehearsed speech. And to start, he praised the support of liberators, the patriots that had fought against the Nazis, and then he began to expound his own philosophy:

> Beloved citizens of our island. We finally got rid of the enemy. Now we are free people, and we promise you a good life for everyone. We don't need a God who is a myth. Has your faith in God or your church ever done anything to enhance your life? Communism promises equality, freedom, good life, and abundance of good things. Marx, Lenin, and Stalin, our powerful trinity, are the strong leaders who can liberate us from the yoke of plutocrats and political sharks. They are the powerful trinity that will make this world a paradise in our time.

Sadly but gently, Papavasile, hearing Seraphim's speech, took the cross from my hands and asked George and Patroklos to take the banner and flag and follow him back to the church. Confused, the altar boys silently walked away from the agitators and followed their priest. A small group of older men and women followed behind them, all with bent backs, staring at the ground earth as though it could reveal to them what was going to happen next to their homeland.

Disturbed yet curious, I stayed behind unnoticed in a corner to hear what else my former teacher had to say. Seraphim's voice echoed across the square, causing my temples to throb and making my stomach tight:

Under our leadership, your faith in God is no longer necessary. We promised and now we deliver what all of us needed, freedom from almost four years of Nazi occupation, freedom from a God that does not even exist, and a religion that is a myth. As your new leaders, we will provide equality and quality of life, justice for everyone, and an abundance of good things. We have your best interests at heart. The curse of exploitation by the plutocrats will no longer threaten you. Religion promises a life in heaven, but we promise a great life here on earth. Religion is the opium of the masses. It numbs, controls innocent people with guilt, and gradually kills. It is meant to intimidate you and to make you feel guilty and sad. We want you to be happy citizens and free thinkers. We no longer need churches or priests. The main part of St. Basil's Church will be used for theater, dances, games, entertainment, and lectures of interest for you and for our children.

Mesmerized, some members of the crowd were applauding. I wondered if they understood or believed what they were hearing. I hurried back to the church to visit Papavasile, feeling anxious, angry, and confused. What would the people do without a place of worship and without a leader to encourage their belief in God? Was it possible that communism would replace Christianity? I wanted to hear what our good priest had to say about the situation.

"It would be a terrible thing to remove God, the greatest source of support and consolation of our life," Papavasile said sadly. "Taki, a curse has fallen upon us. Dark days are ahead for our homeland. Just leave Moria as soon as you can. Go to America, the country of your birth, where there is freedom, and pray for us. When you get there, tell our American friends that the Greek nation will always be their faithful ally."

Communist leaders seemed determined to destroy even the ruins that the Nazis had left behind in Greece. Now the danger came from within Moria itself and spread like wildfire throughout the island. Civil war broke out, dividing families and demolishing sacred buildings, images, and items. Brothers fought against brothers, and sons rebelled against fathers, causing thousands of deaths across the country.

Later that day, with Papavasile's admonition that I should leave Moria and go to America resonating in my mind, I hurried to Patroklos's house.

"Well, my friend, we are not going to take Seraphim's propaganda to heart," I said. "The question is: What can we do?" Patroklos said, shrugging his shoulders sadly.

"We are going to organize the young people of our village and protect them from this communistic propaganda," I said. "I spoke to George already, and he likes the idea."

"How can we do that?"

"We will form a Boy and Girl Scout program to expose young people to sound ethical and patriotic principles, such as truth, faith in God, kindness, and brotherly love."

"I'll do anything to help," Patroklos said, as the sadness slowly faded from his face and was replaced by a hopeful smile. Later, I discovered that he was thinking that his older sister, Asimina, a well-known seamstress in town, would make a great Girl Scout leader.

"Starting Monday we are going to knock on every door of every house in Moria and ask mothers to donate some olive oil."

"And what are you going to do with the olive oil? The mothers will ask."

"Well, George, my friend, we are going to take a bath in it," I chuckled. "We'll tell them this oil will buy fabric to make scout uniforms for their sons and daughters."

"Where will we get this fabric to make the uniforms?" Patroklos asked.

"We will barter the oil with the Kallamari Fabric Factory."

"Will the factory really give us fabric for oil?"

"Of course they will. They need the oil to run their engines."

"How did you get this idea?"

"After I witnessed this morning's fiasco and saw how Papavasile was insulted by what was said against God and the Church, I knew we had to do something to protect the youth of Moria."

"You can count on me." Patroklos said, with a surge of enthusiasm.

"Taki, you always have good ideas," George added, and flexed his muscles.

"Okay, Hercules, get those muscles ready for action."

21

THE UNHOLY TRINITY

Early Monday morning on October 1, 1944, Patroklos, George, and I—"the unholy trinity"—met in front of St. Basil's Church. I brought three two-gallon aluminum buckets, one for each to carry, that I had borrowed from Alexis's tavern. Leaving the buckets at the narthex, we went inside the church and lit three candles. Silently, I prayed that the people of Moria would be generous and willing in donating the olive oil we needed to exchange for the fabric to make uniforms.

My two friends looked at me curiously for they had noticed that—for the first time in my life—I wore long pants. They still wore shorts even though we were all at the age when Greek teenagers traditionally traded in their short pants for long ones.

"How do you like my trousers?" I asked.

"Oh, they look great. Where did you buy them?" they asked in subtle sarcasm.

"I altered a pair of my father's discarded summer pants that he had brought from America. I did the alterations myself, using a needle and thread as well as any tailor. I ripped apart the seam at the back and took in the sides to eliminate the fullness over my father's belly. Now the side pockets fall in the back around my buttocks."

"Taki, you are a genius!" George said, picking up his bucket and avoiding looking at me, apparently suppressing laughter.

"Do I look like a jerk? Just tell me the truth," I asked. I also wore one of my father's old caps that he had thrown away. I could still sense the odor that permeated that cap, my father's personal scent.

"Taki, all I see is a dear friend with noble intentions," George said.

"And you don't look like a jerk," Patroklos added. "I'm just envious that I don't have long pants to wear."

"You'll be even more envious when you hear what else has happened."

"Something good, I hope," George said.

"A week ago, as I was returning home from my father's olive grove with a basket full of olives, I saw a huge pile of refuse by the river, all discarded domestic items that the Nazis had confiscated. Several people were picking through the pile, looking for objects taken from their houses—beds, tables, chairs, ceramic urns. 'Good riddance!' I whispered and began to look through the pile. Then my eyes caught the skeleton of a bike. I could tell from the shiny red that it was *my* bike."

"You must have felt terrible," my friends responded in sadness.

"I did, seeing that fragment of my precious bike. Like a baby, I lifted that piece of metal in my arms, as the ugly memory of the Nazi officer who grabbed my bike surfaced in my mind. He had grabbed my brand-new bike from my hands and ridden it away. The Nazis may be gone but I still hate them."

"What did you do with the bike frame?" Patroklos asked.

"It was useless. Keeping it would only remind me of the Nazi's harassment and invasion in our home. So with a heavy heart, I took it to Mytilene and sold it to an iron merchant. With the money he paid me, I was able to buy a pair of used blue trousers that were hanging outside of a tailor's shop. It was a sailor's winter uniform, made of heavy, navy blue fabric. When I tried them on, I noticed that they stopped at least four inches above my ankles. Seeing my disappointment the tailor said, "No problem, I can fix it to perfection." He measured my height and said, "Come back in a week, and I'll have it ready for you."

When I put on the repaired sailors' pants and looked in the mirror, a bittersweet thought came to me. My once-cherished red bicycle, rendered useless by the Nazi occupation, had now been transformed into a very useful pair of pants. At the age of 18, that was only the second pair of pants I had owned, and I took very special care of them. Each time I wore those pants, I would take them off carefully at night, remove any dust, and then place them under my parents' mattress to maintain their pressed appearance. *Eventually, it is that same pair of pants that I would wear someday when I returned to America*, I thought.

"Shall we get started?" George asked. Then, looking at me seriously, he said, "Taki, your idea of defying the communists by forming these scout groups makes me look up to you as an older and wiser brother."

"Okay, brothers and friends," I said, "It's time for action. Take your bucket and let's go for the olive oil."

"What will I do, once my bucket is full of oil?" George asked naively, looking for some reaction from me.

"All of us must first drink the first full bucket," I said, and Patroklos and I could not control our laughter, knowing that I always teased George.

"Did I ask the wrong question? Why are you guys laughing?"

"It's good to start our day laughing; we have had enough tears in our time," I said. "Now, let's get going and act with confidence. Once our buckets are filled, we have to take it to

Alexis. He's provided a barrel for us in the backyard of his tavern. That's where we will gather the olive oil we collect."

It so happened that the olive harvest that year was unusually abundant. Every family was blessed with a surplus of this liquid gold. And each person whose door we knocked at generously poured olive oil into our buckets. While we were beyond exhaustion physically, by the end of the week we were elated to have the barrel filled with an estimated 80 to 85 gallons.

Koukoutas, a short and shrewd peddler, whose donkey had died, allowed us to use his two-wheeled wagon to carry the barrel to the city. The next question we had to face was: Who was going to take the role of the donkey and pull the wagon? Patroklos and I looked at George in silent appeal. He was stronger than the two of us put together.

"Okay, partners, I'll be the donkey to pull the wagon," he said, flexing his muscles. "You both can push the wagon from behind with all your strength. And you, Patroklos, you can sing some of your love songs on the way." George was a bit shorter than me, but he enjoyed challenges that proved his strength.

22

FROM OLIVE OIL TO FABRIC

On Tuesday, October 12, 1944, a barrel of olive oil, escorted by three teenage friends, made its painstaking way to the Kallamari Fabric Factory in Mytilene. Pulling and pushing the heavy wagon was incredibly exhausting. Nearly four miles later, tired and drenched in sweat, we arrived at the factory. We parked the wagon in front of the manager's office. An older man came out and introduced himself as Mr. Anthony Stevens. "I'm the manager," he said, "and Taki this must be the oil you told me about and that you wish to exchange for fabric." He offered us cups of cold water and asked us to sit in his office to wait as he excused himself. "I'll have your oil weighed, and I'll be back shortly."

On the wall behind a desk, there was a colorful painting of the factory building. And on each side of the painting were pictures, probably members of Mr. Stevens's family. One picture showcased a tall young man dressed in a decorated scoutmaster uniform. I pointed at that picture and said to my friends, "If this is his son and he is a scoutmaster, Mr. Stevens may really help us."

"What if the upper management decides not to barter?" George said.

"Drink the cold water and bite your tongue! Don't be negative," Patroklos said. The thought that Mr. Stevens's boss might refuse to barter made me anxious, but my eyes suddenly caught sight of a Byzantine icon of Christ behind Mr. Stevens's desk. Mentally, I prayed "Lord make this bartering possible. We need the fabric."

Finally, Mr. Stevens returned, in his right arm he held proudly a huge piece of snow-white fabric. It looked like the size of a small tablecloth. He handed it to me, saying, "Your 85 gallons of olive oil will get you 160 yards of this top-quality fabric."

I took the fabric in my hands; it was soft and looked perfect for making shirts, but I hesitated, not knowing whether to thank Mr. Stevens with a smile or to be sad, for I had been hoping the fabric would be khaki-colored. Noticing my lack of response, he said, "Aren't you satisfied with our fabric?"

"Of course, I'm satisfied, Mr. Stevens," I said, "but I was hoping the fabric would be khaki."

"The fabric we produce, and we are famous for, only comes in snow-white. But you could have it dyed khaki."

"We could, but how?" All three of us said with a sigh of relief.

"Yes, you can, and I will give you the name of a place that can dye it for you. It's named Nausika's Dry Cleaners and Restoration. And you can find it at the center of Mytilene's market. My sister-in-law is the owner. I'll call and tell her to help you."

"We cannot thank you enough, Mr. Stevens," I said, and as I firmly shook his hand and looked at the picture on the wall I asked, "The young man in scoutmaster uniform, is he your son?"

"He's my son. His name is Jason, and now he's a high-ranking officer in the Greek army."

"You must be so proud of him," I said.

"I am, I am," he said, nodding in agreement. "But you boys, are you strong enough to carry the fabric? It's very, very heavy."

Patroklos and I turned and looked at George, who proudly flexed his muscles again. "No problem, Mr. Stevens," he said.

As we prepared to leave the manager's office, three strong muscled men appeared at the door, each carrying a bolt of fabric. George grabbed one and threw it up in the air. "Light as a feather!" he said.

Once again, we loaded the wagon, this time with the all-white fabric, George agreeably took the donkey's place again and started to pull the wagon toward the center of the market.

When we arrived at Nausika's Dry Cleaners, to our surprise we were pleasantly received. "I've been expecting you," the owner said as if she knew us. "My name is Sophia. Mr. Stevens called me on the telephone and told me about your project."

"Thank you," I said. "My name is Takis, and these are my friends, George and Patroklos.

"Nice to meet you boys," she said. "You may bring in the fabric." I bowed my head in thanks, but I snuck a longer look at Sophia. She was a shapely, middle-aged woman with a heart-felt smile and blond hair tied into a bun with a blue ribbon. Her blue eyes spoke of kindness, and her light complexion gave the impression of a woman from Scandinavia.

Cautiously, we carried in the three bolts of fabric and placed them on a shiny dark marble counter. Gently, she unfolded each bolt of fabric and shook her head. "Beautiful material. And you want this beautiful fabric dyed khaki? Why?"

"We need to make scout uniforms for the boys and girls of Moria," I said.

"That's wonderful," she said. "Aspasia and Daphne, my twin daughters are both scouts. They love their scout meetings. And by the way, there's a very good seamstress here in Mytilene who made their uniforms. Her name is Asimina. She's one of my customers, and I could talk to her. Maybe she can help you."

"That's my sister," Patroklos proclaimed joyfully. "I know she will help."

As I winked at my friends, I said, "I'm so glad to hear about that. Now with Asimina's help, our goal is in sight."

Meanwhile I was trying to think of the best way to ask Sophia about how much it would cost to have our fabric dyed. I asked my two partners to go out and move our wagon out of the way and wait for it, so I would be alone for the negotiation.

"Mrs. Sophia, how long will it take to have our fabric dyed?" I asked.

"I'll have it ready for you in two weeks," she said.

"Will you be able to dye twenty-five yards in sky blue? We'll need that to make scarves for the scouts."

"That would be no problem," Sophia said.

"Much obliged, thank you! That's great," I said, and my heart began to pound anticipating my next question.

"Mrs. Sophia, I need to ask you another important question."

"Please do," she said graciously.

"Would you accept olive oil in payment for the dying?" I groaned inwardly thinking we could soon be knocking on doors again, asking for more olive oil.

"Olive oil for payment?" She pursed her lips, "Well, I would say half a gallon for each yard," she responded, looking at me straight in the eye.

We have 160 yards, I thought and that means we need to go back and ask the people of Moria for more olive oil, something like 80 more gallons. I felt a sudden tightness in my stomach.

"Mrs. Sophia, excuse me for a minute, I need to go out for a few minutes and discuss this with my friends."

Noticing the anxiety in my voice and discomfort in my face, she said, "You have good friends. It's good to discuss our deal with them."

"I'll tell them that we need more olive oil than I thought."

"Wait a minute. I have a better idea," she said with a smile. "Tell your friends that your fabric will be dyed at no cost, courtesy of Nausika's Dry Cleaners and the Kallamari Fabric Factory."

I couldn't believe what I was hearing. "Wow! Do you mean what you have just said?" I nearly lost my balance and waddled backwards.

"Of course, I mean what I said. My girls and Mr. Stevens would be happy to know that Moria's scouts, both boys and girls, will be wearing uniforms that Kallamari Fabric and their mother's store, Nausika, have provided.

"Mrs. Sophia, you are a saint. How can we ever thank you?" I asked.

"I'll tell you how," she said warmly. "When the Moria boys and girls are all dressed up in their khaki uniforms, take a picture of them and bring it to me. That's all the thanks I want. I will enlarge that picture and put it in the front window of my store."

"That's a promise," I said and dashed out to announce the good news to my friends. When they heard about Sophia's and Kallamari Fabric's donations, they jumped out of the wagon and began dancing and singing:

A scout is a young boy or a girl who lives by a code
To protect their honor, and take the high road.
They face temptations, but don't just give in.
The scout law gives them the courage to win.

From Olive Oil to Fabric

Scouts are trustworthy, faithful to the end
In keeping their promises, you can depend.
They are loyal to family, school, and to friends,
And to our great country that they defend.

23

ELIAS, THE TAILOR

Tall, thin, and slim, Anthony and Stanley, both in their late teens, were apprentice tailors working under Elias Passalis, the master tailor of Moria. Big-belly Elias, himself in his mid-thirties, had the gift of a good voice and was a cantor at St. Basil's Church. His chanting was vibrant and inspirational. We had become good friends and he was eager to teach me the Byzantine chant so I could accompany him in church services.

One evening, I decided to visit his tailor shop when his apprentices were not there. I was happy to find him alone. After my initial greeting, *kalispera* (good evening), I said, "Elias, I came to talk to you about something very important."

"Not about Eleni, that pretty girl you love?" he said with assumed concern.

"No, not about Eleni," I said. Six months before, I had confided to him that I was in love with Eleni, and told him that I was not so sure if she felt the same way about me.

Then he said, "Well, dear friend, I have some love poems for you. If you send them to your Eleni, she would be crazy about you."

"Did you send these poems to Elpis, before you married her?"

Elias, the Tailor

"I sure did, and she fell in love with me and wanted to marry me. Fifteen years later, we still love each other."

"Elias, I didn't come to you this evening to talk about love poems. I came to talk to you about action."

"You sound serious," he said, his hazel eyes reflecting a ray of interest. "Tell me what's on your mind."

"Elias, do you remember what happened last September 10, after the Nazis left our island?" Suddenly my heart began to pound rapidly, as Seraphim's communistic speech echoed in my ears again.

"You seem upset," Elias commented.

"Enraged is the word." I responded. "As I heard Seraphim, my former teacher, telling the people of Moria that God is a myth, that religion is the opium of the masses, and that we don't have to go to church anymore, I hated him. He also claimed that Marx, Lenin, and Stalin are the powerful trinity, the strong leaders who would liberate us from the yoke of plutocrats and make the world a paradise in our time. 'We promise freedom and equality!' he said, and ended his speech saying that the church of St. Basil will be converted into a large auditorium for entertainment, dances, and lectures. Elias, tell me, how can anyone accept Seraphim's communistic soap bubbles?"

"Taki, I'm a man of faith, and I'm glad I was not there to hear Seraphim. He is one of the poisonous snakes of communism," Elias said.

"What do you think we can do about these communist agitators?"

"Perhaps nothing immediately, but my friends and I have decided to protect Moria's young and innocent boys and girls from the communist ideas, and teach them principles and values, such as: truth, faith in God, help, love, kindness, gentleness, and respect for our country and our parents."

"Taki, you sound like Papavasile," Elias said with a smile,

"and you and your friends have good intentions, but what if those communist leaders prevent you?"

"I'm not afraid of them. Already my cousin, Mitsos, a fanatic communist, has threatened to put me behind bars because I did not attend one of their comrade meetings."

"How did you respond?" Elias asked.

"Angry and disappointed that my own cousin was *one of them*. I looked at him defiantly in the face, gave him the scout salute, and recited,

> On my honor, I will do my best
> To do my duty to God and my country and to obey
>   the Scout Law;
> To help other people at all times;
> To keep myself physically strong, mentally awake,
>   and morally straight,
> and I will faithfully abide with the rules of the scouts.

"I have one question for you," Elias said. "Why are you telling me all this tonight?"

"I have secured enough fabric to make thirty-two Boy Scout uniforms. I am hoping that you will tell your apprentices Anthony and Stanley that they can work at your store after working hours to make these uniforms."

"And who is going to make scout uniforms for the girls?" Elias asked.

"My friend Patroklos's sister, Asimina, is already in charge of the Girl Scout uniforms. It is my hope that a couple troops of boy and girl scouts can bring good spirit back to their families and to our little town of Moria."

"I could say that to Anthony and Stanley, but would they listen? They may be already converts to communism, themselves. Why don't you ask them yourself?" Elias said.

Elias, the Tailor

"I did approach them earlier today to ask if they would be willing to make uniforms for a troop of boy scouts."

"What did they say?"

"And who is going to pay us?" Anthony asked, and Stanley waited to hear my answer.

"Money, I don't have," I said, "but I do have the best quality cured olives to give you."

"Cured olives?" Anthony reacted with a smirk.

"Oh, I love cured olives and so does my family," Stanley said.

"If each of you can make sixteen uniforms, I will supply each of you with one jar of cured olives each week for the next four weeks," I said.

"And you have that quantity of cured olives?" Anthony asked in disbelief.

I reassured them that I have stored eighty jars this year in a cool place in our basement. For each week that they work, I was sure I could bring one of those jars to each of them.

"Did they accept your offer?"

"'Okay,' they said. 'We'll think about it, but we might want something more than your cured olives, like money.'"

"Elias, I wonder if you could persuade them that this is a worthwhile cause."

"After what you told me, I plan to do exactly that," said Elias with a determined confidence. "It would be good experience for them in learning their trade. And you don't have to give them anything. They work for me, and your project will be realized in my store."

"Then we should make you our Honorary Scout President."

"Thank you," Elias said, "but no honors for me. Let this be our secret."

"And how can I pay you?" I asked.

"A couple jars of those quality cured olives will be enough."

"What about your apprentices?"

"One jar for each of them will be just fine." Elias shook my hand and said, "Now get home and get some rest. You look exhausted. Tomorrow bring the fabric to my store, and I will start cutting it down for the uniforms. But I'll need each of the boys to come to the store for the correct measurement. Just bring four boys at a time."

"Elias Passalis," I said, still holding onto his hand, "you are a God-sent saint."

"You must have just seen the halo around my head," Elias grinned.

24

HAIL, OH LIBERTY, HAIL!

"Expect the unexpected, or you won't find it," wrote the Greek philosopher Heraclitus some 2,500 years ago. His words became a reality for me in February 1945. The scout movement had caught on quickly and had already spread like wildfire, bringing new life to several other towns and villages on the island. I had worked with joy to develop the scouting program, and as Papavasile praised my effort, he said, "I'm glad to hear that young girls are part of the scouting movement."

Patroklos's sister, Asimina, with a small group of skilled mothers, prepared twenty-four uniforms. The big question was who would be the Girl Scout leader?"

"Electra Englezou is a high school senior," Papavasile said with conviction.

"Do you think she would accept the office as a scout leader?" I asked.

"I will speak with her about taking an active part in our scout program. She is a person of many talents and interests and has a very strong faith," Papavasile said. Knowing that her brother, Lefteris, is a staunch communist and would be against the idea, Electra did accept the challenge. She, too, had heard Seraphim's speech the previous September and was still shocked by what he'd said against God and the Church.

The month of March is the harbinger of summer days for Greek people. Young and old begin wearing lighter and more colorful clothes. Since my elementary school days, I have looked forward to March 25, the national holiday. The entire Greek nation celebrates that day in March as a double holiday: Greek Independence Day, a historical holiday commemorating the start of the War of Independence against the Ottoman Empire in 1821; and the Annunciation, a religious feast day, commemorating the Archangel Gabriel's appearance to the Virgin Mary, when he told her that she would become the mother of Jesus Christ, the Son of God.

March 25 that year was a sunny but not-too-warm day and there was not a single cloud in the sky. The people of Moria were ready to commemorate their independence from the Ottoman Turks after four hundred years of captivity and were also excited to celebrate the fact that Nazi forces no longer occupied their island.

Early that morning, ignoring the hostile looks of a bunch of noisy communists, thirty-two boy scouts and twenty-four girl scouts, dressed in their new khaki uniforms, entered St. Basil's Church in two straight lines and came to a halt by the altar. Slowly, older men and women filled the pews. Many men and young adults were not present. Papavasile, in his festive vestments, raised the Gospel high and chanted in stentorian tones, "Today salvation has come upon us. Let's glorify the One who has risen from the dead and restored our freedom."

In another part of town, a larger number of rebellious men and women attended a rally of the communists in front of the town hall. Under the Soviet flag, a group of them raised their voices:

Rise young and older people,
And come out in every street.

Hail, Oh Liberty, Hail!

With loaded gun on hand,
Kill every fascist you meet.

They sang many more well-rehearsed songs in a Russian tone, promising freedom and equality for everyone in the audience.

When church services ended, Papavasile blessed the scouts and touched each one on the forehead with a silver cross, as they formed a line and marched out in the courtyard. There, at the front of the line, George tested his bugle softy, and Patroklos hung the drum over his shoulder. I nodded at Electra, the Girl Scout leader. I then took a deep breath and shouted joyfully, "Forward. March!"

Vigorously, we all marched to the center of town, just as I had dreamed a long time ago. The scouts knew what we planned to do. In a meeting the day before, I'd told them, "Boys and girls, tomorrow we are going to parade through the Moria marketplace. We will pause in front of the town hall, salute the Greek flag, and sing our national anthem. Should you see or hear anything against you, ignore it. Keep your head straight, and keep marching. We may face opposition, but there is no need to worry."

Once we arrived at the town hall, a number of communist rebels raised their voices in a Soviet song, but George blew his bugle forcefully and drowned them out. In view of the noisy reaction that our presence evoked among the rebels, we began to sing courageously the Greek national anthem:

Ap'ta kokkala vgalmeni   (From the sacred bones,
Ton Ellinon ta iera,   Of the Hellenes arisen,
Ke san prota andriomeni,   Brave again as you were,
Here, o here, eleftheria!   Hail, oh liberty, hail!)

An unexpected pandemonium broke out, followed by a thunderous applause. And as we continued with the next verse, all the people present joined us in singing,

From the Hellenes of old,
Whose dying brought us
Life and spirit free,
Now with ancient valor rising,
Let's hail you, Oh Liberty!

I returned home that day with great joy, proud of the impression our Boy and Girl Scouts had made. I believed that my intention to defy the communist leaders and plant the seeds of love and respect for our country was off to a very good start.

But when I arrived home, I found my father sitting on the sofa with Ma, Kiki, and Jimmy on his right, and staring at a piece of yellow paper that he held in his hand. "This is a telegram from the American government," he said, looking at me for my reaction.

"Taki, good news, we are going to America!" he said excitedly.

For some reason, the news did not impress me, and the thoughts I could not express were: *But I don't want to go to America. This is my homeland, the place that I have grown to love. I don't want to leave Eleni, the girl I love, and my friends behind.*

I excused myself and ran out of the house to meet my friends. I found George and Patroklos at the back of Alexis's tavern, still wearing the scout uniform, drinking ouzo, and having a fun time. When I saw them, I burst into tears, crying inconsolably. "Hey, Scout Leader, what's going on? Why are you crying?" George asked.

"My father just got a telegram from America, and he said

that soon we will be going to America." Tears rolled down my cheeks.

"Taki!" Patroklos grabbed my hand affectionately and said, "You are going to America, and you are crying? You should be happy, and *we* should be crying for having to stay in this accursed land."

Then George took over the role of comforter and began to hammer at me. "First we had the Persians, later the Turks, then as late as yesterday we had the Nazis, now we have the communists." He stretched his arms, hugged me and said, "Taki, I will miss you very much, and you may miss us, but get out of this place as soon as you can. Go to America and find peace. Be happy!" Then with a semi-smile, he said, "Just don't forget us—or better yet, send an invitation and bring us to America."

"I'll remember that," I said.

"Now sit with us and have some ouzo," Patroklos said.

25

A TIME OF CHAOS

The communistic chaos with its confusing promises—freedom from the plutocrats and a better life for the innocent population—lasted several months. Anger, hate, hostile fights among Moria's families—sons against fathers, young women, even sisters against each other, wives against husbands and daughters, husbands against wives, and one family against another family. During this emotionally agonizing period, our priest, Papavasile, availed himself and tried to counsel and comfort people who were despondent and hurting every day, with his kind words and presence.

How well I remember his loving and fatherly advice, "Taki, our country has been accursed, dark days are ahead. Leave Moria and return to America, your birthplace, and tell the Americans that Greece will always be their faithful ally."

It so happened that a month after the initial invitation, the America Embassy in Athens informed us that there will be a delay of seven or eight months for our departure to the United States. I was very delighted about the delay. This gave me ample time to visit Papavasile, attend church services, and be with my friends.

Christmas time was around the corner, and I was feeling very upset that three of my adult cousins—two males and one female—had become communists and tried to spread their political propaganda. I liked them very much and wanted to reconcile my feelings with them before leaving Moria. I spoke to Papavasile about this and with interest he asked, "Taki, how are you going to approach these cousins?"

"I need a creative plan," I said. "Thank God, the celebrations of Christmas and New Year are about three weeks away. I should come up with some attractive plan."

"Let's pray to our Lord for guidance," Papavasile said. Approximately ten days before Christmas, I woke up one morning smiling with a sudden idea that surfaced in my mind to get the communists and nationalists together. An attractive invitation was needed, I thought, such as: On behalf of the Boy and Girl Scouts, your sons and daughters, you are invited to meet at the school auditorium on New Year's Eve, at 8 p.m. to celebrate the arrival of the New Year, 1946. Vasilopita and Cherry Cognac, a special liqueur will be served.

I had the invitation printed and sent to every family in Moria. But my plan needed action. I met with my friends, Patroklos and George, and discussed the plan for the New Year celebration. "Do you think the communists will be there?" George asked doubtfully.

"Perhaps, out of curiosity, they will be there," Patroklos said.

"I sent the invitation to every family," I said, "and it was signed by Electra and Takis, The Scout Leaders of your sons and daughters."

Noticing my friends' hesitation, I said, "Guys, I need your help. George, can you take care of St. Basil's Vasilopetas sweet bread?"

"Where will I find the flour?"

"Some from your father's bakery," I said, "and you can knock on a few doors in your neighborhoods. Ask each mother to give you a cup of flour and tell them about the celebration. Simple enough, guys?"

"Patroklos, do you think your mother can knead and bake a few of St. Basil's bread?"

"She will be honored," Patroklos said.

"Okay! Okay, scout leader," said George, and looking at me in defiance asked, "And what are you going to do next?"

"I'll be eating the sweet bread alone and I will not give you even a small piece, dear friend, George."

"Guys, we have a little more than a week ahead, so let's get busy. And I promise you, it will be the best-ever New Year's celebration."

Eagerly, George knocked on many doors and brought pounds of flour to Margo, Patrokos's mother, who welcomed the idea to knead and bake the Vasilopitas. "The flour that George brought me," she said, "was enough to make at least five huge pieces of St. Basil's sweet bread."

My parents, who were preparing for our departure to America, seemed to ignore my plans. But late on New Year's Eve, when my father saw me holding the big bottle filled with Cherry Cognac, he asked, "Where are you going with that bottle?"

"Dad, you know tonight is the 1946 New Year's celebration."

"I do know that, but did you know that bottle was used for olive oil?"

"I did not know," I said in utter shock and realized the olive oil had risen as high as the top of the bottleneck. Being very upset at my oversight, I said angrily, "Dad, I had asked Alexis to give me a big bottle, and he pointed at three dark bottles on a high shelf. I picked one and anxiously ran straight to a liquor store to have the bottle filled with Cherry Cognac, a special liqueur."

"Now, at this late hour, all the stores are closed," my father said.

"Well we still have to use this expensive liqueur," I said, and hurriedly, I put the bottle on a table and went to look in our medical cabinet in the next room. There I found what I needed, a huge piece of cotton. I made the sign of the cross on the cotton and asked for God's help. I rolled a few pieces of cotton into braids. After a deep breath to settle my anxiety, I lowered one braid gently into the bottle's neck where the oil had accumulated. The anticipated miracle happened. The cotton began to absorb the oil. Within a few minutes, I shouted joyfully, "The Cherry Cognac is ready to reach every human heart in Moria."

By the time I arrived at the school auditorium, my friends were there already setting up a huge table for the five fragrant Vasilopetas and lining up small glasses, which we borrowed from Alexis's tavern, for the Cherry Cognac liqueur.

The school auditorium was filled to capacity. Moria's men and women noisily sat in anticipation for what was to take place. Electra and I stood behind the table and bowed as Papavasile offered a brief opening prayer.

Directed and rehearsed by Electra, youthful voices of Boy and Girl Scouts started a New Year's song:

The old year has come to an end,
It is time for joy and celebration.
We no longer need be concerned
For past disagreements and hurts
The New Year has ended them.
Good Year, New Year, Joyful Year is finally here.
With no hesitation, enjoy our New Year's celebration.

This refrain was followed and repeated more times by the audience and the applause thundered through the auditorium. As I looked around, I spotted my three cousins who were applauding. In salute, I raised my hand, and they slowly found themselves near the big table. I walked closer to them and wished them a Happy New Year. We embraced and kissed each other, and Iphigenia, my oldest cousin, whispered with a smile, "Taki, you never cease to amaze me. Thank you."

Electra and two young mothers kept cutting St. Basil's Vasilopita bread in small pieces, and George and Patroklos distributed them to each person, along with a shot of Cherry Cognac liqueur. It was 1 a.m. and more New Year's songs were sung by the participants as they all cheerfully embraced and kissed each other and shouted joyfully, "Happy New Year!"

Part II
GROWING

26

THE PROMISED LAND

And so it was that my family escaped the chaos of post-World War II. Fortunately, the American government had invited all American citizens who were residing in other countries during the War to return to the United States. Because my father and I were American citizens, the rest of the family—my stepmother and her two children, Kiki and Jimmy who were not citizens—were also included in the invitation.

The news that I would soon be leaving for America prompted my friend, Eleni, to share with a couple of her girl-friends that she loved me. They, in turn, informed me of the news, which gave me both joy and sadness. Before my family and I departed from the island, I managed to meet secretly with Eleni a few times. She told me that she had always loved me, but her mother had other plans for her. There was an older man, a realtor whom her mother had wanted to be Eleni's husband.

"I'm just going to America for a short time," I told her, "but I promise you, once I make enough money, I will return and marry you and make our home in Lesvos, in our little town Moria." Tears of loving feelings rolled down Eleni's cheeks, as she whispered, "I shall be waiting for your return and will pray to God for your safety."

Did I really have any idea at the age of twenty, what kind of job I could find or what amount of money I would earn? Yet I made a promise. Where did I find the courage for this undertaking? Where did I get the strength to say goodbye to my youth in Greece? How was I able to leave behind loving relatives and intimate friends? And how would I endure the heartbreak of parting from my first love, Eleni? Would I ever be able to fulfill my promise to return to her some day?

After we arrived in Athens, where we had to wait our turn to embark on a transatlantic American ship, I began experiencing excruciating pain in my testicles. Frightened, I put off telling my father. I feared that he might misinterpret my pain, and he might be upset that my situation could delay our departure to America.

Perhaps, God is punishing me for my sins, a thought that was the result of growing up among uneducated, yet kind-hearted people, who believed that anytime we did something wrong, God would punish us. This belief was confirmed whenever I went to church. There was a huge eye over the altar. It was the eye of God, I was told, which could read our minds and see all our actions. As the pain increased, I carefully reviewed my past actions; whatever I could remember.

When I was 5, I found a coin that a poor girl had lost. I never gave it to her. I saw her crying and felt terrible. Thinking about the heartless thing I'd done, now at the age of 20, I could not forgive myself. When I get a job in America, I'll be sending her lots of money, I thought, and felt some relief. But more sins surfaced in my mind. *At the age of 6, I learned how to open my stepmother's secret closet and stole sweets that she kept for her guests. And during war and famine when Moria's people were dying of starvation, I jumped in a neighbor's garden one night and stole some artichokes. Yet, another sin kept nagging me. This was the worst sin I had ever committed. When my stepmother punished me for going swimming without her consent,*

I attacked her with rage and yanked off her necklace. What a terrible thing to do, I thought.

In recollecting these horrible wrongs, I went to church and confessed. The priest prayed for me and reassured me that our God is a loving God and does not punish. I felt better when he said, "Our sins or bad choices cause problems and emotional pain; they punish us. But when we realize the bad things we have done and repent, God forgives." He paused, looked fatherly in my sad face and said, "Taki, it's time to forgive yourself."

So it was that I let go of my village beliefs and chose to believe in a God of love who loves us all unconditionally, not because we deserve to be loved, but because God is love. As I prayed, "Lord be not mindful of the sins of my younger years," the swelling increased, and so did the pain. It was time to tell my father about it. In seeing my pain, he asked to see my genitals, and when he did, he whispered unsympathetically, "Have you been to a brothel?"

"No!" I screamed indignantly. I knew brothels legally existed in the capital city of Lesvos, but I had never been to one. I had never so far seen a nude female body, not even my sister's when she was an infant. My stepmother appeared before us always fully dressed. My problem was beyond the range of my father's knowledge, so he took me to a doctor. As the doctor examined me, my father leaned over his shoulder worrying, I am sure, that I might have caught somehow a serious disease. But the doctor diagnosed me as suffering from the mumps, an infection that can be serious when it affects the testicles of young men. To avoid further complications, the doctor said that I should be isolated in a dark room and stay in bed. "Don't let him get up. Get him a bedpan, and don't let him come out of the dark room."

I was very frightened. No one was allowed in the room other than my stepmother, who tiptoed twice near my bed to place some food—boiled rice sprinkled with dry mint—on a night table. As I prayed to God to make me well, scary thoughts kept interrupting my prayers. What if I didn't get well, and when it was time to embark for America, I could not go? *After all that pain, this scenario might not be so bad*, I thought. *I could go back to our island and be with Eleni.* Then other, more frightening, thoughts came: *Will I ever be able to get married or make love to a woman? Will I ever have children?*

Medicine and rest in a dark room helped to reduce my pain. A few days later, when I was feeling much better, my father brought us the latest news. The Marine Shark, a huge military ship, had arrived in the harbor of Piraeus to take us to America. "We need to get ready for departure, most likely tomorrow or the next day."

The Marine Shark took eleven days filled with anxiety and anticipation to make the trip from Athens to New York. One evening, while we were still in the middle of the Atlantic Ocean, I sat alone in the stern, immersed in a thick fog of memories, reminiscing about the life I had left behind. As the ship plowed the waves, Papavasile's sad voice echoed in my ears, *Taki, a curse has fallen upon us. Dark days are ahead for our homeland. Leave Moria as soon as you can and go to America.* As the priest's voice faded, it left me with a smile and a sigh, a bittersweet melody. I felt as if I were on Noah's Ark: God had spared my family's life and myself. I gazed at the swirling ocean, awed by the magical wonders and secrets of its depths. The foaming swells shook me back to reality—I was on a huge ship bound for the New World, embarking on a new beginning. It was a similar journey in 1929 when, as a small unhappy child at the age of 3, I had crossed the Atlantic in the other direction on the way to a different totally unknown world, Greece.

As the Marine Shark's ferocious whistle signaled time for dinner, the whole ship vibrated as people emerged from their cabins. Here I was, the olive picker, embarking on an adventure that promised even more than Moria's communist leaders had promised—heavenly life while on earth. I stood up to stretch my legs, still gazing at the waves. I felt no appetite. Mixed emotions wrestled within me, making me feel weak. I began to tremble like a frightened child.

Each step forward, required me to let go of something, thus my way was paved with a series of surrenders. I had to give up some of my deepest and most meaningful relationships, cherished experiences and places. I struggled to adjust to an unfamiliar land and establish new relationships. I had to let go of so much—ideas about my life, plans that were no longer feasible—yet holding tightly to my belief in God's presence in my life brought some relief.

The changes, although difficult to accept and implement, helped me to mature and to discover who I really was. As the journey of life continues, most of us have difficulty handling endings. Yet all of us must learn to do so, for we will all experience many endings throughout our lives. While it was difficult for me to leave the colorful land of Greece where I had spent my formative years, burying forever many of my youthful dreams and plans, I had to travel across the Atlantic to find my future.

27

MY BIRTHPLACE

When my family and I arrived in New York, we took a taxi to my Uncle Nick's house in North Philadelphia, Pennsylvania, on June 21, 1946. And thus began the second part of my life. Uncle Nick's welcome was warm and enthusiastic. His wife, Karen, had prepared a luscious dinner for us that included an array of delicious foods. Excited, my father, Uncle Nick and his wife rumbled on endlessly, speaking a language that the rest of us did not understand.

Adjacent to the living room was a dining area with a big table that was covered with a light-brown tablecloth. The table was set with knives and forks placed symmetrically on each side of porcelain plates, and next to each setting was a folded napkin. Uncle Nick and my father had begun to savor tall glasses of cold beer and munched on crackers that were spread with a smelly pâté. I could tell that the brothers were happy to be together after so many years. But what was that bad odor coming from their drinking? My father, noticing my sour face expression said, "You probably would not like this cheese. It's famous and expensive, and it's called Limburger cheese." I swore under my breath, thinking, *I would not ever taste that kind of famous cheese as long as I lived.*

Finally, our two families sat down to eat our first meal

together in America. Uncle Nick asked me to sit on his right, and his wife sat across from him. His wife, Karen, a big woman with a light-complexion and silvery short hair, sat silently after serving each one of us. Glancing gently at what was served, I noticed that there were no cured olives on the table, a familiar tradition for me. Olives always accompanied even our holiday meals in Greece.

Uncle Nick paused to teach me table etiquette, insisting that I learn to handle silverware. He pointed out that two knives and a spoon must be on the right and two forks on the left of my dish. Next to it should be a smaller dish for bread and butter.

In the last four years, we had had no bread at all, and butter, if it was ever available, was rarely used for cooking. My eating utensils had consisted only of a fork and a spoon. At this special occasion, there was an abundance of food on the table, but I had a hard time eating. It smelled different and did not appeal to me, even though I was hungry. For the first time in my life, I saw slices of turkey meat, sweet potatoes, and cranberry sauce. Noticing my nervous hesitation in using the knife to cut the turkey into smaller pieces, Uncle Nick offered me a Coke. While he probably observed me eating slowly and not drinking the Coke, he surely could not have been aware that I was praying that this meal be my last one in this house.

After a few sad goodbyes, Uncle Nick directed my father, stepmother, and siblings to take a bus that will easily take them to an apartment that he had found for them on South Broad Street. A couple hours later, as the rest of my family had already left, Aunt Karen cleaned the table and worked in the kitchen. Uncle Nick escorted me into the living room and pointed to a comfortable chair. He sat across on a leather recliner. "This is my favorite seat in the house," he said with a pleasant smile. He was a swarthy man, tall like my father, and austere. "A giant of knowledge and wealth," according to my father, his older brother, and had been in America since 1905. My father adored him and had convinced me that Uncle Nick would be my guardian, and the overseer of my education. For what seemed to me a long time, we sat in the living room where he asked many questions, mostly about our eleven days of travel. Mindful of my lack of table manners and unable to imitate my uncle's dexterity, I remained silent. Uncle Nick carried his glass of beer, drank it slowly, wiped his lips, and rested on his favorite recliner.

"America...America!" he said, "the land of wealth and opportunity! A great country, Peter, my dear nephew." He paused, taking another sip of his beer, "Do you mind being called Peter?" Uncle Nick had decided that Americans would have a hard time calling me Taki.

"I prefer being called Peter," I said, smiling and hoping somehow to connect with him.

"How lucky you are to return to America!" he said, pausing for another sip of beer. "You can even become the president of the United States if you want. But I would not be satisfied with you even if you did become the president. I want you to be more than a president."

More than a president? Is he drunk? I had no frame of reference for what he was trying to tell me. I kept staring at him without blinking, trying to read his mind. I was but a village boy, an olive picker who had survived starvation, four years under the Nazi occupation, and the communistic propaganda. I couldn't speak a word of English at this point, and yet he expected me to be more than the president of a nation! I smiled nervously at the very idea.

"You are my brother's son. I have high expectations for you," he said. As he continued talking about his ideas, it became evident that my uncle wallowed in megalomania. He considered himself an authority on many aspects of life—socioeconomic, political, religious, and philosophical—and he was taking it upon himself to plan my future, although he knew nothing of my life or even what kind of person I was.

I kept looking at him, waiting to hear what other plans he had in mind. He cleared his throat and in a more serious tone of voice he said, "Remember who you are. You and I come from noble ancestors, Socrates, Plato, Aristotle, Alexander the Great." I had some elementary knowledge of these famous names from a history course in high school, but what did they have to do with me, at this time in America—a village boy, who aspired only to get a job, save enough money, return to Greece to be with his friends and share his life with a beautiful woman, the love of his dreams?

I decided that if I could endure and survive the winds of World War II, I could and would survive being under my uncle's rule until I could plan a strategy of escape.

28

TEMPLE UNIVERSITY

Two weeks later, my uncle and I walked on North Broad Street, crossing the city of Philadelphia on our way to Temple University. I was in awe and felt ecstatic, energized by my new surroundings. The flow of straight streets and avenues, the symmetry of trees planted along sidewalks, the majesty of the buildings—what a fantastic sight! This mythical elegance was the product of what the New World called industrialization.

This is the promised land! This is my birthplace, the city where I spent the first three years of my life, I kept thinking with joy. Why did my father ever leave this earthly paradise and take me to a little Greek island? It seemed that now I was making a transition from yesterday's agony to today's ecstasy.

Uncle Nick and I arrived at the gate of the university. I was dumbfounded at the size of the buildings and the swarms of people, both young and old, nicely groomed, and well dressed, moving to and fro, carrying books, talking and laughing, and speaking a language foreign to my ears. My heart pounded rapidly as all my yesterdays flooded my mind. I suddenly felt homesick for my little town of Moria with its narrow streets and whitewashed houses, where every stone had been put in place by human hands, and where people were bound together by invisible ties—*memories sweeter than honey.* Philadelphia was a different world of sights, sounds, and smells; it was a world where multitudes of well-fed and well-dressed people bustled about their business.

When we entered the registrar's office, we were welcomed with smiles and amenities. My uncle introduced me to several important people. With a grin on his face, he rambled on, turning periodically toward me. I smiled and shrugged my shoulders. I didn't understand a word, but I assumed it was about being accepted as a university student. After our brief encounter with school authorities, Uncle Nick told me that this university expected me to become fluent in the English language before being accepted for premedical studies. "After you learn English," he said, "you can be accepted in this school, and someday you will make a fine doctor and I will be a proud uncle."

"A doctor!" I objected in amazement. A few days ago, I was to become more than a president; today I am to become a doctor! What had given him such an idea? What made him think he had the right to decide what I was going to be? Medicine? A doctor? Such professions had never crossed my mind. As far as I was concerned, any career decision had to be exclusively mine. Yet, I decided that the time was not appropriate to confront my uncle. I realized that my stay at his house must be short. I had come to this great country to enjoy freedom only to find myself under this man's domination. I needed a plan of escape.

On our way out, on both sides of the corridor leading us back to North Broad Street were columns that served as pedestals for the busts of important historical personalities. Uncle Nick pointed to the busts of "our ancestors." I recognized the names and was duly impressed. More interesting to me was a bust of a sphinx. Engraved in ancient Greek, on a shiny plaque below was a riddle:

> What walks on four feet in the morning?
> On two feet at noon, and
> On three feet in the evening?

I had come across this riddle in high school. It seemed to me, then, to be merely humorous. That day, however, the sphinx's riddle struck me as much more than a mere test of wit. *Walking on four feet* symbolized infancy, a state of dependency. *Walking on two at noon* implied adult years. *Walking on three* referred to old age, when a person might need a cane for support. Proud that I could read the Greek inscription, I understood its valuable lesson of wisdom. It was time for me to *stand* in the world on my own two feet and to make my own decisions. The time had come for me to lead a truly adult life, to discover who I was and what the meaning of life was all about. What was it that lay behind the world's facade, animating it, ordering it in a particular direction? I needed to find out.

After our visit to Temple University, it was evening and the three of us sat at the dinner table eating the meal Uncle Nick's wife had prepared. He buttered his bread and spoke to his wife in English. She responded oddly, saying, "Oh my gosh! Oh my gosh!" as her face mirrored his disappointment. With the exception of a few words—*good morning, hello, goodbye, thank you*—that I had already learned and remembered while I was still on the ocean liner, I understood not a single word of their dialogue. His periodic glance toward me with a grimace implied that I was the subject of conversation. I thought he might be expressing his indignation that he had taken me to one of the best universities in the country. His advice was that

I could become a doctor, but he probably realized that I was not impressed with the idea.

Not being able to sleep that night, I thought of running away. But where could I go without direction, money, or knowing how to speak English? In the mornings, as Uncle Nick and his wife were preparing to leave for work, I said, "I don't feel well...a little nauseous..." while pressing my hand against my stomach, feigning discomfort.

29

STANDING MY GROUND

I was aware that my return to America offered me a special kind of opportunity to break with the social conditions that had carried me thus far and to do something really new and different. I felt an urge, a force, a deep prompting of my spirit, pushing me to pursue a life that made sense to *me*. I aimed to live a life of simplicity—to be socially useful, ethical, and productive—and to earn enough money to return to the island of Lesvos, where I had experienced my first love. How could I ever explain such thoughts to Uncle Nick, who in forty years had not even once visited his native land?

One day I mustered enough courage to tell him my decision: "I want to become a priest." This was a yearning that my heart had nurtured since childhood. The Church and its rituals had always fascinated me. I saw it as a sacred source of comfort. It was a place where I felt welcomed. When I learned to sing the church hymns, it became a place where I felt recognized. I wanted to be a priest. It felt as if the priesthood was my mission in life and my destiny.

"A priest!" Uncle Nick objected angrily. "What's wrong with you? You're turning your back on a promising future in the world of medicine. I took you to one of the finest universities in America! It doesn't make sense at all."

I stood my ground, "I've always wanted to be a priest."

Disappointment cast a shadow over his face, and not looking at me, he said, "Peter, that's really too bad." He didn't say another word to me that night. In the morning when I said, "Uncle Nick, I don't feel well," he responded with, "That makes two of us. I'm going to work. You can stay home and think about your decision." He shut the door angrily without even saying goodbye.

Regardless how good my uncle's intentions were, I wanted to follow my inner voice. I needed to be the one to decide what my career could be. I kept reminding myself as I followed my journey that I was a worthy human being and I could do good things for myself and for others. I tried to understand that my uncle projected on me his own ideas. Ideas of becoming a doctor could ruin other people's lives and my life. It was important for me to follow the desire of my heart. I was not aiming for the stars for I knew I could not reach them, yet I appreciated their light that made the nights delightful.

I admit that sometimes I did admire certain priests who seemed better, more gifted, more talented, more of everything. One of them had a great melodic voice, another was an eloquent speaker, still another was a prolific writer. At least that was my perception. But before I had succumbed to comparisons, *wishing I could be like anyone of them,* simply I realized that I cannot be like anybody else. I can only be who I am, and that's okay. I had to accept my true self, love and respect my being. Today, not tomorrow or next week, but today at this hour, accept and be grateful to God for His gift of my life. I chose to look deeper into myself and saw my real wish for my life. *I wanted to become a priest.*

By the third week in Uncle Nick's house, the atmosphere had grown thick with tension. One day he said coldly, "Okay, okay, why don't you stay home today? There is a bottle of coca cola in the refrigerator...It might help your stomach," and he hurried out of the house. His wife was already outside waiting for him. I got off the short, narrow couch where I had been sleeping uncomfortably at nights for the past two and a half weeks and tiptoed in circles around the living room, trying to come up with a viable escape plan.

Accidently, I spotted a small desk in the corner of a little side room. A ray of sunlight from a nearby window fell across a desk, spotlighting a magical object—a telephone. *Wow, maybe I can call Aunt Victoria*, I thought, approaching the desk with slight trepidation.

I knew my Aunt Victoria's story from my Yiayia. She was my mother's younger sister who had become a teacher. Years ago, while in America, my mother had found a potential husband for her, a Greek immigrant named Louis Christophas. She'd told him about her sister, and before too long, Louis, who wanted to marry a Greek woman, went to Greece, met Victoria, and married her a month later. He brought her back to the United States where the two newlyweds settled in Media, Pennsylvania.

A little leatherette booklet lay next to the phone. The faded letters on the cover could hardly be read, *"St. George Greek Church, Philadelphia, PA. Phone numbers of Greek immigrants.* I opened the booklet and flipped through the pages and found the letter *C.* Several names started with *C*, and there I saw "Louis and Victoria Christopher." I thought that Louis Christophas might have Americanized his last name to Christopher. Under their names in bold print was a phone number. I made the sign of the cross and prayed to God for help. As my heartbeat accelerated, my trembling index finger dialed the number.

After the fourth ring, I heard a high-pitched female voice, "Hellooo."

"Is this Victoria Christophas or Christopher?" I asked with hesitation.

"Yes...Yes, yes, it's me! And you must be Takis, my nephew. I could tell by your voice....Oh, my God, I'm gonna faint," she cried. "My mother, your Yiayia, wrote me that you were coming to America, but she didn't say when."

"Aunt Victoria, please don't faint and don't cry, but can you come and get me out of this house?" I said imploringly.

"Sweetheart, you sound upset. Is anything wrong?"

"I don't like living in this house."

"I'll come today, but where are you right now?" She asked with concern.

"I'm at Uncle Nick's house in North Philadelphia. I've been here for almost three weeks. If I have to live here for another week, I'll go crazy."

"I know exactly where your uncle lives. A long time ago, I was invited to his house along with some other Greek immigrants," Aunt Victoria said, "I will be there later this afternoon."

"How long will it take you?" I said, already feeling some relief.

"About two hours," she said. I detected excitement creeping into her voice.

"I'll be waiting!" I said happily.

I did not have much packing to do. I had come to America with one extra pair of pants, two khaki shirts, and two sets of underwear.

Aunt Victoria arrived around 4:00 p.m., at the same time Uncle Nick returned from work. As he opened the door, allowing my aunt to enter first, I heard him saying with faint enthusiasm: "Victoria...Victoria what a wonderful surprise to see

119

you. God, I haven't seen you for years. But you look younger now than when you first came from Greece."

"The American climate does miracles to newcomers," my aunt said with a smile and began to open a heavy-looking carryall bag.

Uncle Nick sniffed and said curiously, "Something smells fragrant."

"I brought you something special," my aunt said, uncovering a large ceramic dish piled with bite-sized meatballs seasoned with Greek aromatic herbs. She gave the dish to him saying, "Wait a minute," and with the dexterity of a chef, she brought out a big square clay pot wrapped in foil. The pot contained two huge pieces of moussaka—layers of eggplant, potatoes and seasoned ground beef, topped with béchamel. Uncle Nick was struck with delight at the sight of all this wonderful Greek food. He stood bemused, inhaling the smell of the meatballs, still puzzling out the reason for my aunt's unexpected visit.

"Victoria, you must stay for dinner with us tonight. My wife should be home in less than an hour. We would love to have you."

"Nick, I want you to enjoy what I brought you with your wife. But I need to get back to my family, and if I may, I would like to take Taki with me for a while, that is if he would like to come. I want him to meet my children, Harry and Margie and my husband. Media, where I live, is a nice little town, just like our hometown Moria, in Greece." She handed me the clay pot, still hot. "Taki, take this to the kitchen and put it on the stove."

"Victoria, I have plans for our nephew. You call him Taki, but I call him Peter, and he likes his American name. I took him to Temple, one of the best universities in America."

"Wonderful! I can tell you have the best intentions for our nephew," Aunt Victoria said. "But, Nick, don't you think that Taki—I mean Peter—also needs to rest and recover? Less than a month ago, he came from a war-beaten country. It's good to let him get a feeling of our American life and environment, relax a bit, and then he may be ready for your plans. You know that schools don't start until September, two months away."

"Well, you can take him with you this evening, but don't keep him in Media for too long," he said, keeping his eyes on me as if I were his slave.

"I wouldn't think of it," she said with a gracious smile, then looked at me and winked.

As Uncle Nick took the meatballs into the kitchen, I winked back at my aunt and whispered, "Aunt Victoria you are a master diplomat," knowing that she had brought this delicious food as a bribe for Uncle Nick. I reached and touched gently her arm, wanting to remind her of an old Greek slogan that she probably already knew, *"Beware of Greeks bearing gifts."*

30

A WARM WELCOME

On June 29, 1946, I arrived at 132 South Orange Street in Media, Pennsylvania. The moment Aunt Victoria brought me to her home, I felt warmly received and relaxed; a foretaste of inner joy and happiness. When we entered her door, her husband, whom Aunt Victoria introduced as Uncle Lou, welcomed me with a great smile. With joy and a little curiosity, I looked at this short and unpretentious middle-aged man, who had traveled from America all the way to Lesvos, Greece, to marry my aunt Victoria. He had unusually bushy curly hair, slightly graying at the temples, and a well-trimmed mustache. His dark gray eyes reflected youthful joy and a sense of mischief.

With me now in my early twenties, our meeting brought him unexpectedly back to his own early twenties. "Welcome to our little palace. I'm happy you decided to come and be with us," he grabbed my hand and held it tight. "Your aunt and I are glad to have you stay with us as long as you want. This is your home, and we love to have you."

Then he turned to his wife and said affectionately, "Victoria, now I have our nephew as my partner to share the wine I made last year."

"Lou, not too much wine for you today, you hear?" she said with evident concern. "And don't give Taki too much wine either. I have prepared some very good food for dinner, so just a little wine. Okay?"

"Okay, princess," he said and reached again for my hand. "Taki, just follow me. Don't listen to your aunt," he said laughingly, leading the way. At the deep end of the first floor, there was a small, cozy, freshly painted room, decorated in an oriental style with chestnut-brown drapes, a thick carpet on the floor, and a round table in the middle that was covered with a bright multicolored tablecloth and surrounded with four comfortable chairs.

"Sit in one of these chairs," he said, as he began filling two glasses of wine. "We're going to have a little wine for starters, and then dinner." He placed a square box in front of me and said with an inviting smile, "This is a little welcome present for you. Feel free to open it now."

I could smell a spicy fragrance coming from the kitchen and felt hungry. Seeing what my aunt had brought to Uncle Nick's house, I knew that she would have prepared something very special for me as well.

As I unwrapped and opened the little box placed next to my wine, I saw a beautiful brown wallet, made of soft leather, with separate sections in which to keep—or even hide— important notes.

"I hope you like it," Uncle Lou said.

"Thank you very much," I said, "I love it. Never in my life have I had anything like this before." Then I saw him pull something from his back pocket. He opened an old black leather wallet and extracted some dollar bills. "Take this money," he said with genuine affection, "and put it in your wallet, along with a prayer and my personal wish that your wallet will never be without money."

"Thank you, Uncle Lou, for your wish and for such a generous present," I said. He handed me a new ten-dollar bill and five new singles, which for me in 1946, not having any money of my own, was lots of money.

Aunt Victoria came from the kitchen to serve us. She brought a big bowl of fresh-cut tomatoes sprinkled with feta cheese, oregano, and parsley and placed it first on the table, along with a ceramic pot filled with cured green olives. Then she brought forks and knives and gave us each a red napkin. Dinner etiquette was not a part of her hospitality. She gently placed dishes in front of each of us filled with stuffed grape leaves covered with yogurt. She sat across from her husband who made the sign of the cross to bless the food. As he was eager to start eating, he said once again, "Taki, welcome to America and to our home."

Aunt Victoria added, "Welcome, and I hope you enjoy your stay with us."

Already overwhelmed with their initial hospitality and kindness, I said, "Thank you very much. I'm truly happy to be with you."

"By the way," Aunt Victoria said, "I have also baked lamb, garnished with potatoes and carrots. I hope you have a good appetite this evening."

The days that followed with Aunt Victoria were relaxing and fun. After breakfast, which was also complemented with a special milkshake for me, each day started with music and dancing. She wanted me to teach her some of the recent Greek dances and songs. I tried to teach her the sailor's dance, but she had a hard time doing those fancy steps. An outside person, a passerby, who may happen to see us from the window dancing and singing so early in the morning would probably think that we had just escaped from some mental asylum. We did not care. And we both seemed to enjoy that morning ritual. It made my days go by joyfully.

Periodically, I did get up early in the morning to sit at the table with Uncle Lou and keep him company as he had his first cup of coffee. He used to tell me a humorous story or an event of his life every morning, and we enjoyed laughing together. He always had a story to tell, and we both laughed, while Aunt Victoria went back to the kitchen to check the coffee.

"Taki, you won't believe what happened to me and my friend, Steve, a few years ago," Uncle Lou said as he began to giggle. Steve was one of his buddies, with whom he shared a room, when they first came to America. They worked and traveled together and shared expenses. Now eager to tell his story, he started: "One weekend," he said, "Steve and I decided to go to Reading, Pennsylvania, to meet two other newcomers to America. We had no car, so we got on a train. In those days, the trains had no air conditioning, and because it was a hot August day, we opened the window. Steve wanted to sit by the window. He lit a cigar and kept blowing the rings inside of the train." "Steve," I said and elbowed him hard, "Blow your smoke out the window." He suddenly began to cough, and as he did, his dentures fell out of the window." It was funny seeing my friend toothless, and I began to laugh non-stop.

But I felt sad for Steve. I could not laugh, and wondered how Uncle Lou's friend would be able to chew his food.

Then Aunt Victoria joined us and asked what we were laughing about. Concerned that Uncle Lou might be telling me one of his dirty jokes, she scowled, "Lou, if you say any of your bad jokes, I'll put pepper on your tongue."

But Uncle Lou smiled back at her and said, "The sky is cloudy again this morning."

31

A CHURCH VISIT

On the Sunday morning following my arrival, Aunt Victoria took me to the church to which she belonged in Chester, Pennsylvania. We passed by many churches along the way with spires, steeples, brick facades, and huge signs announcing the churches' names. The church we went to was dramatically different. It was a simple two-story residential house with a porch, a kitchen on the ground floor, and bedrooms that had been turned into classrooms for children to attend Sunday school. There were approximately 75 people, both young and old, sitting around in anticipation of the service to start.

The priest, an impressive-looking older man with a beard, and who obviously knew my aunt, extended a kind welcome and asked us to sit in the front row of chairs. Aunt Victoria respectfully introduced me to the priest, "Father Sophocles, this is Peter, my nephew, who has just arrived from Greece." The priest reached out, shook my hand and said, "So nice to have you in our church today. I hope you find the United States a welcoming home."

In response I said, "Father, this is the country of my birth, and I'm happy to be back."

After he spoke to a few more people, he came back to me

and asked, "Peter, would you be able to read the Epistle of the day?"

"Yes Father, I would be honored," I said enthusiastically. "I have read and chanted the Sunday Epistles since I was 12."

"Happy to hear it," he said and walked back to his part of the sanctuary.

When the Sunday Liturgy ended, my aunt said, "Taki, *she always preferred to call me by my Greek name*, I have a ritual. Every Sunday after I attend church, I pass by the cemetery.... It's not far, and...we can walk there." She choked up for a second before asking if that was okay with me. I nodded, a silent "yes" not knowing what she had in mind. As we arrived at the cemetery, she paused for a few seconds, embraced me tightly and said, "Taki, this is the place where your mother has been buried. I come here almost every Sunday and offer a prayer. Sometimes I talk to my sister, and it makes me feel good."

"You talk to my mother?" I smiled, concealing the fact that I was wondering if my aunt was losing her mind. She was too young for that.

"Yes, honey." She called me *honey*, an adjective I had never heard before, and added, "For me, your Mom is not dead. She is alive forever in my heart. She was the one who found Uncle Lou for me, and he came to Greece, married me, and brought me here."

I knew Aunt Victoria's story, but I kept silent, watching her facial expression and movements, perhaps repressing an avalanche of emotions. We walked silently among the graves until she suddenly stopped and pointed to a particular monument. I took a closer look and saw my mother's photograph encased in a white marble tombstone. Under the photograph was an inscription—"Mersene Kalellis, died at the age of 26, February 7, 1929. Memory Eternal."

As I looked at the tombstone, I felt sad for a few seconds, but I realized that I no longer had any strong feelings toward my mother. I didn't even know her. Katerina, my father's wife, had raised me. She was a good woman and I used to call her Ma. Directly across from my mother's grave, there was a marble bench. It seemed a good place for us to sit for a while. Silently, I perused the area surrounding my mother's grave, but my eyes kept returning to the picture on her tombstone. No memory of my mother. Aunt Victoria sighed deeply, clearly wanting to say more, but not sure where exactly to start.

Eventually, she talked to me of my mother's death and the early days of my return to Greece at the age of 3. She was there the day my father and I arrived in Moria and was able to fill in many details that had been lost for me in the ensuing years. As my mother's sister, she had been upset that my mother was too soon replaced by Katerina. She believed it was likely to have a negative effect on me, who was only a young boy, three years old at that time.

32

SEARCHING DEEPER

"The wise person looks beneath the surface and chooses what is real." I memorized T. S. Eliot's quotation that hung framed on the wall of the principal's office in our high school. More impressed then with the calligraphy, the advice to look beneath the surface and choose what is real spoke to my heart later in my early twenties.

My father's and Uncle Nick's wish that I should become a doctor was not "real" to me. My first jobs earlier in my country of birth were dishwashing and later becoming a busboy. Do I remember the experience of how busboys were treated those days? From Thanksgiving Day until Christmas, lunch was a turkey neck and a large serving of mashed potatoes. After the celebration of the New Year, again the lunch for the busboys was leftover turkey necks and carrots.

On August, 10, 1946, Aunt Victoria found a job for me at a restaurant until I decided what I wanted to do. The owner, Mr. Emmanuel, who was from Greece, had named his restaurant Arcadia and he wanted to be called Mr. Manny. Two boys from South America worked in this restaurant as busboys. My employer suggested that I should wash dishes at least for a month; later, he would make me a busboy. I accepted this job for a while, but I had other plans in mind.

At lunchtime we ate eggs. Lunch every day for the busboys and me was eggs—scrambled eggs, boiled eggs, eggs over medium, eggs benedict, fried eggs. One day, we just threw our lunch in a garbage can. Knowing that the boss was a Greek, I approached him one day, and politely asked, "Mr. Manny, in the last three weeks, every single day we have eaten eggs for lunch. Is there some time that we could eat steak?"

With raised eyebrows he fired back, "What did you say... steak?" His glance scared me.

"Did I say a bad word?"

"Steak is not a bad word," he said. "You have to work at the Arcadia at least two months, and then you may have a hamburger."

He smiled and as he turned to go about his business, he said, "I'll tell you what I can do for you. As of tomorrow, instead of washing dishes, you can work as a busboy."

When I arrived home at Aunt Victoria's house, I said, "Dear Aunt, today I have been promoted, from a dish washer. Tomorrow, Mr. Manny will advance me to a busboy."

That was it. I couldn't see how I could ever make enough money as a busboy and return to Greece and marry Eleni if I stayed on that route. But I still loved to sing in church and chant the Sunday Epistle. In fact, a number of people, who heard my singing and chanting every Sunday, approached me and said, "You should become a priest."

I had always wanted to be a priest, and that wish had not changed. That was real. As a priest, I believed I could fulfill most of my dreams. On December 12, 1946, I applied to the Holy Cross Greek Orthodox Seminary in Brookline, Massachusetts, and was accepted by the end of that month. So, on February 1, 1947, I said goodbye to Philadelphia, and relocated to Brookline, Massachusetts. I felt excited! My new path was designed—the fulfillment of my dream to become a priest. But when I wrote to Eleni to tell her of my plans, she wrote me back in disappointment. She didn't want to be a priest's wife.

Despite Eleni's choice, the seminary was my decision of what I thought could be my future. It also became part of my definition of who I was: impressed and fascinated by religious pageantry and joyful variations of Byzantine music, drama, and chants. Because I had been an olive picker and still had my village manners when I arrived in Brookline, I thought of the seminary life as the place that will hone me, remove my impurities, negative feelings, bad thoughts, and polish my rough spots.

In the seminary, there was consistent obedience to the dean's expectations—rising at 6:00 a.m., making sure your bed is made and your room is intact, church services every morning from 6:30 until 7:00, and breakfast at 7:30. We had compulsory and supervised study from 8:00 a.m. until 10:00 a.m., when students had to attend their individual classes until noontime. Luncheon was served at 12:30 p.m. From 1:00 p.m. until 2:00 p.m. we had a free hour to rest and get ready for three afternoon classes. Vesper services took place faithfully at 5:30 p.m. and dinner was served at 6:30 p.m. From 7:30 to 9:00 p.m., it was time to do our homework and by 9:30 p.m., we had to return to our rooms. At 10:00 p.m., the rooms were checked and lights were out. Sleep time. On Thursdays between 1:00 p.m. and 5:00 p.m. we could get a haircut and buy shaving cream and toothpaste.

Time was very important to the dean of the seminary. Furthermore, every student had to make sure that his appearance from the morning church service through the rest of each day was immaculate—dressed in a black suit, white shirt, black tie, well-shined black shoes, shaved and hair combed to perfection.

I faithfully went through my theological training, embracing the discipline, fasting and prayer, biblical studies, and daily rituals, amid clouds of fragrant incense. I completed the five-year course of study in three years and emerged—glossy and shiny, like a car completed on the assembly line—from the Holy Cross Greek Orthodox Seminary. Now I was almost ready to become a priest, to serve my Church in the best way I could, giving direction to people's lives, educating them about a godly life, saving their souls, and performing my duties with absolute devotion and forthrightness.

How alive and clear my daily life at the seminary surfaces in my mind, and I keep smiling as I think of attending my theological courses. Abstract, theological concepts of faith delivered eloquently by Ezekiel, bishop and dean of our school who we thought as the giant of spiritual life. But for our youthful minds some of his theological knowledge was too difficult to conceive.

Performing the Sunday Liturgy or the Sacraments of Marriage, Baptisms, and preaching the word of God, were pieces of cake, delightful services to look forward to. And those innocent youthful days seemed to me what a priest is supposed to do. Days that the bishop Ezekiel was to conduct his class of theology, even some of the most interested students were anxious. Thank God for the presence of our classmate, Tom Roman, a tall swarthy young man, a terrific basketball player, a bright and serious student that I admired. He always asked important and serious questions to our bishop. I knew that all my classmates loved him. One or two of Tom's questions and the possible answers he might receive from the bishop would take over the class hour. The remaining sixteen of us in that class would feel relieved on that day. We renamed Tom, the new Thomas Aquinas. In private he admitted to some of us that he had studied Aquinas with a passion and admired him, because he was a dedicated student of Aristotle's philosophy. As I write this chapter, I recall only a few of Roman's questions: "Your Grace, at what point of his life did Jesus know that he was divine? Did he know that he was the Messiah? What did he think about the miracles he was able to perform?" Dean Ezekiel, as professor, and spiritually exceptional bishop, listened carefully, smiled for a few seconds and paused. "Mr. Tom Roman, we really don't know," he said gently. "Any other question for today?"

"Yes, your Eminence, when Jesus was on the Cross, did he feel the pain, knowing he would die, but would rise on the third day?"

"I believe you do know the answer. Now, please turn and tell your classmates, what was the response of Jesus while on the Cross?" Turning to the rest of the class, Tom Roman said, "There are indications in the Gospels, that while Jesus hung on the cross he cried out in pain. In his physical self being totally human, he must have felt excruciating agony and he painfully cried out in a loud voice, *Eloi, Eloi, lama sabachthani*, which meant 'My God, my God, why have you forsaken me?'"

"Thank you, Mr. Roman," Bishop Ezekiel said. "Of course, Jesus trusted God so completely that He knew that even in the midst of unimaginable suffering, in His divine nature would somehow rise into a new life and bring new life to others in ecstasy and joy on that glorious day of Easter."

On that day, the theology class ended in a good and positive spirit. Bishop Ezekiel cleared his throat and in his familiar gentleness, he said, "Young men as our future priests, bear in mind that the life of Jesus Christ is the central metaphor for your mission, it is also a metaphor for your life's journey as clergy. It is time to let God transform your true selves into new life for others. In this journey you are not traveling alone, you have the Holy Spirit inspiring you and guiding you. And you have the love of God the Father, and you have the companionship of Jesus Christ.

"Gentlemen, I'd like to end our class today with one of my favorite quotations from H.G. Emelow: 'Nothing in human history is able to equalize the love which Jesus inspired, the solace which He spread, the compassion which He engendered, the hope which He kindled in the breast of humanity.'"

33

ORDINATION APPROACHES

As ordination approached, the yearning to go out into the world and bear witness to what I had learned kept burning in my heart. I thought I was ready, but was I? The high ecclesiastical authorities dictated, "You must find a wife and get married." Greek Orthodox priests have to be married *before* their ordination, if they are to marry at all. Once a priest is ordained, he is no longer permitted to marry. This was the rule, and it had to be obeyed. Along with this rule, the definition of a priest's wife had been hammered into our minds during our training:

> She has to be modest and dedicated to the church; she must be above reproach in manners and dress; she must be unconditionally devoted to her priest-husband; she has to be or to have the likeness of being a good mother; and she has to be an exemplary wife, a role model in the parish.

How can anyone decide in their early twenties who could be their mate for a lifetime? I was fresh out of the seminary, and since leaving Lesvos, I had seldom even been alone with a woman. Eleni was already planning to marry the son of a dentist back in Greece. With her definitely out of the picture, I was faced with the formidable challenge of finding the ideal *presbytera*—a priest's wife. Despite feeling the physical drive to be with a woman, the thought of the permanence of marriage made me panic, so I decided to continue my education and postpone any decision about marriage.

My seminary training emphasized theology, church history, biblical studies, and dogma. These were necessary courses to lay a strong foundation for an authentic priesthood, but there were no courses that taught us how to channel the spiritual energy and vitality that exist in every parish. There were no courses teaching family dynamics, what it means to be a married person, or how to help dysfunctional families in crisis. Several of my classmates and I felt the need for more training in dealing with our present-day issues—helping young people to find direction in their lives, helping families that are facing difficult relationships—and most of us needed a deeper spiritual connection.

We wanted our studies to lead us into an ever-growing communion with God, with each other, and with our fellow human beings. Rituals and symbols were impressive, but we wanted something more, yet not knowing where to start. That *something more* caused anxiety in our young, naïve minds. How were we to offer and make real the rich mystical traditions of Christianity amid a materialistic civilization? Isn't that still our challenge today?

The anxiety and stress of daily life seem to be increasing for many people. Not finding relief anywhere in their present life or in the pursuit of material possessions, they search for a new life. The Church can be that source of "the newness of life." It can be very effective in transforming human lives, but only if every piece of advice and every message offered comes from hearts that understand and love Jesus Christ and his mission on earth.

In the process of developing a deeper faith and understanding of who Christ really is—God in human flesh—I gained a better understanding of the reason *why* God chose to reveal himself in human form. His incarnation and engagement with the world was evidence of his unconditional love and concern for a faltering humanity. He chose to become one of us that we might learn to emulate his human life.

My present reality was clear—totally aware that I was not yet ready to enter married life. In seeking a deeper spiritual understanding, I decided to pursue further studies at the Philadelphia Divinity School and later at Princeton Theological Seminary. I invested three years in studying pastoral psychology, which for me was the study of the soul. I envisioned a synthesis of psychology and theology bringing new life to our society, as promised by Christ. As an instrument of God's grace, I wanted to offer people practical steps in building a life of spiritual freedom, joy, and peace that the world alone could not offer.

34

CHRISTINA

With my master's degree in hand three years later, I was eager to enter the real world and offer my services as a priest. Yet I still lacked one thing: I had no prospect for a wife. To divert the attention of the hierarchy from my marital status or lack thereof, I started a vigorous fundraising drive for our seminary in Brookline, Massachusetts. With such an important activity, I figured I could delay marriage for at least another year, claiming that I was still in search of a wife.

During the time as I was still doing post graduate studies, I was helping Father George Roussos, a warm and devout priest, at St. George Cathedral in Philadelphia. He was encouraging me to get married, so I could be ordained, become a priest, and serve as his associate. As his congregation increased, he tried to convince me, not to delay but to be ordained and become the second priest at his cathedral. But he knew what the hierarchical rules dictated. I had to get married before my ordination. In his fatherly heart, he came up with a solution.

"Well, Peter, how long are you going to wait?" he said to me after a wedding that he performed, and I had assisted in chanting hymns pertinent to marriage. "There are many nice girls in our community, choose one that you can love and feel love in return, and marry her."

Among two or three young women that he suggested, each of them would have been a good wife to a priest. He favored one, in particular, who used to be the director of the Sunday school program for four years. Her name was Christina, the only daughter of the Christou couple, devoted members of the congregation.

"Thank you for thinking of my future, Father George," I said. "I know Christina. She's very pretty and kind, and I have seen her diligent work for our educational program. But would her parents ever want their daughter to marry a priest whose life is controlled and designed by the hierarchy?"

"Her parents are very fond of you. I don't believe they will have any objection. But I know them well enough to ask them at an opportune time."

As I reexamined my thoughts of marrying Christina, some questions emerged regarding the marriage. Would she love me? Would she want to be the wife of a priest? Three weeks later, still swimming in my insecure thoughts about marriage, a most painful and shocking event happened, beyond my human imagination.

In the early dawn on a Thursday morning, a phone call woke me up. I jumped out of my bed to answer the call. I heard a familiar yet groaning voice.

"Peter, it's me, Father George. Sorry to call you at this early hour, but something very sad has happened in our community. Christina, our Sunday school director died last night."

"Dear God how...why?" I asked. "I saw her in church last Monday evening at a meeting, talking to a group of Sunday school teachers. But how in the world did she die?" I was in such a shock and wanted to cry but an instant tightness in my stomach held back my tears.

"I have no idea. Last night, her mother found her dead in the bathtub."

Christina

"What a painful loss, *dead in the bathtub*, her parents must be devastated."

"They are! Last night, around 10:00 p.m., her mother called me at my house crying inconsolably. I rushed to her immediately. I stayed with Christina's parents the rest of the night. I just came home this early hour. I'm beyond exhaustion. I'm calling you to prepare you."

"Prepare me? Father George, I'm not sure I know what you mean." I said.

"Tomorrow, Friday, 4:00 to 6:00 p.m. is the wake at the cathedral, and I want you to be there at 3:30 p.m. to receive people in a spirit of sympathy."

"That I can do," I said.

"On Saturday morning, 10:00 a.m., I need you to chant during the funeral service and at the end of the service to offer the eulogy. I'll be there myself but in silence."

"Would her parents agree to that?"

"They will understand," Father George said and hung up.

Every week, different sacred services and sacraments took place—and Father George Roussos needed help with the Sunday Liturgy, weddings, christenings, and funerals. That day, I began to worry about my choice to become a priest. Could I perform funerals, especially for young people? In my younger days, I thought that only very old people die.

Both days, the congregation was the largest ever, as if it were Palm Sunday or Easter. That Friday at the wake and again on Saturday morning, I looked around with tearful eyes. Glancing at Christina's family, relatives, and friends, I saw not just a deep sadness about her death, but also a real fear of everyone's destiny after death. At the wake, her father whispered closer to my ear, "Father Roussos has told me that you are going to do the service. Please pray for my Christina's soul."

Random rumors, faster than lightening had spread among the people of faith: She must have committed suicide;

she probably had personal problems that she could not admit to herself or to her parents or to anyone, maybe she was a sick girl.

In painful tears, Effie, Christina's first cousin approached me the previous evening at the wake and said, "May I speak to you for a moment?"

"Of course," I said, "let's walk toward the narthex." At the far corner of the narthex, there were a couple of chairs where we could sit. Effie, older in years than Christina, burst into tears, saying, "How painful and unfair! She had such a loving heart. She had good friends and loved her church, the children she taught. Why did she have to die?"

What I wanted to say as a student of theology was "*Someday when we get to heaven, we will know the answer,*" but that would be of little comfort here. Instead, I responded, "Honestly, Miss Effie, I don't know the answer. Nobody really knows why kind people of loving hearts and sometimes very young people, like your cousin or young children, die unexpectedly."

At that moment, I paused for a few seconds, closed my eyes, and meditated. I visualized myself in heaven standing before our Lord Jesus. I looked at his eyes and saw compassion and love. Then with evident humility and less courage I asked, *"Lord, why do you permit young children or young men or women to die? Forgive me Lord, but when we pray, 'Thy will be done,' is this really your will for these innocent people? I don't think so."* As Jesus listened to my questions, he gently shook his head compassionately. But his words, clearly and gently resonated in my heart: *"Peter...Peter, someday when you get to heaven, you will know the answer to all of your questions."*

Effie's question, "Why did she have to die?" And my silent response, *when we get to heaven, we will know the answer,* became the basis for my eulogy the next day. At the end of the funeral service, I walked near the coffin, I controlled my tears and glanced at the congregation—the largest church attendance I had ever seen. These people were her family and her many friends. These were good people, people of faith, and good church members. Suddenly, more questions crossed my mind: *Were some of these people sad about Christina's death? Or were they more concerned about her destiny? Or were they thinking about their own death? Would God ever even allow a bad person to enter heaven?*

In the silence of my pause, my audience sat in wonder; their faces reflecting a deep sadness. My intention was to assure everyone present that this young woman was already in heaven. As a director of the cathedral Sunday school, she had spent precious hours and days preparing faith lessons for our young children. Christina had a loving heart and a strong faith. Where else could she be but in the presence of our loving God? But after my thoughts and many questions that kept surfacing, I decided that my eulogy should be short:

Dear Mr. and Mrs. Christou, our pastor, Father George Roussos and I wish to offer you our deepest sympathies. No human words can possibly wipe the tears of your grieving hearts over the sudden loss of your daughter. This major loss is an event that has caused you the ultimate pain. It is only our Lord Jesus and his Blessed Mother to whom we pray diligently today, that will sustain you in these critical hours. Our sympathetic presence this morning is our most limited way of offering comfort. People who are here today share your feelings in full awareness of your current grief. We are all human and pain exists for all of us. We may not know what to say to you, the grieving parents. But all of us here are able to say with our heart, "We are right here with you." Believe us, we care, even if we are unable to express it.

Our faith in a loving God reassures us that Christina is and shall ever be right now, lovingly and joyfully embraced by God, our Creator. If we, with our weak understanding and imperfect compassion, are able to see this young woman's commitment and the goodness of her loving heart, how much more so can our God see? Can we really enter into the joy of God today at this critical hour? Can we really hear his voice, through St. Paul who writes in his Letter to the Philippians: "Rejoice in the Lord always; again I will say, Rejoice. Let your gentleness be known to everyone. The Lord is near. Do not worry about anything." (Phil 4:4–6).

Now, beloved members of our cathedral, it is time this morning to let our gentleness and profound condolences be known to Christina's parents; as we approach the altar to pay our respects, say gently: *"Christina, Eternal Be Your Memory. Amen."*

35

DEATH

Christina's unexpected death had a tremendous emotionally paralyzing impact on my life. Although, I had liked her very much and had wished that, God willing, she could be my wife, her sudden death perplexed me and my participation at her funeral left me confused. I tried to recollect the eulogy I gave at her funeral, and doubted if my words had brought any comfort, especially to her grieving parents. The deeper I reflected, the more I realized my subconscious fear in dying.

This fear started when I was a child. Nickolas, a much older boy who had excelled in his class as a senior in high school and planned to go to college, suddenly died. A week later, Lazarus, one of our best young goalkeepers died. The entire town of Moria grieved for many days. As a result of World War II, many older and some young people died of starvation. All these deaths gave me a fearful and recurring nightmare that I had died and was buried in the ground beneath tons of dirt but was still alive and scared. Not being able to breathe, I began screaming until I woke up.

While training for the priesthood, I accepted my fear of death as part of life and began to read the New Testament. I wanted to know what was written in the Scriptures. Did Jesus Christ say anything about death? Was he afraid of death? These

143

were questions also asked by several participants in one of my Lenten Retreats in Virginia Beach, VA, a number of years ago.

The entire audience then turned and looked straight at me, anticipating my response. I paused for a few seconds, then picked up the Bible that was placed on the podium. I opened it and said humbly, "You have asked certain serious questions: A quick look at the Gospel narratives provides a most convincing answer." In the garden of Gethsemane, Christ said to his disciples: "I am deeply grieved, even to death; remain here, and stay awake with me." And going a little farther, he threw himself on the ground and prayed, "My Father, if it is possible, let this cup pass from me; yet not what I want but what you want" (Matt 26:38–40).

Obviously, in his human nature he felt the bitterness of the cup. He was a Man of flesh and blood, living and breathing like one of us. Alone in the night, alone before God, He knew that his death on the Cross was near. He would be mocked and scourged, and then his body would be pierced and nailed to a cross. Did he have any fear as he prayed? According to Luke: "In his anguish he prayed more earnestly, and his sweat became like great drops of blood falling down on the ground" (Luke 22:44).

As a man, he was mindful of the impending tragedy. But as God, he was not afraid. In his divine nature, he knew and reassured his disciples that he would rise in three days.

Our rational minds perceive birth and death as two ends of life. *Where there is life, there is death*, I kept telling myself in my younger years and then I dismissed the thought. Later, during my middle years, I used this metaphor to comfort grieving people: *As the butterfly frees itself from its cocoon and enjoys a colorful field, likewise the soul frees itself from the body and finds everlasting joy in the presence of a loving God.*

Our human perception of the mystery that lies beyond life is limited. Here, faith reassures us that, at the end of our days, God has plans for each of us. How can this be? My faith tells me that if God created the universe out of nothing, if God created life and made humans his co-creators, would he not be able to bring us back to his presence? If this life, in its pure form is so beautiful, one can imagine what kind of life a loving God has prepared for us.

I do not claim to be an authority on what will happen after death; I can neither ignore the reality of death nor be preoccupied with it. How I approach death is crucial in living my present life. In other words, how I perceive the afterlife affects how I live today.

Often times, especially when I am physically ill or sense unusual symptoms that affect my wellness, disturbing thoughts cross my mind. What if this is it? Then my own mind interprets what God's response might be: *Peter, all these "What ifs" can only stop you from living your present life. Some day you will die, and you will leave behind unfinished tasks. But I have plans for you, as I have plans for all humanity. Trust that I am a God of the living not a God of the dead.*

Furthermore, I know that my body will eventually return to its elements. But what about my soul that has kept me alive this far? My faith responded, *Death has no dominion over the soul. By his death and resurrection, Christ destroyed death and gave life to those who have died.*

The story of Mary and Martha has always intrigued me. On his way to Bethany, a couple of miles from Jerusalem, Jesus met Martha, whose brother had died and was four days in the tomb: "Jesus said to her, 'Your brother will rise again.' Martha said to him, 'I know that he will rise again in the resurrection on the last day.' Jesus said to her, 'I am the resurrection and the life. Those who believe in me, even though they die, will live, and everyone who lives and believes in me will never die'" (John 11:23–26).

At the tomb, *Jesus wept*. These are the two most powerful words about the *Theanthropos*—the God-Man, Jesus. The Jews present said, "See how much he loved him." Then Jesus approached the gravesite with the full assurance that he will raise his friend from the dead and he did. The raising of Lazarus is the most daring and dramatic of all the Savior's miracles. It revealed that Jesus was who he said he was—the resurrection and the life. But it revealed the *tears of God*. And which is more incredible: a man who raises the dead or a God who weeps?

Finally, with the realization that death will happen to each of us, I live with the awareness that life has a beginning and an end. The last article of the Christian Creed says, "I look for the resurrection of the dead and the life of the ages to come." As a Christian, I anticipate a time when there will be a resurrection and there will be no more death, pain or sorrow, but everlasting life. Will I retain some identity of who I am after death? At his transfiguration on Mount Tabor, Jesus appeared in dazzling white clothes—a foreshadowing of his resurrection. With him were Moses and Elijah. These two prophets died hundreds of years before Christ, and yet they had an identity which the disciples recognized. As Peter said to Jesus, "Rabbi, it is good for us to be here; let us make three dwellings, one for you, one for Moses, and one for Elijah" (Mark 9:5).

It is of great comfort to accept the truth that death is another beginning of a different life. *We will be like angels in heaven.* Our body will take on a spiritual form like Jesus when he appeared to Mary Magdalene and to his disciples who, out of fear, were hiding in a room with closed doors.

Three days after my stepmother died, I had a dream where I saw her face that looked youthful and beautiful. I recognized her although her body was smaller. In the dream, I tried to embrace her. I was amazed that she was as light as a feather. She smiled and said, *"My son, just put me on that sofa.*

It's my favorite one. I used to sit there and do needlepoint." I did what she said and carried her to her sofa. I saw her smile and heard her say, *"Leave me on this sofa. It is the place where I would like to be."* When I woke up, I pondered my dream thinking that this is the kind of body we might have after we die.

36

THE INNER JOURNEY

Recently, in my daily prayers, I sensed something missing. Sometimes my prayer is clear and slow, and other times it is quick and not as meaningful. Reflecting on the vocabulary that I often use in prayer, I became aware that although my words are often poetic and sincere, they lacked depth and substance.

That same night, I decided to discuss my concerns about my prayer with Father Seraphim, a priest who has heard my confession. He is a humble and well-known spiritual man, who, for a number of years, has helped me to develop a more effective spiritual life.

A week later, I decided to go and see Father Seraphim in his newly built church in Roseland, New Jersey. After the initial jovial welcome, we went into the main part of the church. In due reverence, we sat before the altar and Father Seraphim offered a brief prayer, thanking God for the blessing of our meeting that Friday morning.

After a couple of deep breaths, I said, "Father, I'm soon to be ninety-three. Thank God, I'm healthy and so far most of my plans and wishes have been moderately fulfilled. I have Pat, my loving wife, who has regained her health and vitality, two lovely daughters and two sons, five kind-hearted grandchildren and two great grandchildren. Through writing books that hopefully help people, I have connected with many churches, and several clergy have invited me to conduct retreats for their congregations. I am grateful for all these blessings, but why is it that I'm not happy?"

"What else is it that you need to be happy?" Father Seraphim asked kindly.

"Well, regardless of my public achievements, I still feel that my inner private life is not rewarding or fulfilling."

Taking my hand gently, he said, "Dear Father Peter (in my eyes you are still a priest so I can call you, Father), I'm aware that you are no longer in active ministry, but you are a priest-psychotherapist—a much needed and sensitive ministry.

"Father and dear brother, you and I live and have two separate lives, although in different parts of the State, together we are running parallel to each other. One is an invisible, inner, personal life and the other is an outer, public life, as you and I relate with the community or with friends and relatives.

"As a younger priest in a small church, I was interested in educating the young people of our community. The different and large programs that I developed—visual aids, films, and publications—were colorful, visible, and attractive. Soon my small church attracted more parishioners and increased in number. Newly formed PTA, the Ladies Auxiliary, and a married couple's group invited me to speak at their meetings. But while my outer, visible self became highly praised and increasingly complex, my invisible, inner world had not grown at all. My inner life, my secret thoughts, repressed feelings, hopes and wishes, was totally neglected. My personal prayers were words of inspiration written years ago that I had memorized. Reciting them was easy, but I felt they lacked depth.

"Peter, my dear brother and friend, you have described in detail my own early life as a priest. When I first decided to become a celibate priest, I took an emotionally costly and deep journey into my inner life, examining my inner life honestly and removing the poisonous ugly events and thoughts. Consequently, I felt much better once I had left all my past history behind me."

"You mean that you forgot everything of your past?" I asked.

"When an ugly memory surfaces, I repeat King David's words, 'Lord, be not mindful of the sins of my younger life.' I took three months leave of absence and did not attend any church services. I travelled alone into the deepest part of my soul. As you know, many people talk about life being a journey, and it must mean something for them, but for me, travelling into the deepest part of my soul, has special significance."

"Will you ever tell me about it?"

"I might...!" he said, "but let me hear from you about the true reason why you wanted to see me this particular Friday morning."

"Since dawn this morning a part of me kept bringing you to my mind, I wanted to see you. What truly drew me here today was that I did get to know you when I came to you for my confession. People of this community speak with pride about your priestly life and spiritual accomplishments."

"Peter, I don't mean to be arrogant, but at this point in my life, I don't care about what people think, feel, or say about me. My concern is what our Lord's thoughts are about me thus far. Am I on the path that leads to Him?"

"Father Seraphim, attending your Sunday Liturgy, hearing your sermons, and knowing how effectively you have helped me in my confessions, I do believe that you are someone who masters the inner life, or has at least advanced much farther down that road than most others, myself included."

"Peter, your physical presence, as important as it is, is not the real you; it is only part of you. The true you, the unseen part of you, your spiritual self cannot be seen by anyone else.

The Inner Journey

You and I came into this world by God's love, wisdom, and power. You belong to God's family, you are one of his beloved children. Your presence here today signals a different type of journey which I have also taken and am still taking every hour of the day. I call it my special and deep inner journey."

"I think of my life as a journey," I said.

"Peter, this inner journey is unusually complex. There's hesitation and fear because it penetrates our illusions. Taking it seriously leads you into some very shadowy places. You're going to learn things about yourself that you'll wish you didn't know. There are enemies, monsters on the way—monsters you can't control—and trying to fight or keep them hidden will only give them greater power."

His emphatic description of this mysterious journey made me skeptical of taking it, and to diffuse my doubt, I asked, "Why is there such value and mystery to this journey?"

"Because of this tiny, fragile, vulnerable, precious thing we call the self. We are in God's caring and healing presence. The Lord God who created each of us out of the earth and dust, breathed into our nostrils the breath of life. Simply ask yourself: Who is making your life possible each day? It is not your thoughts, your feelings, or your intentions. It is God who gives you the daily bread of life, the essence of life: it is God who is in charge."

"Father Seraphim, I really need help to be more compassionate. While in active ministry, I followed St. Paul's advice in being emotionally available, rejoicing and being happy with those who were happy and sharing the sadness of those that were going though grieving times. Now, when I hear that a family or someone has lost a beloved relative or a young child, it is hard to stay connected—to empathize—with those who are grieving. Is that normal?"

At that moment, I saw a glitter in Father Seraphim's eyes giving me the impression that he understood my concern. He said, "Jesus's compassion prompted Him to act with love—healing the sick, forgiving the sinners, and raising the dead. His very presence in the world is the ultimate act of compassion and mercy."

"Well that was Jesus in His divine mission," I said, "but what about me or you becoming more compassionate?"

"Peter, as you know, my rectory is near the cemetery. Over the years, I have seen many funerals, sometimes twice a day. I feel the family's pain, and initially, tears would fill my eyes. But after a few years as a priest, I realized that I could not cry for each funeral that crossed the cemetery gate."

"And how did you deal with your feelings?"

He stood up reverently for a moment and pointing toward the sky, he said, "It's God's people, Peter, and like for all of us, God is in charge!"

It was time for me to return to my office, and as I shook his hand, I said, "Father Seraphim, thank you for your time today. I would like to come back and meet with you again. Will you be available next Friday?"

"God willing," he said and shook my hand warmly.

However, over the weekend, Father Seraphim had to be rushed to Morristown Hospital. Through his secretary, I learned that, over the previous three months, Father Seraphim had been treated for cancer, but he did not want to burden anyone with his condition.

A week later, while still in the hospital, he submitted his resignation to the president of his church and the parish council along with the details of his chemotherapy treatment. The cancer had seriously metastasized from the lungs to his pancreas, and he was transferred to Boston University for intense treatment and total isolation. Less than a month later, his secretary called to inform me of his death.

Unfortunately, I was unable to attend his funeral, but I attended a most inspiring memorial service in his honor presided over by one of his clergy friends. The reality of death in losing such a good friend evoked in me deep feelings of depression. I also realized that I had to continue on my deep inner journey alone, however, I still carry in my heart my dear friend's healing presence.

37

THE DREAM

Earlier we explored the topic of death. While many people are afraid of death, is it possible that death could be a *friend*? There is a popular Greek song that says, "When death comes to you, welcome him with joy, let him sit on your right side on your leather sofa and offer him a glass of wine." This rather romantic idea makes us consider how death could be a friend to welcome. In some cases, when a person has been suffering for a long time with no hope of recovery, then death could be considered as a friend.

I recall having a most disturbing dream that woke me up one night and kept me wondering about its message for days.

In the dream, Michael, my eldest son who had recently retired, came to my office and found me busy tapping on my computer. In an unusual caring tone, he said, "Dad, you have written more than twenty-five books in your lifetime. You are now in your mid-nineties. Why are you still so passionate about writing more?"

"I love writing books that help people," I said with a smile.

"I was about six or seven years old," Michael said, "when you told me that you had begun to write self-help books. You were then twenty-seven years old yourself. Now some seventy years later or more, you are still writing. Aren't you tired?"

"I never get tired. When I get a call from two or three people who have read one of my books, I get a great deal of satisfaction and motivation to continue writing still another book."

"But when are you going to have some fun in your life?"

"Oh, I have lots of fun. Once I see another book in print, I become excited."

I turned and took a profound look at my son. Suddenly, he looked different. I knew he had retired at sixty-three and seemed happy. Curiously, I noticed his unordinary dress code and said, "It's still February and very cold. Why are you wrapped in such a light and all-white coat?"

"It's my official garment," he said. "I never feel cold and I always wear a white coat each time I have an important message to announce." His voice had suddenly changed into a light baritone that made me very skeptical. *What's going on with my son?* I thought.

With increasing heartbeats and instant anxiety, I said, "In that case, you must have some important message for me. What is it? Tell me."

"You thought I am your son, but I'm not your son. I have called you dad out of respect for your age. I did not want to scare you."

"Who are you anyway?" I asked as I felt a sudden fear and my blood rushed up to my temples. My heart palpitations soared high. I began to worry.

"I'm Michael, one of God's messengers. And today, I'm not sure if you would be happy to hear what I'm about to tell you."

"Tell me," I said, as I became instantly possessed with fear.

Michael who I thought to be my son was not my son. Abruptly, his whole appearance changed—long, dark chestnut color hair, dazzling big striking eyes, and a darker and glowing face. A flowing garment whiter than snow enveloped his body and as he stretched his arms, I saw a tunic under his garment that was brown at the top, red around the waist, and ending in deep gray below his knees. He no longer looked like my son and his voice had changed into a vibrant sound totally strange to my ears.

Ecstatic at the sight, I mastered enough courage to say, "I'm content enough with my life and I want to hear what you came to tell me."

"You may not be aware, but serious and sometime painful symptoms of your body have already prepared you to return to your Creator."

"At my age, some physical discomfort, aches and pains are normal but I do take good care of myself. I exercise, maintain a good diet and keep my brain active always writing another book. Honestly, I'm not ready to return to my Creator."

"I have orders that I need to follow. And at this hour, St. Peter will be standing by the pearly gate of heaven and waiting to receive you."

"That's very nice of St. Peter, but I'm not ready to go to heaven."

"Your time on earth has come to an end. I have no choice but to take you with me now," he said firmly.

"But you don't understand. I have a wonderful, younger and most loving wife. My sudden departure will break her heart. I cannot just leave her. And I have four children—two sons and two daughters—five grandchildren, and two great grandchildren—my whole family loves me and I love them dearly. How are they going to feel, if I suddenly disappear from their lives?"

"Our loving God and Creator of our lives knows all that and has plans for each young or older member of your family. You do not need to worry."

"How can I not worry?" I even forgot to mention that I'm still working on my new book.

God's messenger did not hear me, and as he lifted his

shoulders, two enormous wings spread open. He reached and gently embraced me with his long arms and we both flew through the air with no effort. Under my arm, I managed to carry my laptop computer, reams of paper and a small bag with three of my best books. In no time, I found myself fearlessly rising higher and higher, passing through clouds. Within seconds, God's messenger and I landed in front of a huge gate arrayed with millions of brightly colored pearls.

Behind that gate, I saw a tall and thin man in a snow-white tunic, a velvet sky-blue belt wrapped and tied around his belly. His long hair rested on his shoulders and a sweet fatherly face stood graciously near the gate and said, "I'm Peter and I am here to welcome you."

"Could you be that Peter who was one of the Apostles of Jesus Christ?" I asked nervously.

"I am," he said with a smile.

"Are you that same Peter who denied Jesus Christ three times?"

"Yes. I am he," Peter said lowering his head and his big brown eyes becoming moist.

"And now you are in heaven? How come?" I asked courageously.

"Because, Jesus Christ is a God of love, he forgave me and made me one of his chosen Apostles."

"So, now you are St. Peter," I said, still in doubt.

"Now I am in this part of the universe that we call heaven. And this is where you are going to be."

"I need to get back to earth, I have important things to do that I have left unfinished."

St. Peter shook his head and said, "Earthly life is a life of unfinished business. But in heaven, all the unfinished business of earthly life is completed and perfected with our Creator's loving presence and power."

"That's good to hear, but..." (I didn't tell St. Peter that I had a hard time believing him.)

"I know what you are thinking," St. Peter said. "All your life, you have been a good man. You did some truly wonderful things in your life and some bad things but not so bad as to be called a sinner. You have also helped thousands of suffering people through your profession."

"Thank you," I said, still hoping to get back home.

"Well, for all the good things that you have done, our Loving Lord has prepared here behind this gate a special place for you. But you cannot cross this gate with the things that you are still carrying under your arm."

"Why not?" I protested. "This computer is a light tool that saved many lives. It is a harmless hobby that I have writing books to help people who face mental and sometimes physical problems."

"When you go through this gate and you will be already in heaven, you will know why. It's too difficult for me to explain. Have faith and trust that our Lord God will give you something better than your computer and the reams of paper and your books."

Reluctantly, I dropped everything I was holding on the ground and, like a dusty wind, it all disappeared into the air. A darkness fell and enveloped me. As I approached the gate, it began to slowly fade. Then I heard the most beautiful music I had ever heard. As it slowly grew in volume, a pure white light descended upon the pearly gate. In an instant, I entered the open gate and found myself in a completely new world. The strangest, most beautiful world I had ever seen. Instantly I realized that I was more than my physical body. A melodic sound, like a glorious chant became a background to a hymn familiar to my ears. *Holy, Holy, Holy, Lord Sabaoth, heaven and earth are filled with your glory. Hosanna in the highest!* I remembered how happy I was singing this hymn in our church.

The Dream

As I looked around, I could see thousands of winged beings; some had six wings and others had many sparkling eyes. These huge white-feathered birds, created a divine breeze shifting the world around me into a higher vibration that moved my being. The sky had embraced me, giving me a feeling of warmth and comfort.

St. Peter held my right hand tight, and I felt secure that he was guiding me. Walking alongside me was a beautiful girl with beautiful dark brown eyes. She was wearing similar yet brighter clothes that people wore in Lesvos. She looked at me for a few moments with a glance that suddenly made my life, a life of joy, similar to what I had experienced on earth, when my cousin, Galatia, had brought me two sweet, loving kittens.

Without using any words, she communicated with me through her eyes, and I instantly realized that it was Galatia but with a younger, smaller body and a gorgeous face. Her message came via St. Peter, who said, "We are going to see your mother. She has been expecting you and she is eager to see you."

"My mother died almost ninety years ago," I responded in anger. "I was not yet three years old then, and...I felt abandoned."

"As a young child, not having the warmth of your mother's arms, you naturally felt abandoned and angry," St. Peter said in a most affectionate and compassionate way. He glanced at me and said, "Your mother has always loved you. But she had a terrible accident that brought her life on earth to an end much earlier than she expected. But being here, she has never stopped loving you."

"Great! You are a man who lives in heaven." Now my anger rose high and I screamed as loud as I could, "Can't you understand me? I don't want to see her. I don't need a mother anymore." My guttural scream woke me up. I found myself in my own bed.

"Dear Lord, what a strange dream!"

Pat, my caring wife, rushed into our bedroom, and anxiously asked, "I heard you screaming...are you okay? You look so upset."

"I'm not okay. I had a terrible dream, please leave me alone," I said.

"You sound so angry. Why?"

"Because, I'm still human and weak."

"I'll make you a cup of herbal tea and some breakfast."

Eventually, shocked and emotionally drained, I got out of bed and sat on a cushioned chair, laid back still pondering the meaning of my dream.

"How could I be angry at my mother who died ninety years ago? I don't even remember her. She had a fatal accident and died. I don't think she would have abandoned me. *Mothers just don't abandon children.*

My dream revealed my feelings of abandonment and anger. It's hard to believe that a part of me is still weak and I cannot move forward and become what God expects of me, to be a forgiving and loving human being. Obviously, I still live in an imperfect world where evil seems to be triumphant, although I believe that at the end it will be defeated. And in God's larger picture of the world, love will be overwhelmingly dominant and ultimately triumphant for all humanity.

Since that dream, my whole being changed drastically. I began to question how I perceived our human reality and the mysteries of life and my mortality became more real. For example, does anyone really know what happens to our being after our death? No human knowledge can give an answer to the mystery of death.

Personally, I feel comforted in my conviction that the all-wise and loving God, who allowed me the privilege of visiting this planet for many years, will include me and every human being that he has created in his divine plan. What comforts me and continues to inspire me is simple: My knowledge of life after death is limited; the eyes of my soul are currently dim, but it is enough to know and believe that Christ arose from the dead, appeared to his disciples and eventually returned to his kingdom. And I pray that, when the time comes to leave my present life, I shall be with him and be happy in his divine presence.

In our everyday life, how excited we feel when we are about to meet an important person. We groom ourselves, we dress well, and mentally, we rehearse what we might say to that person to make sure we will be received favorably. Now, imagine meeting our Lord God, Creator of heaven and earth and of all things visible and invisible, the Giver of life and Sustainer of the Universe. What an exciting meeting that will be! No joy on earth can possibly compare with the delight of such a divine encounter, as well as the amplified ecstasy in meeting our loved ones.

Family is important in heaven, and the family members we knew well on earth will still have great bonds of love in heaven. Family members, relatives, friends, coworkers, fellow church members will know us in a special way in heaven.

Nevertheless, we must put our worldly affairs in good order. Some of us know people who have departed from this life and left behind confusion for others to sort out. This is not the way to treat those we love. We should not add our unfinished business to their distress and grief. The mark of a mature person is to express clearly to our family members how they wish their possessions to be distributed and how they wish their funeral service to be and where their body could be buried. Often, family members do not want to listen to or to discuss such serious issues. However, having a will can be peace of mind.

In addition to a will, we should take time to write a paragraph describing and acknowledging our fear. Fear of death is natural, but *what exactly is there to fear*? An initial fear often concerns the events leading to death—failing physical and mental powers, illness, prolonged pain, helplessness, and leaving tasks unfinished. A second fear in dying is the emotional anguish that it may cause to loved ones. Should I be conscious when my death is approaching, I would want my wife to be near me and be able to say, "Goodbye! I love you very much. Be at peace. In time, we will be together again in our heavenly home."

If we are blessed with time to prepare for death, it can help to write one's own obituary, plan aspects of the funeral: Who would you like to perform the funeral service? Who would you like to give the eulogy? Who are the people you want to be present? For me, it is of great comfort to know that my loving family, my wife and children, and the gentle presence of good friends will be present to wish me Godspeed, to rest in peace in the promising adventure of our eternal home.

38

DISCERNMENT

In subsequent years, the emotional impact of Christina's death and my own fear of death caused both passivity and sadness. It challenged my faith in God and despite my theological training, I could not visualize myself as a priest dealing with suffering, visiting the sick and dying, the grieving, and performing funerals.

Fortunately, the Institute of Religion and Psychology which I attended for three years offered me courage and strength to move on as a responsible person with a mature and adult life. When I trusted and revealed my feelings to Dr. James Murphy, a respected psychiatrist of the Institute, he provided a much-needed dose of reality:

> Peter, I have known you for three years, so I can speak to you openly with my thoughts and words that come, not out of books but out of my heart. As a priest or as a future therapist, there is only one life that you can save, and that's your own. So start now. If you are dealing with other aspects of your life that seem important to you at this time, go after them, but make sure you know what you are doing with your time today.

Like every other human being, you have only so much time on this planet. Make it meaningful. You are at a point in your life that you have heard many voices around you shouting, "Do you know what you are doing?" What they wanted to give you is advice pertinent to what they think you should do. They might mean well, but do they really know what is best for you? Even the best advice may interrupt the course of your journey. Do not stop. You know what to do. Start today. Little by little as you leave those voices behind, your mind will clear and you will regain inner peace. It is time for you to decide and save the only life you can save, your own which is God's gift for you. Only then in full confidence, can you reach out and minister to others.

Hearing Dr. Murphy's words, I left his office feeling relieved. I knew I wanted to move forward in confidence and hope of better days ahead. But I also wanted to move forward with stronger faith, purpose, and passion. There was so much to do, and I needed to move from reflection to action.

Most of my classmates who also graduated in 1949 were aware that our Holy Cross School of theology needed funds for survival. We talked it over, and many ideas for raising funds surfaced. Some graduates promised to help, others moved on in search of wives. Personally, I felt profound gratitude toward the school that had educated me. So when I returned to Philadelphia, I thought of starting a drive. I began to knock on the doors of families that I knew and ask for donations. Many people gave generously, others made annual pledges, and some skeptics requested time to consider giving.

In the course of my fundraising efforts, I met Mary, an attractive young woman, who was a radio announcer. Her chestnut hair was combed to perfection. She was modestly dressed and had a strong handshake. And though she wore no makeup, she possessed a radiant glow. She received me graciously, gave me a donation, and invited me to speak on her radio program. Excited by her offer, I accepted the invitation. She gave me the address, and we met the following Sunday at WKDN radio station in Camden, New Jersey.

At the station, Mary tested my voice and explained the mechanics of the program. She noticed my nervousness and gently demonstrated how to approach the microphones: "Nothing to it. Relax and talk to the mike as you would talk to a friend." She started the program at 2 p.m. with enthusiasm and informed her audience that she was pleased to welcome a special guest. She turned, looked at me and with a pleasant smile she blushed. My heart raced. "Was *I* the special guest? Would my prepared speech appeal to her audience? Would it appeal to *her*?" I was so wrapped up in my thoughts that I totally forgot the written contents of my prepared talk. I looked down to read what I had prepared, but my vision blurred as the blood rose to my head. I was more nervous than ever when I saw her gesture to me to come and sit next to her in front of the microphone.

At 2:15 p.m., she announced my name with extraordinary charm, saying that I was the special guest, a theologian and future priest. She turned the microphone toward me and nodded for me to start. I took a deep breath and rolled my tongue around in my dry mouth. It is moments like this that God's grace comes to our assistance, especially when our intentions are good. I began to feel more relaxed, as I started:

> I'm one of the sixteen students that graduated in 1949 from the Holy Cross School of Theology, located in Brookline, Massachusetts. Today I feel honored and happy to inform you that this school which prepares young men who have decided to become priests, is totally supported by the faith and

generosity of people like you that are listening to this radio program at this hour. In our times, there is a need for clergy, and our theological school needs your financial support at this time and in the days and months to come!

Out of the corner of my eye I saw Mary nodding her head and smiling, obviously approving of my message, and I began to feel more confident. As soon as I finished my presentation, the phone began to ring off the hook. Listeners were calling the station, eager to make a donation. Mary answered the calls with enthusiasm, acknowledging the names of the donors and tabulating the amounts donated. By the end of the program, the total had risen to over three thousand dollars, not a small amount for the early fifties, and the phones kept on ringing. More donations came through even as we sat in the lounge to chat. Mary wanted to know more about the seminary life. Then her questions took a different, more personal, direction. "What made you decide to become a priest?" she asked.

I told her that I had been fascinated with the Church since childhood, and as I grew older, my desire to become a priest had become stronger.

"Isn't a priest's life somewhat restricted?"

"To some extent," I said.

"Does the Church permit you to get married and have children?"

"Of course! I have to get married before my ordination."

"So you must have found someone who wants to be a priest's wife."

"Not yet," I said, wondering if she was thinking of being a priest's wife.

As if she'd read my mind, she said, "I would not want to be a priest's wife. Nothing personal, but I see that life as being too conservative, too much under the public eye."

Discernment

Mary called me the following week to tell me that more donations had come in, and, if I wanted to make another presentation on WKDN, I would be more than welcome. I thanked her for the offer and said that I would like to give it some thought. Again she changed the subject with a more personal question, "Why do you want to be a priest? You could be a professor and teach in a college or university. Then you could really be free to enjoy life." Her many questions raised doubts in my mind. Does this woman need to get married? I began to wonder if behind her interest in me, she had other expectations.

I tried to explain to her that I visualized a great future in the Church, and I was happy with my decision. It was obvious to me that she liked me, and she continued to find reasons to call me. During these calls, we discovered many similarities in our background. We were both born in the United States but, at a younger age, we had both been transplanted and raised in Greece, and lived there during World War II. Furthermore, we found out that we were both motherless and had both traveled to Greece on the same ship in 1929, the Edison. Then we had both returned to America in 1946.

I didn't think these similarities in our backgrounds were coincidental. The more we talked about our lives, the more I thought that it was God's way of pointing her out to me as a possible mate. Despite her initial resistance to the thought of being a priest's wife, Mary became regular in her church attendance, and whenever I preached a sermon, she managed to find a seat in the front pew. One Sunday, she invited me to her house to meet her father and brother. It was a pleasant visit, and I felt welcome.

As I was leaving, she escorted me to the door and in a soft voice said, "I'm curious. Is a priest's wife permitted to dance?"

"Of course! She is not the priest," I said, looking straight into her eyes.

"I love to dance," she said and lowered her eyes with a sweet flirt.

I recalled again the T. S. Eliot quotation, "The wise person looks beneath the surface and chooses what is real," and how my father and Uncle Nick, both with good intentions, wanted me to become a doctor. However, pursuing studies at Temple University was not "real" to me. Deep down in my heart I believed I made the right choice. I wanted to become a priest. When I wrote to Eleni of my choice, she responded forthrightly, "In no way could I be a priest's wife. I had a premonition that being thousands of miles away from Greece, you would forget me. So, think of me no more. Good luck to you."

On one hand, I felt anger for being rejected by my first love; on the other hand, I felt relieved that I didn't have to travel back to Greece to get married. These two mixed emotions gradually made me realize the truth that I was not yet ready for married life.

Between my seminary assignments, I had time to meditate and reflect. Why am I still confused and indecisive? Is Mary really the right person to be a priest's wife? Why would I want to get married anyway? Am I really a love-stricken person or is it because the church dictates that marriage must come before ordination into priesthood?

One day I went to see Bishop Ezekiel, who had come to Philadelphia for his annual visit to our local parish. Gracefully, he welcomed me. I thought that he would be happy to know that soon I could be one of his priests. At that time, he needed to have more priests to serve the needs of his expanding diocese. I wanted to share my thoughts that, at twenty-six, I did not yet want to get married, and hoped to gain some understanding. His smile instantly faded as he asked, "Why not?"

"I could serve a parish as a layperson and learn more about the different functions of the church."

"Become an ordained priest and learn as you serve our people."

"Your Eminence, I want to be a priest now, but the church rules demand marriage first before ordination and I have not yet found the right person to marry."

"Do you expect to marry an angel or a human being?" Annoyance surfaced on the bishop's face. I did not answer. Why was I so naïve in expecting Bishop Ezekiel to understand how I felt about marriage? Bishops in our church are never married. That is the rule for the bishops.

"Your parish must have several young women. Choose one."

"Your Eminence, I met one, but I'm not so sure I want to marry her."

"Why not?" He said.

"She has too many expectations," I said.

"Don't you have any expectations?" he asked.

My visit with Bishop Ezekiel was in vain and I could see that maintaining a dialogue with him was counterproductive. I needed to hear the human voice of God telling me what to do. After a long silence in prayer, I put my hand on my heart and listened to a whisper from my inner self that said, *Peter you are responsible for your life; you are responsible for your mind, your thoughts, your feelings, your actions and your current confusion. Faith or doubt, hopes or fears, all are yours. Be in charge and decide. It's time for you to move forward.*

39

THE PROPOSAL

Soon afterwards, I met Dr. Joseph Hopkins, our theology professor and my spiritual counselor. He was short in stature but superb when it came to spiritual issues and an inspired and inspiring counselor. For the past three years he had been my counselor and the director of my theological studies.

"Dr. Hopkins, I need a couple minutes of your time," I said. He pointed to a chair across from his desk and said, "You seem worried, tell me, what's on your mind?"

Dr. Hopkins showed personal interest and genuine sympathy as I described the dialogue that had transpired between Bishop Ezekiel and myself.

Looking at me straight in the eyes, he shook his head and said, "You have been a good student and in the three years that I have seen your involvement at our Divinity School, I know that you honor and love your Orthodox Church." Then he said, "Well, by now, you know the church rules. What are you going to do?"

"I don't want to get married yet."

"Not wanting to get married is not a sin. But you still want to become a priest."

"That's correct."

"Well, have you found someone that you could love?"

"I did, but I'm not sure that I'm in love with her."

"In love, falling in love? What a fantasy," He smiled. "As if love exists in a large pool that people fall into and swim forever in ecstasy."

Nervously, I smiled to hide my reaction to what I heard from Bishop Ezekiel and wondered what other words of wisdom Dr. Hopkins was going to tell me.

"I have been married to the same woman for fifty-two years," he said. "I was twenty-three and my wife, Barbara, was nineteen when we were married. All I can tell you is what I have experienced."

"Thank you," I said, still concerned and wanting his advice.

"Married life needs to be faced realistically. Imperfect people make imperfect marriages. Romance is replaced by the responsibilities of daily living. Often, unfulfilled expectations, financial problems, and parent-child conflicts cause emotional upheavals. No matter how rich our personalities or attractive our bodies, none of us can indefinitely excite and generate novelty, sexual electricity, and psychological pleasure within a marriage. No matter how wonderful the other person may be, we always find ourselves somewhat disappointed. Yet respect for each other for the years we spent together seems to maintain a favorably stable relationship."

"What can I tell my bishop now?"

"I don't know," Dr. Hopkins said, and scratched his head.

"Could you suggest something?"

"Yes. If I were in your shoes, with respect, faith, and love, I would get married and be ordained. You want to be a priest, and you have been trained to be a priest, this seems to be your goal. Now, you must decide."

Decisions, decisions! I walked out of Dr. Hopkins office, still undecided. I thought of calling Mary. Soon enough, I found a phone booth. I dialed her number but once it rang the first time, I hung up. I truly need more time to think about this.

The following Thursday, I received a phone call from the Archdiocese. Thalia, the Archbishop's secretary said, "His Eminence, Archbishop Michael wants to see you. Friday morning at 11:00. Be at his office."

I did not dare ask her why the Archbishop wanted to see me. "Thank you," I said nervously and froze, afraid that I might be reprimanded for delaying my ordination. On Friday morning, dressed in a black suit and wearing a black tie, like a graduate seminary student, I met Thalia on the first floor. She politely escorted me to the third floor to see the Archbishop. As the door opened, a sweet fragrance of incense permeated his office. Behind a huge, dark chestnut desk, sat the giant, a spiritual shepherd of the Greek Orthodox Archdiocese of North and South America. His bright eyes turned from a leather bound book, which he was reading, to me. He took off his glasses, placed them on his book, and, pointing to a chair, he said, "Welcome."

I bowed and said, "Thank you."

He cleared his throat and with a gracious fatherly smile said, "It is my personal wish that next time you enter my office, you will be wearing a clerical collar."

I nodded, but silently shook my head.

"I have been informed how persistently you initiated and pursued a fundraising drive to help the needs of our theological seminary." He paused for a few seconds and the subject changed. "I know that you have done some postgraduate work."

"Yes, Your Eminence."

"How old are you now?" he asked.

"Twenty-six," I said.

"It's time to be ordained," he said, "and there is a young lady waiting for you."

The Proposal

In shock and silence, I waited to hear who the young lady was that the Archbishop had chosen for me. He stood up, combed his long beard with his fingers, and walked around his desk. He came and sat next to me. He reached and took hold of my right hand and said, "Peter, Mary was the young woman who helped you, through her radio program, to collect thousands of dollars for our seminary. She left her work and came all the way from Camden, New Jersey, to New York City to see me. She loves you and wants you to marry her. She wants to be your wife. I asked many questions and she answered them with confidence." He squeezed my hand, looked at me directly, and still holding on to my hand, said, "I believe you should marry her and serve your church as a dedicated priest. She promised to be a good wife for you. And when you both have decided the date for your wedding, I plan to be there to bless the sacrament of marriage for you."

Stunned, I left the Archbishop's office. For several days, his fatherly voice resonated in me as I kept asking myself, Is this God's will or the Archbishop's?

Two weeks later, after constantly considering what the Archbishop had advised, I decided to contact Mary. She sounded happy to hear my voice. I took a deep breath and said, "I have a question for you."

"I'm listening," she said.

I didn't know how to phrase my question, so I remained silent, thinking as always, am I doing the right thing?

"We haven't spoken or contacted each other for weeks. What's the question?" she asked politely.

"I have thought about us and prayed," I said. "So here is my question: Would you consider becoming my wife?"

"Are you still planning to become a priest?"

"That's what I plan to do."

"I understand," she replied.

I was hoping she would reveal her visit to the Archbishop,

but she didn't. I didn't mention my encounter with him either. There are some aspects of life that are better left sacred and special, I thought. Sunday morning before going to church, I called her. "Are you coming to church today?"

"Of course, I am. But why are you asking me?"

"Because, I want to ask you, after church services, if you still want to be my wife."

Mary's response was an enthusiastic "yes."

40

MARRIAGE AND FAMILY

On June 8, 1952, Mary and I were married. Archbishop Michael performed our wedding ceremony, and at the end of the service, he shook our hands and greeted us with affection. He spoke eloquently about the solemnity of the Sacrament of Marriage and ended by saying, "I'm aware that both of you have been deprived of a mother's caring love at an early age, but God has always been present in your life, loving you and caring for you. Today, at this sacred hour, our Lord has brought you together and united you with his love. I wish you a long life together, a fruitful ministry, and lasting happiness."

On December 9, 1952, I was finally ordained, and the following Sunday, I was assigned a position in the parish of St. Nicholas in Newark, New Jersey. From the start, I wanted consciously to apply the wisdom of St. John Chrysostom, a Church Father of the fourth century, whom I admired during my theological training. He wrote that the church is like a clinic.

It was my daily prayer that my church would be that spiritual clinic for my parishioners. Parish life was demanding, but preaching the gospel in eloquent sermons, administering the sacraments, and celebrating religious services were visible tasks that any priest could perform. I was determined to create something more; something different and deeper. I want my parish to be a community of love, compassion, forgiveness, and service, reaching beyond the boundaries of the church building. My faith dictated that I should be mindful and that I needed to be loving and humble enough to accept guidance from the Lord in whose service I had enlisted.

The following year, my wife and I were blessed with the birth of a little girl, Mersene, whom we named after my mother. Two years later, we were blessed again by the birth of our son, Michael. Inside the Church, I was the spiritual father to many; young and old called me Father. But at home, I was the natural father of two beautiful children; a family man. By the age of twenty-nine, I was both a full-time priest and a family man. It was very inspiring being a spiritual leader for an army of parishioners, but it became increasingly difficult to give equal attention to both Church and family.

Two years later, I was transferred from the East Coast to the West Coast. It was an honor to be sent to the Greek Ortho-dox Cathedral in Los Angeles, but along with the honor came a multitude of responsibilities. Every week, I had to perform two weddings, three to four christenings, and funerals. Wed-dings and Christenings were two sacraments that I enjoyed celebrating. I felt truly rewarded seeing happy faces; the joyful reactions of most people. During this time, my wife and I were blessed with a third child, a boy with blond hair and dark blue eyes, whom we named Basil. His christening was followed by a lavish reception: a big time of celebration and entertainment, a delicious meal served with refreshing cool drinks. A Greek desert, baklava attracted the attention of the participants with its sweet and fragrant taste. It was a rewarding experience for me to see my parishioners honoring my family and my newly christened son.

One Saturday during Lent, I entered the Cathedral, as I did every Saturday from a small back door, to prepare the altar for Sunday Services. The main door was open till 5:00

p.m., when people could enter and pray. As far as I could notice this particular Saturday there was not a soul inside the main church. Suddenly, I heard the echo of a young voice. Unable to discern the words, I stood behind a partition that carried the icons of saints and listened. It was a young boy voicing the following prayer:

> "Lord, you have taken my dear father away," his words were punctuated with deep sighs. "Can't you send him back, oh Lord? We love him—we need him….Please, please, please, dear Jesus, may I return home and find him seated with my little brother and sister, with my Mom placing dinner on the table. And please may I hear all my family laughing and laughing, my Lord God, Creator of earth and skies? It would be simple for you, and I know you want us to be happy. We would adore you and sing you praises every minute….Wouldn't it be glorious, oh Lord, to bring my father right here, right now? And I'll take him by the hand and take him home and knock on the door and then when Mom opens the door, I'll say, 'Mom, here's Dad'—Oh Lord, don't you see how wonderful—?"

Touched by the prayer of this innocent soul, I stepped out of the altar slowly and recognized little Johnny, the six-year-old boy whose father had died in a car accident on the Hollywood freeway two weeks earlier. I remembered performing his father's funeral; a sad day. I reached out and gently took his hand, lifting him from his kneeling position. "Johnny, how did you get here?"

"My Mom went shopping at the Greek store across the street, Father. So, I told her that I wanted to light a candle, and she said, 'Just be careful as you cross the street.'"

Unable to say anything about his prayer, I said, "Johnny, let's walk back to your Mom....I want to buy a couple things for myself at the Greek store, some feta cheese and olives." In my heart, I knew and believed that when the father is absent, God is present. I had even written a book on that theme, yet I had no idea how to convey that belief to Johnny's innocent heart. I had the greatest difficulty conducting his father's funeral. That Saturday night, I lay awake for a long time, thinking that there is so much suffering in life.

41

MAN, PRIEST, HUSBAND, FATHER

Recalling my earlier years in the ministry, I naively offered grieving people sweet and comforting platitudes: "Death is the gateway to Paradise. God has a plan for each one of us, and brings us back into his presence, when our time on earth has comes to an end. But when God takes children away, he is protecting them from the world of evil and corruption. God wants to have innocent children in his kingdom."

More than a month after conducting Johnny's father's funeral, a five-year-old girl died. Her young parents were inconsolable. Lisa was their first child. At her funeral, my anxiety rose high enough to dry my tongue. Words would not come to my lips, and I tried to imagine what God could say about the death of this young girl, Lisa. So I improvised what God might say,

In view of the ultimate pain that little Lisa's parents feel today, I can hear God's gentle voice, who in His loving heart claims: I want only children in my kingdom. I like children because my image has not yet been tarnished in them. They are new, pure, without a blot or smear. I like them because they're still growing, they are still improving. They make mistakes as they grow, but they don't mean any harm. In my heaven, there will be children and only adults with children's hearts, for I know nothing more beautiful than the pure eyes of a child. I, your God, live in children, and it is I who look out through their eyes. It is I who smile at you through those innocent eyes. When death occurs, I am with you to bring back to life the innocent child's heart in you.

As I reflect on myself as a man, as a priest, as a husband, and as a father, I realize that I had exaggerated expectations of myself, of my wife, and of my children. I think I did better as a priest than I did as a husband, respecting my wife, loving her, and supporting her ideas. Even when we had differences of opinion or disagreements, I strove to be a positive figure in her life and a reasonably caring husband. As a father, I suffered from bouts of anxiety when I noticed any of my children's shortcomings or witnessed some of their risky choices. I wanted my children to make good choices and be happy, in full awareness of my own and their human vulnerability.

Today, one of my lasting joys is to sit with my two daughters and two sons and their spouses, and chat during casual visits or celebrations of important holidays. Our conversations include humor and serious talk; we relive memories, they tease me about things they got away with, and they commented on how strict or flexible I was during their growing years. Their presence in my life is rewarding. We interact with each other, less as father and children and more as friends. For me, this is God's ultimate blessing. Often I remind them of their growing years, and we laugh remembering the mischief that they used to get into and how I used to discipline them.

Man, Priest, Husband, Father

Recently, I notice that they are interested in learning about my growing years. They want to know in what ways my father influenced me and what methods he used to discipline me. Selective as memory tends to be, I choose episodes from my past that are sometimes humorous and sometimes not. For example, I was late for church one Sunday and my father slapped me in front of other churchgoers. The hurt of that Sunday's slap was not as painful as it was embarrassing. Another vivid recollection is the corrective belt he used whenever I failed to live up to his expectations; he would pull off his belt to strike me. I was terrified. I can still remember how much it hurt.

One day my father had made plans to take me to work to help him trim olive trees. He woke me up early and said that we would be leaving in half an hour. Quickly, I rolled up a quilt, an imitation of myself, and placed it on my bed under the covers. I hid in the closet and heard him yelling, *Peter! Peter! Aren't you up yet? Now, you are going to get it!*

From a chink in the closet door I watched him as he dashed angrily into my room. He yanked off his belt and struck the rolled quilt again and again. Not hearing my usual cries of pain, he pulled back the covers and saw the trick. Beneath the harsh punishments, then, was a sense of humor.

His New Year's message to me when I was nineteen still lives in my memory. I came home in the early morning hours as happy as ever. I had been out with my friends celebrating the arrival of the New Year and we had been singing love songs to girlfriends. This was the custom in the Greek village where I grew up. I saw a cloud of anger in my father's face, as he asked, "Where were you until this early morning hour?"

"Out with my friends."

"With losers. Doing what?"

"Nothing."

"I give up on you. You're hopeless! You'll never amount to anything."

On hearing this story, my daughter Mersene exclaimed, "Wow! Dad, you did your share of mischief."

Mike added, "I don't think that Dad caused as much trouble as we did. He was pretty normal."

"Thanks Mike," I said. "As I recall, there were times I used my belt to punish you when you came home late. I still feel bad about it. I want to apologize and ask you to forgive me."

"Dad, I don't remember the belting as much as I remember that never once did you ask where I had been, who I was with, or why I was so late in getting home."

Mike's reply was a lesson. I was eager to punish him without asking where, how, and with whom he spent his time. I had inherited that method of discipline from my father. It was cruel and I should have known better, but where did *my* father learn that method? When he told me how his father disciplined him, I was appalled. One time, he arrived home in the wee hours of the morning and when the sun came up, his father tied him with a rope behind a donkey and paraded him through the marketplace. It did not matter that the boy was late because he was chanting at a church vigil, assisting the priest of our parish. My father's punitive methodology somehow had a positive influence on me. As an adult, I learned that difficulties and obstacles in life sharpen our skills to face life's challenges. I have worked hard all my life; I have a home and a happy wife; and I have raised a family.

In addition to my children's wish to hear what kind of a father I had and my desire to tell them, they probably want to know what I think of my relationship with them. My recent evaluation of myself as a father has been modified over the years. I have admitted to my sons and daughters the fact that I was not a perfect father. As a Christian father, I tried to teach and model for them what I believed to be the values of the

Christian Faith: love, joy, compassion, generosity, patience, and forgiveness. I want them to be grateful to God for what they have, to accept and love those who are not able to return love, and to find inner joy and peace even in difficult times. I want them to show patience, even when things are not going as well as expected, I want them to practice charity and to be ever mindful of the needs of others.

Of course, I no longer have any control over their lives. They are mature, responsible adults, not because of my anxious hovering but, at least in part, because they know I love them. I know my children love me and respect me. They no longer need my wisdom to design their lives.

42

A BEGGAR AT THE DOOR

In 1954, on the Sunday after Thanksgiving, a Pontifical Liturgy was scheduled at 10:00 a.m. to be celebrated by His Eminence, Archbishop Ierotheos. It had been an annual tradition of the cathedral for many years. I had already told Johnny not to come into the sanctuary that day. "Respectfully, you and your mother, sit in the second pew on the right, enjoy the liturgy, and observe how the archbishop blesses the people."

"Father, when can I see and speak to the archbishop?"

"I'll take you to him later, after the services," I said. Johnny nodded with a smile.

The archbishop was respected as a holy man by the simple and humble believers of the Greek Orthodox Church. They obeyed him and bowed reverently before him as he spoke to them in church, and after the Liturgy, they each kissed his hand. Whenever he visited one of his parishes, he praised the Patriarch of Constantinople, as the highest spiritual authority of our times. He emphasized the virtues of the Fathers of the early church, suggesting them as our models to emulate. His mansion in Napa Valley, California's wine district, was located near those wealthy Greek-American businessmen, who invited him to dinner on major Holy Days.

The archbishop favored only certain clergymen, who were his allies in reviving the spirit of stern obedience among his believers and in evoking the generosity of the wealthy. There had always been a magic message in his voice that magnetized the interest of his audience. The women were especially moved by the sweetness of his words and looked upon him as a messenger of love, and their eyes were rich with tears.

During this visit to the great Greek cathedral, he raised his hands and said, "My brothers and sisters, I ask you in the name of my love, respect, and friendship for you, do not associate with nonbelievers, for you will not find their support. If I deserve your kindness and love, let me live among you and share with you the happiness and sorrows of life. Let us join hands and work together, for if I cannot make myself one of you and help you, I would be a hypocrite who does not live according to his principles."

An hour after the church services, the local bishop had prepared a special lavish lunch for the archbishop to be served by his butler at his rectory, an elegant building adjacent to the cathedral. Young Johnny, overwhelmed by the melodious chanting and the archbishop's sermon told his mother to stay in the church. "The priest and I are going to see the archbishop," he said softly. He got up from the pew and walked around the corner of the cathedral. The priest arrived as they had agreed. Johnny's heart palpitated fast, as he rang the bell of the rectory. The door opened and an older man, the butler in a black suit appeared through the half-opened door. Purposely, I stayed a few feet behind Johnny, allowing him to be in charge of his visit.

The butler could not see me, but I could hear his voice when he said, "What do you want?"

"I want to see the archbishop."

"He's about to have his lunch."

"I must see him," Johnny said.

"What about?"

"It's...Oh, I can only tell him."

"Does he expect you?"

"No, but I know he will see me."

"Perhaps after his lunch."

"I cannot leave until I see him."

The door was closing.

"You will have to come back some other time...perhaps tomorrow or next week when he is not too busy." The butler's voice sounded firm and angry.

Hearing the butler, I felt a sudden rage, but when I saw Johnny put his right foot in the doorway, I stood where I could see the outcome.

"Oh, if you only knew how serious it is...!" Johnny pleaded.

The old butler hesitated.

"Is somebody dying...?"

"No. My father died in a car accident four weeks ago. My mother and my little brother and sister still cry. We need help."

"This is a cathedral house," The butler said.

"That is why I must see the archbishop," Johnny insisted.

"You are too young to come here."

"I do not understand."

"Let your mother come...next week when the archbishop may be still here."

As the butler was closing the door, Johnny screamed, "I must see him...."

"Not today!" the butler shouted.

When I heard Johnny's voice: "I must see him"...and the butler saying "not today," and closing the door, I jumped out of my hiding place and approached the butler. Angry and disappointed, I shouted in scathing Greek, *"kyrie oikonome yiati ferese toso akartha s'afto to paidi pou ehase to patera tou* (Mr. Butler, this child has recently lost his father. Why are you treating him in such a heartless manner)?"

With teary eyes, Johnny looked at me and said, "Father, I just wanted to see the archbishop. Maybe, he can help my family."

The butler turned and looked at me arrogantly, and said, "Sorry, Father. You and this boy may come in, but His Eminence is resting."

A couple times I had been inside the bishop's rectory. It was richly decorated with expensive furniture and portraits of important benefactors on the walls. It was a mansion donated by another wealthy man to be a home for the local bishop. We were led through a tall heavy door into a room with thick walls, soft dark red rugs, solid chairs and a broad table. There was the smell of woodwork, candle incense, and clean...cleanliness...*have there ever been in this place young children crying with empty stomachs?* I kept pondering and thinking of Johnny, *a young grieving boy that had gone inside that wealthy rectory to see the archbishop, hoping for help.*

The archbishop came through the kitchen door with a napkin around his neck, wearing a rich black and shiny cassock. He approached the big table, sat and smiled at the beautiful slim candles that shone a warm glow on the shiny porcelain plates, containing baked potatoes and cuts of brown dripping lamb chops and fresh peas and platters of hot fragrant food. I saw Johnny inhaling the fragrance, his mouth drooling. I thought of his young brother and sister sitting at that table and eating.

The archbishop pointed gently at a leather chair in the corner away from the dining area where I could sit. He sat in a large cushioned chair, closer to the dining table, smoothed his apron, and looking at Johnny, he asked, " Young man, why do you insist upon seeing me?"

"Pardon me, your holiness, but hearing your words of love today...."

"And..."

"What?"

Johnny, somewhat tongue-tied, noticed the butler's hands placing on the table a wide and high shortcake with big perfect strawberries staining the pure white whipped cream.

"Well, why don't you speak?"

Johnny began to speak, but could not find the right words to say exactly what he wanted.

"Ah! Yes, yes," said the archbishop. "But tell me, what can I do for you?"

"My mother needs help," Johnny said, as his mind ran back to his family, *"My Mom could sit at the head of that wonderful table and hand to my little brother and sister the beautiful food...."*

"Has your mother applied at the Welfare?"

"They said my father wasn't a citizen."

"Your mother is entitled to workmen's compensation."

"That's what they say. We got a letter from them."

"Good. So?"

"But it will be a long time before the case comes up."

"Has your mother tried to get some help from your local church?"

"But you, your holiness have food on that long table, wonderful food, and clean white hands picking it. Who is eating that wonderful food?" Johnny could not verbalize his thoughts, and for a few seconds he remained silent.

"Your holiness...."

"Yes?"

"Could you please help us?"

"How?"

"We need..."

"I have nothing to do with the charities. There is a board of trustees who appropriates funds for people in need. Do you understand?"

"Yes..."

Then there was silence.

Then the butler emerged from the kitchen again, and bowing with respect he said, "Dessert is served, Your Eminence."

Without looking at Johnny, the archbishop said, "Cut a good portion of the cake, wrap it nicely and bring it here.... Does your family like strawberry shortcake?"

"Yes..."

A soft package was placed into his hands from the glowing round and smiling face of his holiness.

"Thank you..."

"God bless you."

As a withering flower is brought back to life by a few drops of water, so the young Johnny's anxious heart felt enlivened by a piece of cake that the archbishop gave him. Out through a tall door and strong walls, he whispered, "*Will they ever protect me and my family?*"

Unreasonably annoyed, the butler shut the door.

Touched deeply at what I had witnessed in the presence of His Eminence, only a few minutes before, I placed my hand on Johnny's right shoulder and said, "Let's step in my office for a few minutes. I need to do something. *It was the end of the second week of the month, and I knew that an envelope would be waiting for me, containing $250.00; half of my monthly salary.*

"Father, my Mom would be still waiting inside the church."

"I'll take you to your mother," I said.

Johnny's mother, still sitting at the second pew, was happy to see us both approaching; Johnny was holding the cake wrapped in foil, and I was holding an envelope. "This is a small Christmas present for you," I said, and I gave her the envelope. After a hug and a kiss, and a heartfelt *thank you*, mother and son left.

The mixed emotions that I felt propelled me into the

sanctuary, where I knelt before the cross, thought of Jesus, and began to pray, *Would the hierarchy, dear Lord, ever be willing to translate their rich and colorful words into action? Their elegant sermons are impressive and evoke enthusiasm on Sunday mornings in church, but is there any action? Does the enthusiasm produce any positive results through the week?*

I stayed there and pondered these thoughts for a long time.

43

THE TRAP OF PRIDE

To avoid falling into the dangerous trap of pride, it was important to discern between positive pride—good feelings of doing something worthwhile in the eyes of God—and negative pride—pursuing projects for personal glory and failing to acknowledge God as the Giver of all Blessings.

I had to minimize my impact upon people, cease trying to impress them, and acknowledge the Holy Spirit working through me. I was simply an instrument in God's hands—Isn't that what we all are? God's tools in bringing about our salvation. Our well-being, peace and happiness on earth prepares us for the ultimate reward once our earthly life comes to an end.

Despite my theological education, it took me a long time to see myself as an instrument of God. What I needed was a large dose of humility and spiritual maturity. I had to learn to live compassionately among people. The Lord was very clear when he said, "The Son of Man did not come to be served, but to serve." Humility permeated his entire ministry. In the hours before his crucifixion, Jesus washed the feet of his disciples. Was that a sign of weakness? Or was it the ultimate example of humility? From his birth in a stable, his presence among people, and his final entrance into Jerusalem—not riding in a chariot or on a horse as a king, but on a simple donkey—to his tragic death on the hill called Golgotha, we see a life of utmost humility.

As Christians, it is worth becoming aware of the Lord's presence in our life, his acceptance of us, and his love and forgiveness. He directs us away from personal pride and points us to a simple way of living where there is peace and contentment. It is through simplicity that our hearts become tender to the needs of the afflicted. There is an old saying: "The one whose stomach is always full can never understand how a hungry person feels."

Granted, living in a competitive, *me-first* society and wanting to climb higher and higher up the ladder of success makes it difficult to be humble. Humility may be regarded as a sign of weakness. We may lose out and be left behind in the corporate world, while others gain success. Christ's message is reassuring: The one who is humble shall be raised high. When we choose to live the Christian life, there is one fact on which we can absolutely rely: God has a specific plan and purpose for each one of us. Instead of striving for higher positions or envying other people's apparent success, we can be grateful for our present position and each day do the best we can, experiencing the joy of daily living within God's will, which guarantees peace. God's love and immeasurable mercy are his gifts to us.

I could not abide the hierarchical mentality that tended to make God—and other people, for that matter—into who they wanted or needed God to be. I see the role of the priest to keep his people free for God. But, at the same time, it is the priest's responsibility to keep God free for people. Of course, I could not interpret God the way I perceived divinity myself, either. Can any human, however theologically educated he or she is, define God? The only human knowledge we can have about God is the personality of Jesus Christ, who is God in human flesh.

For a long time, I experienced a sense of personal loneliness, even when I was among gatherings of people who attended church, or religious rituals, or community celebrations. The best way that I was able to diffuse that loneliness was to write books for religious education classes. I had strong faith in the potential of younger people, whose hearts and minds were still pure and receptive.

Years later, still a therapist, I realized that loneliness is one of the universal sources of troubled souls who seek solace. To emerge effectively from our labyrinth of loneliness is the challenge to see the reality of life, face its ramifications, and attempt to make it more humane and simple. There is joy and peace in simple things.

Of course, many realize the influence of the advertising industry with its artificial and deceptive world, telling us how we can escape the malady of loneliness. All we need is a credit card to buy ourselves anything in sight—electronic devices, cellular phones, gadgets, luxuries, possessions, and better and bigger attainments. The clever merchants claim to know what we need.

Perhaps we need some external authority to help us enter our inner self and find the secret of contentment within. The realization that no other person can completely think the way we do, feel or act the way we do, offers us the freedom of choice: either design our life like anyone else, following the unwritten law of conformity; or choose the straight path, living a Godly life.

My choice surfaced gradually. I had to be responsible for my personal life. My life as a priest was already planned by Jesus Christ, who had chosen a handful of dedicated men and changed the course of human history. What a great honor and responsibility for me, to be in line with his disciples and bring the "Good News," the immortal teachings of Christ among his people!

As difficult as it seemed, I had to let God be greater than our theological knowledge, and our own projections. Before I conveyed any authentic knowledge about God to my congregation, I needed to learn who I was; my own reality of being human.

The God who favors certain people while ignoring others, and allows tragedies to occur, was not acceptable to me. The war-minded Greeks had Zeus, a god who could hurl thunderbolts and destroy the evil-doers.

For the Jews, God's chosen people, God responded only to their demands, caused famines, and punished the transgressors of the Law. God created us in his image and likeness, and therefore, it is wrong to make God in our human image and likeness.

It was Jesus Christ and his apostle, Paul, who removed the boundaries and spoke emphatically about a God of love and reconciliation. When I read about the earthly life of Jesus and contemplated his unconditional love through his healing ministry, compassion, forgiveness, and how responsibly he related to all people, I felt inspired. At the same time, I recognized my ineptness, not simply to imitate him but to implement his teachings.

Could I ever discuss or share these concerns, personal dilemmas, with any of my superiors? While being critical of my ministry, I guarded myself from being threatened with suspension. I had a wife and children who needed my support, and the church provided my only income. Shy by nature, I kept my thoughts to myself, realizing, at times, that even noble ambitions cannot be fulfilled. What was I to do? Feel sorry for myself? Our ancestors provided the answer: *Get deeper into your Self and learn from your Self what you must do*. The choice was evident. You must do what your soul dictates and not expect approval or support.

St. Basil, a fourth-century church father, encapsulated the ministry of the church and the mission of every Christian. I contemplated his words slowly, and meditated on how to

make God's unconditional love and mercy available to myself
and to others:

> According to the abundance of Your mercy, fill our
> life with good things; preserve our families in peace
> and harmony; nurture the infants, instruct the youth,
> embrace and support the elderly, comfort the dis-
> couraged, bring back closer to You those who have
> gone astray. Free those who are possessed by nega-
> tive or evil thoughts. Sail with those at sea, be a com-
> panion with those who travel, defend the widows,
> protect the orphans, free the prisoners, and heal the
> sick and suffering. Remember those who love us and
> those who hate us, and forgive those who reject us.
> Lord, extend your mercy to the helpless, give hope to
> the hopeless, for You are the Father of all, the Healer
> of all ailments, the Savior of our bodies and souls who
> knows the name and the age of each one of us, and
> You know our needs even from our mother's womb.
> (A prayer from St. Basil's Liturgy, 330–79)

This prayer places us in the hands of God. We trust God
and we ask him to be in control of our lives. We are all his children, and we surrender slowly to his loving care and guidance.
Once we let God be present in our life, we extend his loving
care to others by kindness, charity, and good attitude. One
may say, well, this is what the church should do. Wonderful!
But who is the church? You and I are the church. As St. Paul
states, "You are the body of Christ and individually members
of it" (1 Cor 12:27).

I asked certain well-to-do parishioners to donate money
for a child who needed open-heart surgery. The parish president said, "Our community has many financial needs we are
concerned about. Missionary work is a project for charities."

It was known on the parish level that some of these well-heeled people spent enormous amounts of money on personal luxuries and entertainment. They drove expensive cars, lived in elegant mansions, took exotic vacations, and dressed in designer clothes. Their lives imitated the stars of Hollywood, embellished by seductive advertisement. Wonderful!

But who gave me the authority to judge? People who work hard deserve the best. Why should they deprive themselves of all these benefits? People are the architects of their lives; they have freedom to design their lives as they please. Perhaps they should not deprive themselves of anything they desire. I find that hard to stomach. Could it be so difficult for them to extend a benevolent hand and help others who are in dire need of food, clothing, or medicine?

All humans are challenged with the question: As one person with little resources at my disposal, what can I possibly do? I can scarcely make ends meet. The answer lies with each individual. There is something that we can do, despite our circumstances. No matter how poor in money, talent, or position we are, there is a gift that each of us can give. Any person whose nature is normal can show love, affection, and sympathy.

The following Chinese wisdom may inspire and encourage us to do God's work in our life:

> If there be righteousness in the heart, there will be
> beauty in the character.
> If there is beauty in the character, there will be
> harmony in the home.
> If there is harmony in the home, there will be order
> in the nation.
> When there is order in each nation, there will be
> peace in the world.

The Trap of Pride

If God's omnipresence included the stars and the whole universe, God must also be right around us—as Jesus Christ put it, "The kingdom of God is among you" (Luke 17:21). In grief, we cannot simply think of God as living in heaven. Whenever we see God as aloof and not caring about our daily realities, we alienate ourselves from God. We need a concept of God that will bring him into our homes, our kitchens, our bedrooms, our living rooms—yes, even when those living rooms are crowded with guests. If God is everywhere, he must be quite as near to us as he is far away.

We need to make God our *immediate* reality. We need to seek God's guidance and inspiration in our most intimate thoughts and feelings, when the world is most demanding of our attention, even in our light undertakings, and behind our silliest jokes. Ultimately, God alone can satisfy our most personal needs. In our dealings with others, God is our conscience; in our work, God is our satisfaction; when we read a good book or listen to melodic music, God is our inspiration. In everything we do, from the performance of serious duty to the most trivial pursuits, God is there, watching, joining in with our invitation, and giving us strength. To ignore God's presence means to go stumbling blindly through life, unaware of innumerable pitfalls on the path before us.

When we think of God abstractly, we distance ourselves from him. Saying that our belief is enough to save us, what sort of salvation could that possibly be? Theological definitions give no comfort to the heart. They are like antique chairs to display but never to be sat upon. Some people remember God during their times of suffering—but otherwise? Sometimes they consider themselves well enough without God, as they go trudging wearily from one crisis to another, their brows furrowed in anxiety.

You and I need a concept of God that will motivate us to *love* him and want to know him. How we relate to God is crucial for our peace of mind and for our happiness.

44

THE ORPHANS

In the early sixties, I decided to visit my aging parents, who upon retirement returned to Greece and settled on the island of Lesvos. Every two years, I enjoyed taking this trip to be with my parents and to visit my friends. I was only three years old when my father took me to Lesvos where I lived for seventeen years. It was on my twentieth birthday that my family and I returned to the United States, the country of my birth.

On one of my visits to Greece, the director of a local orphanage, Theodore Skinas, approached me and asked if I could help his boys. He said, "We have 160 orphaned boys. These were victims of war or children of divorced or no parents to take care of them. We feed them, educate them, teach them a trade, and help them to become good citizens." The words, *orphaned boys*, brought me instantly back to my own childhood, when I was called and considered an orphan. I felt an immediate and unexpected urge to help these boys.

"Mr. Skinas, what kind of help do you think I could offer?"

"You live in America, a very rich country," he said with a gracious smile. "Perhaps you could find one or two wealthy people to...you know...," he paused.

"What is it that the orphanage needs at this time?" I asked.

The Orphans

"Well, for starters, we don't have a refrigerator or a freezer to store food that local people donate. I need to buy fabric to make new uniforms for my children." He always referred to the orphans as his children. "The Holy Days of Christmas and the New Year will be here in another six weeks, and I want my children, besides the familiar uniforms that orphans wear, to have something new to wear like other boys."

"Let me think what I could possibly do," I said, "and I'll get back to you."

He thanked me graciously, and we shook hands. It was the first Saturday in November when I decided to visit the orphanage. Conditions were not ideal. The elegant building was old and tired. The dormitories were large, each holding twenty-eight beds. The walls were damp and peeling. The place appeared clean and all the beds were neatly made, but the entire edifice needed to be renovated. The wooden floors were bare but clean; two or three faded pictures of war heroes decorated each wall. In certain rooms, instructors taught classes in carpentry, furniture making, shoemaking, and tailoring.

As Mr. Skinas took me on a tour around each part of the facility, each time we entered a room the boys stood up and bowed. Mr. Skinas asked the trainees to sit down and introduced me as a guest from America. Beautiful swarthy faces with crew haircuts and big dark brown eyes looked at me respectfully. Their clothes were in tatters, and their sandals had seen better days. "Oh! America!" The boys whispered among themselves and smiled. I wondered what thoughts lay behind their innocent exclamations.

After we had seen a few areas, a loud bell rang. Work stopped, and the boys emerged from their rooms and headed toward the dining room. Tactfully, everyone took their places. Mr. Skinas invited me to join him and the personnel for lunch. We sat at the head table. Everyone stood for grace, which was offered by one of the older boys. The whole meal consisted of a dish of fried potatoes for each boy, a slice of dark bread, and an apple. Glasses of water were available at the table, but juice and milk were not part of the diet. While the boys ate silently, their eyes kept wandering across to me, the VIP at the head table.

The potatoes, fried in pure olive oil, were delicious, dessert and salad were not on the menu. My mind played an instant video of American children back home, sitting around the table, eating a variety of nourishing foods. How much these orphans would enjoy an American Sunday dinner, complete with a dessert! Why should our American children have so much and these children so little? The thought saddened me. I drank a little water and noticed it was lukewarm. Mr. Skinas, catching my grimace, said, "Our water is not cold. That's why we need a refrigerator in this place. At least my children should have cold drinking water, especially during summer." Who would have thought such an institution could be lacking in what we consider the most ordinary thing in every American home?

At the end of the meal, the tables were cleared instantly. The boys walked out of the building and stood in single file on a soccer field. An instructor brought out a bike, and the first boy in line took a ride around the entire field. When his turn was over, he joined the end of the line to wait for a second turn. The second in line took his turn, and so the pattern continued. I couldn't believe my eyes.

It was beyond my imagining that 160 boys would wait in line, well behaved and excited, for a bicycle ride. Mr. Skinas informed me that every Saturday he gave each boarder an allowance of five drachmas, equivalent at that time to about half a dollar. "My children, instead of buying ice cream, rented a bicycle." He chuckled and said, "So I bought them a used bike. Now they have a ride here on the premises and can buy ice cream with their pocket money." It was an amazing sight to behold, the excitement of these boys sharing a single bicycle. *What would our American children say if they saw such joy over a simple plaything?* I wondered.

When I returned to my post at the cathedral in Los Angeles, the images I had witnessed at the orphanage remained vivid in my mind. On Sunday mornings, the radiant faces of children who got so much pleasure from a used bike continued to haunt me. I looked at my well-fed and well-dressed congregation—men, women, and children.

As I was about to deliver the sermon on the first Sunday of Advent, I glanced at my entire congregation. It was good to see their jovial expectant faces. With Christmas less than a month away, I knew that most of these people would be steeped in the frenzy of shopping, partying, and gift buying. I thought of delivering a couple of brief messages about the mission of the church, focusing on God's love and caring. I reminded my audience of the needs of others and how we might be able to help during the Christmas season.

When I mentioned my visit to the orphanage and their dire need for a refrigerator, I noticed some uneasiness. I remember saying, "The kingdom of God is not just in heaven after we die. It starts right here, as we apply Christ's command: *thy kingdom come.* As we repeat these three words, we become members of God's kingdom now. And that means we have to share God's gifts—our wealth and talents—with the less fortunate while we are still in this life."

That afternoon, I received a telephone call from Despina, an eighty-five-year-old widow who offered to buy the refrigerator for the orphans. Roy Dolley, a convert in his early sixties, happened to be in the cathedral and heard my Sunday message, referring to the needs of the orphanage that I had recently visited. A couple days later, he visited my office and offered to build an additional dormitory so the boys would have more comfortable sleeping arrangements. Unfortunately, a week later, before Roy Dolley could finalize his plans to go to Greece, he had a head-on collision on the Hollywood Freeway and died instantly.

Relatives and friends sent flowers to the mortuary. Sixty-seven wreaths, the funeral director told me. During the eulogy, I praised Roy Dolley's philanthropic intentions and told listeners what he had planned to do for the orphanage. I thanked those who had sent flowers to honor him, but thinking about what happened to the flowers after the funeral led me to say, "How wonderful would it be if, instead of spending so much on flowers, we could appropriate part of this money for charity? Holy Days are around the corner, and the less fortunate would welcome some help."

That was not what the trustees of the cathedral wanted to hear. After the funeral service, Paul Pitches one of the trustees, came to see me in my office. Tall, swarthy, and arrogant, he paused in front of my desk and pointed his finger at me, saying, "If you ever speak like that again at any of the funerals of my friends or relatives, you will no longer belong to this cathedral."

Blood rushed to my face, and I tried hard to control my frustration. "What was so offensive to you?" I asked.

"You spoke about what interests you, charity and orphans."

"Is that so bad for a Christian congregation to hear?"

"Yes, we have national charities; they take care of these needy people."

I looked him straight in the eyes and said, "I am a priest, and an important part of my ministry is to direct our people to love each other and to practice philanthropy."

"This congregation consists of good and generous people who have their own favorite charities," he said. "They don't need to be told what to do with their money. So, for your own sake, I advise you to follow the wishes of the Board of Trustees."

The Orphans

While I knew that this man had no power over me or my ministry, I suspected that he could influence my local bishop and might even be able to have me transferred. So be it! I said to myself. As inconvenient as a transfer would be, I would still have my integrity and my principles to bring to another parish.

For the Los Angeles cathedral congregation, charity did not feature prominently in their character. To a great degree the Hollywood influence was evident in their appearance and lifestyle. Life was taken lightly. Living in a capitalist society, most people find it hard to discover their own spiritual dimension. Affluence brought high fashion and style into the lives of the many cathedral members, but what inner joy did they experience? Yet, who was I to judge? I could only evaluate silently what I saw.

Joy is an inside job, I thought, and when we expect to find it outside, we end up disappointed. Perhaps the yearning of their souls to reach out was stifled by material accumulations. Performing the Sunday services and sacraments well was what most people expected of me. It was the visible part of my ministry, but I expected more of myself, more that might not be visible to anyone but God. In addition to my parish duties, I began to follow a more gratifying path, that of domestic and foreign missionary work.

Initially I had made desperate attempts to live up to others' expectations. But I was not what others thought of me. As a priest, I had to claim the truth. Like anyone else I was a son of a loving God, and I no longer had to beg for permission to do my job. If I were to keep my priestly integrity intact, I had to obey my inner voice. I felt it was in sync with Christ's expectation of me: "Go therefore and make disciples of all nations... teaching them to obey everything that I have commanded you. And remember, I am with you always, to the end of the age" (Matt 28:19–20).

THE OLIVE PICKER

My involvement in educational activities for the youth, in missions, and in the healing ministry of the Church left very little time for my family. I became everybody's benevolent Father, but not a good father or husband at home. My wife and children complained about my long hours at work, and my answer to them was a sign of external compliance, "You're right, I shouldn't work so hard," but that external compliance was coupled with an inner defiance. I followed the command, *parish and serving the people come first*, and I felt satisfied in my priestly commitment. Often, I even envied my Catholic colleagues for being celibate. They had as much time as they needed to do things they wanted, without the responsibility of a wife and children.

45

EXPECT THE UNEXPECTED

Heraclitus's saying again proved to be true. This time "the unexpected" came on August 6, 1966, in the form of a command from Archbishop Iakovos, the Primate of the Greek Orthodox Archdiocese of what was then North and South America. The upper hierarchy informed me that I was being transferred from the West Coast back to the East Coast. "You are to start a new parish in Westfield, New Jersey, as of September 1, 1966." It was a command that I had to obey; otherwise I could be without a job. The reality of packing and moving my family, wife, and three children, didn't seem to matter to the archbishop. But it did matter to me. It also mattered that in taking up a new post in New Jersey, I would be leaving unfinished and serious responsibilities at Agia Sophia—the Holy Wisdom Cathedral of Los Angeles, California.

In 1963, *America, America*, a dramatic motion picture written and directed by Elia Kazan, was screening in most theaters throughout the United States. To diffuse my indignation, I decided to go and see that much-talked-about motion picture.

It was a true American classic in the best sense, one of the best pictures ever made. It was a must see for any first or second generation American. Impressed by Elia Kazan's *America, America*, and having read his book on which this film was based, I wrote him a letter, praising his masterful production, and expressing my wish to meet him. I was writing a novel at that time based on a true story, and I hoped that I could get some ideas from such an accomplished author. Within two weeks, I received a gracious response and an invitation to meet him the next time I was in New York.

In August 1966, I was transferred from Los Angeles, California, to Westfield, New Jersey. I contacted Mr. Kazan and we met in New York City at the Pantheon Greek restaurant, on Eighth Avenue. Initially, he wanted to know about me and why I would leave the beautiful climate of California to come to New Jersey. Briefly, I explained that priests have no choice but to accept the orders of their bishop, who decides where there is a need for a priest.

"So, you are like a soldier," he commented.

"It seems that way," I answered. "But before I'm transferred again, maybe to Alaska, please tell me your story about *America, America*, I have seen the movie twice."

I saw pride in his face when he said, "This was my best film so far, based on my best book of the same title."

"I have also read your book and loved it. Since then, with enthusiasm, I began to write a good story, a novel of my own," I said. "I would like some help and direction."

Firmly, he looked at me and said, "If you are interested in writing a novel, the best advice that I can give you is that with each three pages that you write, try to reduce them to one page only."

I had already written 325 pages. I chose not to tell him.

"You are silent," he said.

"Skeptical," I said. If I follow Mr. Kazan's advice, two thirds of my novel will have to go.

"Tell me your thoughts," he said, smiling graciously.

"I don't think I'm qualified to write a novel," I said.

"Why not?" he asked.

"Too much work, energy, and time, and I don't even know the skills of writing."

"That's all negative thinking," he said, "But writing a novel is serious business, believe me. I'm working on another book, and it doesn't come easy."

"Another book?" I asked, envious of his motivation.

Beyond the Aegean Sea. It is a true story that I have been thinking about since I wrote *America, America.*

"Aegean Sea," I said, feeling excited. "Mr. Kazan, I grew up in Lesvos, an island of the Aegean Sea."

"That's the island where I plan to stage my next motion picture. I may need your help," he said.

"I'll do whatever I can. This August, I plan to be in Lesvos for two weeks. My parents are there, and I have relatives and friends that I will visit."

"Good," he said. "Can you come to my office next Monday morning? I plan to give you a written message for Mr. Yiannis Kalimanis, the mayor of Lesvos."

"I sure can," I said, feeling sure that now I had a connection with an author and movie producer.

After a luscious meal and a glass of Greek wine, we hugged each other, shook hands as friends, and parted.

Bright and early on Monday morning, I arrived at his Broadway office. He was there, sitting behind his desk, flipping through pages of a thick manuscript.

"Come and sit for a moment," he said, "I have a couple of Greek poems. Do you think you can translate them for me? I want to use them in my screenplay."

The poems were short and familiar to me. So I asked him

207

for a pencil and some paper. It didn't take me long to read and translate them from the original Greek into English. He read them aloud and said, "Very good. I do like your translation." He shook his head, and as his eyes reflected pleasure, he said, "You have passed a test this morning, and I'm going to make you a very interesting offer." He took a deep breath. It looked to me like a real sigh revealing emotional pain, as he said, "In my story, there is a major character, Chrysostomos, a renowned bishop of Smyrna." He paused for a few seconds, and, pressing his lips with evident indignation, said, "Bishop Chrysostomos was the spiritual leader of the Greek Orthodox Church and community of Smyrna at the time when, in 1922, the Muslim Turks conquered and destroyed major parts of Asia Minor.

"During their conquest of Smyrna, while Chrysostomos was celebrating the Divine Liturgy, a group of Muslims interrupted the worship service and dragged him out of the church and murdered him. His death ended Christ's church and its community in Smyrna, sealing it with Chrysostomos's faith and his blood. I want you to play this bishop's part in my movie."

"A bishop!" I exclaimed, nearly swallowing my tongue in ecstasy. One by one, negative images of the hierarchy surfaced in my mind. Bishops simply don't care about their clergy. And a question surfaced in my heart, "What kind of a bishop could I be?" Silently, I kept looking at Mr. Kazan.

"Yes, a bishop," he said, in raised voice, and handed me the screenplay. "Read his lines, memorize them, and come to this office in two weeks. We are going to have a rehearsal here."

On the train back to New Jersey, I held the manuscript tightly against my breast, anxiously wanting to read my lines, but I hesitated. Instead, I kept looking out the window; I saw familiar areas of old and new buildings and gigantic trees as the train sped past. The window mirrored my face, and nervously I smiled. Just the thought of playing the part of a bishop gave me a shiver. I blinked joyfully, and controlling my laughter, I visualized myself with longer hair, reaching my long gray beard, wearing a miter, special episcopal vestments, and a gold cross resting on my breast. I shook my head forcefully to come out of my fantasy. "It's only a movie," I said to myself, and began to read the screenplay. I had an ulterior motive and wanted Mr. Kazan to like me. Maybe he could make a movie of my story, I thought.

During the following two weeks, I met Norman Rose, an actor and a gifted narrator for documentary films. In the basement of the Church of the Annunciation on West Ninety-first Street, Norman Rose taught me how to use the tone of my voice and how to present myself as a bishop. Considering Norman's experience in theater, I followed his directives every single day at home and occasionally in my office. I gained confidence that I could play the bishop's part rather effectively.

The day of rehearsals arrived sooner than expected. It was the second Monday of April 1973. I took a seat among a group of six middle-aged men who sat in a semicircle. These must be some of the actors in Mr. Kazan's story, I thought. Each was holding pages of the screenplay, with a blue color cover, same as mine, and telling stories to diffuse their anxiety. I could not think of a story to tell, so I opened my screenplay and glanced at my lines.

"Good morning, gentlemen." We heard the robust voice of the author and director, Mr. Elia Kazan, and all seven men stood up.

"Please be seated and relax. We have some serious work to do this morning." At 10:00 a.m. this master of motion pictures joined his potential cast.

"Today I would like to hear each one individually," he said, and took a peripheral look at us. "In the next room, which is sound proof, I want to hear how each of you interprets his part. I'll start with the major character of the story," he said and pointed at me.

The soundproof room was small but comfortable, carpeted with a colorful oriental rug, two dark brown chairs, placed on one side, across from a podium. Elia Kazan's portrait was hanging on a terra-cotta wall, lit by a tiny light.

He said, "Okay, *Your Eminence*, stand at that podium and let me hear your lines, as the Bishop of Smyrna."

My rapid heartbeat caused intense chest vibrations. Why in the world did I accept to be in a movie? I thought. I'm a priest, not an actor.

"Mr. Kazan, I need to drink some water, my throat is dry," I said.

"You must be anxious, it's a normal reaction. I'll get you some water."

I drank the little bottle of water, took a deep breath, and feeling more relaxed, I began reciting my lines and looking straight into his eyes.

I saw a smile, and my mind quickly tried to interpret. Is it approval or...?

"Relax, relax," he said, "and let me hear more of your part."

I took his remark as approval, and after another deep breath, I recited another verse, "It's better to be an hour free, than to be forty years in cruel slavery...." But before I continued, I saw Mr. Kazan's hand raised, a signal to stop. He came closer to the podium and in a tone of gentleness, he said, "Father Peter, you are a kind man and you have a gentle voice, but I want a bishop who is a bastard with a wild and demanding attitude, one who could scream at the infidels to combat their dominance."

As he probably noticed disappointment in my face, he shook my hand and added, "Worry for nothing, I'm going to give you another part in my movie." I squeezed his hand and with a genuine smile, I said, "Mr. Kazan, I do understand, and

I want to thank you for the honor considering me for any part of your next movie."

To his great regret, the story, *Beyond the Aegean Sea*, was never made into a motion picture. Unexpected obstacles from Hollywood politics and, above all, from the painful and sudden death of his son prevented the production of this movie. Later, when grieving of his most painful loss and the emotional conflicts had subsided, he converted the screenplay into a novel.

Elia Kazan was one of the most influential people in the theater world. He had an amazing life through his art, and at the age of seventy-seven, past the point of modesty. He tells his remarkable story that speaks of his incredible God-given talent in *Elia Kazan: A Life*, published in 1988. The following year, he received an honorary Academy Award for lifetime achievement in films.

46

FIRE IN THE SOUL

The thought of moving from Los Angeles to New Jersey to start a new parish was stressful. I did not want to move back to New Jersey.

That evening, I brought the news of my transfer home. My wife was excited by the news of returning to the East Coast. It was no wonder; she would be much closer to her brother and sister who lived in Cherry Hill, New Jersey. Our children were upset that they had to leave their friends and California's good climate. While I tried to see the transfer as a challenge, I was concerned about the new mission that I had initiated. How could I give up such a unique opportunity? That night I couldn't sleep, and turned to a familiar prayer, "Lord, show me the path in which I should be walking today."

What were these responsibilities that I might have to leave unfinished? Between the years 1965 and 1967, the Ladies Philoptochos Society—the philanthropic arm of the Greek Orthodox Archdiocese of America that cared for the poor and afflicted—had made arrangements to bring three children from Greece to St. Vincent's Hospital in Los Angeles. Johnny was eight, Petrakis was seven, and Billy was eight, and all suffered from congenital heart failure and needed open-heart surgery or else their days would be numbered. At that time open-heart surgery was not done in Greece. It had been my job to coordinate the mission, while Philoptochos had assumed responsibility for all the hospital and medical expenses.

Petrakis survived his surgery, and weeks later happily returned to his homeland. But, unfortunately, Johnny and Billy did not make it. I remember how happy Johnny was playing with my son, Mike, who was of the same age. And then one fatal day, he was no longer there. Even today, I'm nagged by the unanswerable question: *Why do innocent children have to die?*

On the day of little Johnny's funeral, there was an article in the *Los Angeles Times* stating that a team of cardiac surgeons had just returned from Pakistan where they had donated their services to the critically ill. They had performed forty-three open-heart surgeries with forty-one successes. These were missionary doctors from Loma Linda University Hospital (LLUH) in Loma Linda, California. Rebecca, a candy striper who saw me at the hospital, comforting Johnny's mother, had read the article and said to me, "Maybe these doctors can go to Greece and perform heart surgery for children." Her idea was good, *but would these doctors accept my request and do this?* I was skeptical.

In my church office that same afternoon, I called LLUH and asked to speak to the doctor in charge of that heart team that had just returned from Pakistan. Dr. Ellsworth Wareham came to the phone. I told him how moved I had been by the contribution his team had made to the people in Pakistan. Briefly, I related my experience with the two boys who had died and asked if his team would consider going to Greece.

I could not believe my ears when Dr. Wareham responded, humbly and compassionately, "Father, you are a busy man. I shall come to your office in Los Angeles, and we'll discuss your request." That day I thought, *the spirit that nourishes every human soul visited with me, chanting the compassionate song of God's caring and loving presence in human life.*

Soon afterward, Dr. Wareham came to my office, and we spent two hours discussing the possibility of his team going to Greece. A summary of his own words: "A team of seven of us will be able to go to Greece. We will donate our services, and all you have to do is provide for our traveling expenses."

I promised him there should be no problem getting airplane tickets to Greece. *That will be the easiest thing to do*, I thought, and immediately contacted Olympic Airways in New York and related Dr. Wareham's generous offer. "We need a donation of seven round-trip tickets to Athens for seven American doctors who are willing to go to Greece and offer their services gratis to heart victims."

My request was denied with a brief answer: "It is with regrets we inform you that it is against IATA, International Air Transport Association, rules to give free transportation to any individual or organization."

At that time, being a man of the cloth, I had to request permission from the head of the Church to pursue this project. I wrote a letter to the archbishop explaining the situation. His reply was, "Let me remind you that you're a priest. Involvement with doctors and medical problems is not a Church activity. Besides, we have no Church representative in Greece to supervise such a serious project."

Of course, the cardiac surgeons did not really need ecclesiastical supervision. By this time I had learned that when we try to do something worthwhile for a noble cause, obstacles are always put in our way. Even this humanitarian effort, promising health and hope to hundreds of heart victims, had to overcome two major obstacles: Olympic Airways' refusal to give free transportation, and the Church hierarchy's refusal to allow me to pursue this mission.

How could I tell Dr. Wareham that two of my own resources had turned me down? I tried to find meaning in their refusal to help, but I could not. *There has to be another way*, I thought. My frustration ignited a fire within, an insistent call. I had to improvise in finding funds for transportation. The wealth of the Church, whose generosity had made headlines in the news, erecting monuments for themselves, could not extend a hand to help such a monumental project! They referred me to charities. Wonderful!

Why not contact a Greek hospital in Athens? I thought. When I called to explain the American doctors' offer, President Dr. Doxiades, head of the Evangelismos Hospital, seemed offended. "We don't accept charity. We are not an underdeveloped country, and we don't need foreign medical help. We have our own competent professionals here." His laconic answer shut the door. I put my trust in the old axiom, "When one door closes, God opens ten other doors." Each negative response reinforced my need for patience and my persistence was cemented with prayer.

Prayer is my daily practice; patience is my passion and continues to be my best quality. I contacted Rebecca Weiler, a compassionate woman, who was at the hospital on the day Johnny died and saw me comforting his mother. I told her I had spoken to the head doctor and that his team was ready and willing to go to Greece. "However, there is a problem," I said. "I have to provide transportation for them, and so far, I have not been able to find even one person interested in helping."

Without hesitation, Rebecca said, "Don't worry, I'll pay for one ticket. I'm sure other donors will come forward." The following day I received a travel ticket from El Al Airlines in the mail. I was excited. Now I knew what the next step should be. I must visit the headquarters of Olympic Airways and explain the situation in person.

There is a Greek proverb, "The face is like a sword," which means that a face-to-face meeting cuts where it should and brings results. For me, that meant that I needed to visit these authorities in person and say to them, "We have many requests from heart patients in Greece who need heart surgery. They cannot afford to travel to America for help. The Loma Linda University Heart Team has volunteered its services to help at no charge. All we need is transportation." To overcome barriers and get results, I needed divine intervention. On my way to visit the offices of Olympic Airways on Fifth Avenue, I prayed, as I passed by St. Patrick's Cathedral, "Lord, please, I need your help today."

Mr. Love, the manager of the airline, stood behind his mahogany desk and gave me an artificial smile as he offered me a chair. "What can I do for you, Father?" Not knowing my name, he could tell by my black suit and white collar that I was a priest.

"Something very simple, Mr. Love," and I explained the purpose of my visit.

"Of course, I remember. You contacted us about donating tickets."

"Transportation for doctors to save lives," I said.

"Sorry, but my hands are tied. There are rules I have to follow."

"Rules that deprive hope and health to people who suffer from heart failure?"

"Well, I could possibly give a personal donation, but tickets—that I cannot do."

"I know for a fact that you provide free transportation for celebrities."

"I have nothing to do with that," he said in an unyielding tone.

I pulled out the ticket from El Al, and said, "I have a ticket donated by a Jewish woman, Rebecca Weiler. If you're unable to donate six more tickets, I will go from this office directly to El Al office and buy the tickets with my own money. But once we arrive in Athens, I'll write an article for the Greek newspaper and tell them our story."

"I don't think Mr. Onassis would like that," Mr. Love said, coughing nervously.

"I don't think he'd like it either," I said.

In those days Aristotle Onassis, one of the richest people in the world, owned Olympic Airways. I'm sure my face was red to match the frustration I felt, while my hand holding the El Al ticket trembled as I waved it in Mr. Love's face. Mr. Love was infected by the trends of the society to which he belonged: indifference and apathy. He probably enjoyed sitting comfortably on his long cushioned chair, watching sports, attending cocktail parties, flattering, smiling, and exchanging irrelevant stories.

A priest ignited by anger was not in vogue. I had not visited Mr. Love's office to change the rules of his company or his lifestyle. I had a purpose and passion that required fulfillment. The offer of the Loma Linda University Heart Team fired my soul. I felt most alive when caring for and serving the needs of others. Isn't that what the Greatest Teacher of all time had said, "I did not come here to be served; I came to serve"?

47

A NEW BEGINNING

Early on a Friday morning, September 1, 1967, and almost a year since I was assigned to Holy Trinity, a newly established parish in Westfield, New Jersey, I received a phone call from a grieving wife whose husband had died in his sleep the night before. Tearfully, she asked me to talk to Tim, her five-and-a-half-year old son, who did not yet know about the sudden death of his father. "Please, tell him that his father died and somehow try to comfort him." Then she said, "Father, I wonder if later today you could also go and tell the sad news to my husband's mother."

"Of course, I will," I said, "and I'll be over to pick up Tim in fifteen minutes." Soon after the call, I rushed to the widow's house and picked up her son, promising to take him to an amusement park. Half an hour later, after young Tim and I played a couple games, he climbed on a carousel. After he went around joyfully for a couple times, the carousel stopped. I had bought a box of popcorn and said, "Tim, let's sit on that bench and rest before I take you back to your house." As we both were munching the popcorn, I was trying to figure out what I could say to a young boy who had just lost his father. After a few minutes of silence, Tim looked at me curiously and said, "Father, you look sad or scared. What are you thinking?"

"Tim, I'm thinking about you," I said, and paused, trying to phrase the bad news. "Something very sad has happened to your family. Your father has died."

"I don't believe it," he fired back. "I saw my dad leaving for work yesterday and coming home last night."

"Well, during last night, he died in his sleep," I said.

"I want to see him," Tim said. "Take me to him right now."

"You will see him a little later."

"Please take me home, now," Tim said and began to cry.

Silently, I drove him to his home, and his mother, who was in tears and dressed in black, thanked me and said, "Father, please go to Mrs. Savvas, my husband's mother. She doesn't know anything yet about John's death."

When I knocked on the door at John's mother's house, she opened the door and pulled back in shock, wondering about my visit. She was also dressed in black, mourning for her daughter who had died of cancer two years earlier. She looked scared, and with a trembling voice said, "Father, coming to my house unexpectedly, did you come to tell me something bad?"

"Yes, Mrs. Savvas," I said. I reached for her hand. It was ice cold. "During last night your son died."

"My son, Johnny, died?" She screamed and pulled out a handful of her hair and cried inconsolably. My mouth remained open and dry unable to utter any word of comfort. I took her in my arms and held her for a few moments, then we sat together on a sofa. She continued to lament over the loss of her only son, and kept saying, "Why are you punishing me, dear God? Two years ago, I lost my daughter. I haven't done anything wrong, why am I being punished?"

One evening in November of that same year, Rich and Susie, a couple in their early forties, returned home from a church vesper service and found their sixteen-year-old son dead. He hanged himself in the basement. "He was an unhappy child," the grief-stricken parents told me when they both came to my office to arrange for a funeral service. The reality of their son's unexpected suicide threw them into deep depression. Following their son's death, they continued to seek comfort in therapy once a week for several months.

To tell these grieving parents that when a person's soul suffers or is troubled, it wants to escape the body would be of no comfort. I chose to listen to their feelings with patience, understanding, and sympathy, and was simply present in their sadness in the weeks that followed.

Two weeks before Christmas, among three big hospitals that I planned to visit sick members of my parish, there was one particular facility that treated people afflicted with tuberculosis. It was the last hospital on my calendar and I wanted to bring Holy Communion to several patients. Five women of the Ladies Philoptochos Society came with me and brought Christmas presents. I had been at that hospital before and I was familiar with what I would encounter, but the women who came with me were in utter shock at what they saw. A collage of cots, anguished faces, blistered lips, and emaciated bodies, some of them already had one foot in the grave, yet when they saw me holding the cup of Holy Communion, they sighed with relief.

After all the TB patients had received Communion, my part was to consume the remains of the cup. The women that kept observing my movements were in shock once again. Two of them almost shouted, "Father, how can you swallow the leftovers from the cup that is most likely contaminated? Aren't you afraid you may catch tuberculosis and die?"

"Thank you for your concern," I said, "but no disease can contaminate the Body and Blood of Christ. For many years, I have always consumed what was left in the chalice after thousands of people had received Holy Communion. Nothing has

ever happened to me. Look, I'm still here and ready to serve."
It was a special day for me, and I felt rewarded emotionally.

When members of the church who were experiencing
either personal or family problems came to my office seeking help, I was always willing to assist them. However, I felt
inept and not tuned up psychologically. Furthermore, I was
facing my own problems at home—an unhappy wife, who was
frustrated because I was unavailable to her and to our children. With my interest in missions and my commitment to my
church duties and being involved with every possible aspect,
it did not leave much time for my family. I wanted to become
a super-priest, to strive for success and surpass all others.
Was that a latent adolescent dream, or was it the intense theological training at the seminary? Where was my mind? Why
didn't I learn my lesson at the beginning of my ministry, when
I developed an ulcer that lasted for nine years and required
drastic surgery?

48

THE HEART MISSION

As I sat across from Mr. Love's desk and looked patiently at him, he struck me as one of those men who cannot grab life's opportunities with his bare hands and relish it. Instead, he handled it with tongs. He shuffled papers on his desk. I did not say another word but kept looking straight in his eyes. Under my breath I repeated, *"Lord Jesus Christ, have mercy on him and lead a good thought into his mind that he may actualize the true meaning of his last name: Love."* I decided not to leave his office until I got a favorable reply: the tickets for the doctors.

Noting my persistence, Mr. Love said dispassionately, "Let me have the names of those doctors, and I'll see if I can do anything. I'll call your office tomorrow." Somehow, I had a hunch that he might eventually receive the tickets. I thanked him, and with my enthusiasm rekindled, I headed toward the offices of the archdiocese at Seventy-ninth Street and Fifth Avenue, New York. Because I operated under the auspices of the Church, it was imperative to inform the archbishop that we now had transportation, and the heart team would soon be on its way. I would be going with them as a liaison, but I had decided to buy my own ticket. I did not want to give him the impression that my involvement had the ulterior motive of a free trip.

It so happened that I met the archbishop in the lobby. He was waiting for the elevator. I bowed and greeted him. He responded gently and said, "What brings you to the city?"

"Your Eminence, may I speak with you for a few minutes in private?"

"Today I have a very busy schedule. Tell me briefly what you want," he said as he held the elevator door open.

"It's about the heart mission—the outreach ministry to Greece."

"I thought I answered your question in writing. Did I not?"

"Yes, you did, Your Eminence. Now we are almost ready to go."

"Well, I've already spoken with the Greek government. They are not ready to receive the American doctors; perhaps they will be more receptive sometime in the future," his words were pronounced with evident annoyance. He entered the elevator, pressed the button, and the door shut in my face.

I could not follow him to his office and try to convince him to see this effort as a call from God. Facing reality, which strongly indicated that any time I wanted to do anything worthwhile, either for myself or for the benefit of others, major obstacles will appear. I now had a decision to make. If I disregarded the archbishop's negative answer and continued to follow the dictates of my own heart, I would find myself at the risk of being suspended or expelled from the ranks of the priesthood. Despite the strong resistance I'd encountered from several sides, I chose to press on with what I believed to be my outreach ministry.

Finally, on November 1, 1967, Olympic Airways flew us to Greece, and we didn't have to dance in the aisles. Soon after our arrival at the Evangelismos Hospital in Athens, the doctors examined the heart patients. The candidates for open-heart surgery were many, and a day later the operations began. Within six weeks, thirty-two patients had open-heart surgery, and twenty-nine of the operations were successful. Meanwhile, the doctors compiled a waiting list of eight hundred more patients who would need heart surgery within the next two years.

The heart team returned to their base at Loma Linda University Hospital in California, and I returned to my new parish in Westfield, New Jersey. Six months passed swiftly, but even as I performed my church duties, my thoughts kept gravitating to those people in Greece suffering from heart problems. They were awaiting a miracle, and I felt that our mission still remained unfinished. Being three thousand miles from those wonderful doctors in California, what could I do? I could pray, of course, but would my prayers be enough? As powerful as prayer can be, God wants us to be active participants in whatever requests we make of him. Along with my prayers, I had to act on the inner call, the flame that had the potential to brighten many lives with health and hope.

One evening, I called Dr. Wareham and said, "Doctor, when I think of those eight hundred people who need surgery, I have sleepless nights."

"I understand totally," Dr. Wareham said with genuine concern.

"Do you think your team could go back to Greece again?" I asked hesitantly.

"It's possible, but you may have to come to Loma Linda in California and speak with Dr. Hinshaw, Dean of our university. As you may know, we are the university doctors, and he is the one that would have to approve another mission.

"No problem," I said, and the following week I flew to California. The hospital was not that far from the airport, where Dr. Wareham picked me up. That night I had a chance to speak at a dinner honoring the seven doctors who had made up the Heart Team for their major contribution to the Greek people.

Besides expressing gratitude on behalf of the Greek patients who had recovered, I emphasized the fact that Greek hospitals and doctors were not yet equipped to do open-heart surgery, and they still needed help.

After dinner that night, Dr. Wareham and his team met with Dr. Hinshaw and discussed the seriousness of their mission and the plight of the eight hundred Greek patients who still awaited surgery. Dr. Wareham delivered their decision to me in person the next morning: "A team of twelve doctors will go to Greece to continue our work, train local doctors, and establish a permanent heart team there." I was so overwhelmed that tears of joy filled my eyes.

Dr. Wareham put his arms around me and said, "Now, dear Father, we need *twelve* tickets." He smiled. "I know you will be able to get them."

Back in New York at the Olympic Airways office, Mr. Love caused major waves, saying, "We did it once—against our regulations—and we were criticized by other airlines. This time we cannot do it."

Disheartened, I left his office. "Lord God," I whispered, "the patients and doctors are now in your hands." Suddenly, I saw Mr. Aristotle Onassis walking down the hall of his building. I had not met him before, but I had seen his picture in the newspapers when he had married Jacqueline Kennedy. A short man with a dark complexion, he was the giant multimillionaire who owned Olympic Airlines. I introduced myself, "Mr. Onassis," I said, "thank you very much for providing transportation for the doctors."

"You're welcome. You're welcome," he said and sped away before I had a chance to ask for additional help. One of his consultants informed me, "Mr. Onassis is not to be bothered at this time." The high-powered businessman had come to New York on this particular day to discuss the purchase of more oil wells for his shipping fleet. I had to understand that, despite his generosity, the wealthy and famous tycoon had his own priorities.

Late that afternoon, I composed a letter to Mrs. Jacqueline Onassis and sent it by overnight mail to her Fifth Avenue apartment. I explained in detail the success of the first mission to Greece and requested her intervention for twelve more tickets to enable the doctors to return to attend to more patients. The next morning, my telephone rang. It was a familiar voice.

"Good morning, Father. How are you today?"

"Indisposed. I had a sleepless night, Mr. Love," I said with evident frustration.

"You're too emotional, Father, but the news I have to tell you will perk you up."

"I'm listening."

"This morning, Mrs. Onassis forwarded your letter to me. Your twelve tickets will be ready by this afternoon, and there'll be a ticket for you as well, if you decide to go with the doctors."

"Thank you, Mr. Love. I will be there this afternoon to give you the names of the doctors." I immediately went next door and knelt at the altar of our church. "Thank you, Lord, for another miracle."

At this juncture, it is important to acknowledge the generosity and sensitivity of the female heart. Most church leaders today will attest to the substantial contribution of women to their ministry. When women hear of an existing need, they are eager and ready to help. Knowing their consistent commitment to charity, I sent a letter to each state chapter of the Ladies Philoptochos Society informing them of the "heart mission" to Greece.

Once again, women proved to be ardent proponents of the Christian spirit. Within a month, they had sent $68,000 for the heart mission to their main office in New York. That money helped buy a heart-lung machine, a striker's saw to be used for cutting the sternum open, and other surgical tools. Above all, it helped to fund the services of the American heart doctors for five more years, until they were able to fully train local Greek doctors to take over this much-needed project.

For the following three years, a rotating team of heart specialists from Loma Linda University Hospital went to Greece. The system ran like clockwork: every four weeks, four new doctors would arrive to relieve the doctors who were already there. At the same time, local surgeons were being trained to do the work, and George Tolis, a Greek doctor trained in the United States, was the head of the heart team. Eventually, the American heart team was no longer needed in Athens as the Greek team had become competent enough to take over their work. The mission of the Loma Linda team was complete.

In the meantime, I had asked Dr. Wareham to prepare a prospectus outlining what was needed to build a hundred-bed clinic in Athens. When the prospectus was prepared, I took it to Olympic Airlines' office and gave it to Mr. Gratsos who was Mr. Onassis's private secretary and friend for many years. He took the prospectus in his hands and said, "Mr. Onassis is getting older. He cannot eat much anymore, he cannot sleep well, and he probably cannot make love to his wife anymore. It's about time for him to build a clinic. I'll put this prospectus on his desk, and I will also talk to him about it in person."

Another Greek proverb, "A tiny acorn, planted at the right time in a fertile soil, produces a huge oak tree," was proven to be true. In his will, Aristotle Onassis left instructions that a heart clinic be established in Greece. Years after his death, his instructions were carefully carried out.

In 2002, Dr. Wareham went vacationing to Greece with his wife, Barbara. When they returned to the United States, he called me from New York and asked me to meet him for lunch at the Essex House. I took my daughter, Katina, with me. I thought it was a good idea for her to meet this wonderful doctor, a heart surgeon, who dedicated his life in missionary work. I had not seen Dr. Wareham in more than twenty years, but he looked as lively and as healthy as ever, and was very excited to tell me the latest news.

"Peter, there is no hospital in the world, as far as I know, that runs more efficiently than the Onassis Cardiac Center in Athens. I spent two days there, exploring it and learning about its functions. They perform approximately two thousand operations a year, something that no other hospital can do, even in the United States. It is a miracle of human endeavor."

"Thanks to you and your team," I said.

"We can thank God for enabling us to do this work," he replied.

I could not argue with that. I looked at him with admiration and reminded him of the initial obstacles encountered when we first went to Athens—professional jealousy on the part of their Greek colleagues, not enough surgical tools, red tape, and bureaucracy.

But Dr. Wareham didn't seem to remember what he called "small stuff." "What obstacles?" he said with a smile.

I reminded him of the day there was no more blood available—they always needed supplemental blood for each operation.

"We cannot have any surgery tomorrow," Dr. Stathatos, head of the Thoracic Surgery Department, claimed.

Dr. Wareham had looked at the faces of his team and said, "Oh, well! All of us look very healthy here; we will donate blood." Silence had prevailed for a few seconds, succeeded by smiles. Sure enough, surgery continued the next day.

At the end of that day after witnessing two major operations, I stepped out of the hospital for a few minutes to catch a few breaths of fresh air. I saw a long line of young soldiers waiting at the main entrance. "What's the meaning of this?" I asked, and they answered, "We are here to give blood."

"You are smiling, and you're silent," Dr. Wareham said.

"Not silent, grateful," I replied. I kept thinking of a doctor, a priest, a candy striper, and—may God rest her soul—Jacqueline Kennedy Onassis and how each of them responded to tragedy.

A picture of the clinic's benefactor, Aristotle Onassis, hangs in the main entrance. Although he is no longer alive, his tremendous contribution, the untiring and dedicated services of Dr. Ellsworth Wareham and his team, and the ongoing power of the Holy Spirit will continue to make it possible to offer lifesaving health care for many years to come.

On October 3, 2014, Dr. Wareham turned one hundred years old. His centennial celebration was attended by more than four hundred people who came from all over the United States and other places of the world where Dr. Wareham and his team of heart surgeons had contributed their services. I was honored to be one of the speakers, and after expressing my profound gratitude for the tremendous contribution that the Loma Linda University had made to the Greek people, I said, "Dr. Wareham, I came all the way from New Jersey to California to celebrate your hundredth birthday. Twelve years from today, when I become one hundred years old, I hope you come to my birthday."

Dr. Wareham died on December 15, 2018, completing his earthly life at the age of 104. *May his memory be eternal.*

49

WHY ARE WE TESTED?

The question, "Why are we being tested?" is one that my dear friend Dr. Andy McCabe has asked me a few times. Andy is a professor at New Jersey City University, New Jersey, and an author of books that carry messages in how we can improve our lives and be healthier and happier people. For the last thirty years, Andy and I meet for breakfast every Tuesday. While we are always happy to share a couple of hours together, there are times that we both engage in a serious dialogue about major issues of life and living. On one occasion, he suggested that I write a book on this topic.

The suggestion evoked a personal challenge in my current life as I began to ask myself the very same question. While developing an outline for the book, a client that had come to my office for therapy eighteen years ago, returned, but this time emotionally very upset and crying. She stopped crying and tried to wipe her tears as she sat across from me.

Knowing her as being married and having two sons, I said, "Dorothy, what is going on? You seem so upset."

"Frustrated and very angry," she said, her eyes still filled with tears.

"Last night over an argument, my husband said, why don't we get a divorce? I could not believe my ears. After thirty-five years of life together and having two teenage sons, he is thinking of a divorce?"

"What caused the argument?" I asked.

"Something stupid."

"Something stupid and you are so upset? Could there be something else that is bothering you?"

"Lots of things. All my married life I have been trying to please him, to make him happy—keeping our house clean... doing the laundry...shopping for groceries...making good meals—but I do not feel appreciated. No more flowers as he used to bring me, or some occasional dinner in a special restaurant. There is no romance, my heart is aching, and I don't think he cares."

"Anything good about your husband?"

"Well, Johnny works very hard, and financially, we are doing well. He never complains when I spend money for the kids or for myself."

"Dorothy, your emotional pain and anger need to be addressed," I said.

"Let me suggest, next time you make an appointment, you and your husband come together. I do not perform miracles, but having been a marriage counselor for many years, I believe you could use some professional help in regaining peace of mind and making some adjustments to your married life."

Smiling, she shook her head, got up and was about to leave, but as she opened the door, she paused and said, "Doctor, can I come by myself alone once again?"

"Of course, you can, if it is important to you," I said.

"To be honest, I'm not as good as I think I am. I'm bitchy, angry at the world, I don't feel any real joy in my life. I hold a magnifying glass over my husband's reaction to me. I'm irritable, hate my life and blame Johnny for my misery."

"I'll see you alone next time," I said, with evident empathy.

Dorothy was just another person that I could add to my list of several clients who have been tested and have suffered emotionally and physically.

In both the Old and the New Testaments, the word *tested*, means "proved by trial." Sometimes God does test our faith, just as he tested the faith of the ancient Israelites by allowing them to go through hard times in the desert, "in order to make known to them what was in their hearts" (Deut 8:2). God knows our strengths and our weakness. If our faith is weak, it may not be obvious when our life is satisfactory and things are going on smoothly.

When hard times come, a weak faith will be revealed for what it really is: shallow and unable to help us through life's difficulties. It may be anything: an unexpected illness, an accident that was costly, the death of a loved one, the loss of our job, or even a friend who turns against us. But when hard times happen, the true nature of our faith will be revealed.

God tests us to realize our potential and how strong we are. The Psalmist prayed, "Search me, O God, and know my heart; test me and know my thoughts" (Ps 139:23).

The testing of faith can come in small ways and daily irritations; they may also be severe afflictions (Isa 48:10) and attacks from Satan (Job 2:7). Whatever the source of the testing, it is to our benefit to undergo the trials that God allows and that help our faith to be stronger.

The account of Job is a perfect example of God allowing one to be tested by the devil. Job bore all his trials patiently and "did not sin or charge God with wrongdoing" (Job 1:22). However, the account of Job's testing is proof that Satan's ability to try us is limited by God's sovereign control. No demon can test or afflict us beyond what God has ordained. All our trials work toward God's perfect purpose and our benefit.

There are many examples of the positive results of being tested. The many and different biblical examples about being tested bring to mind the words of Philaret, a Russian monk. Here is part of his prayer that I find inspiring:

> In every hour of the day, reveal Your will to me. Bless my dealings with all who surround me. When I feel tested, I pray for strength. Dear Lord Jesus, please teach me to treat all that comes to me throughout the day with peace of soul, clarity of mind, and with the firm conviction that Your will governs all. In all my deeds and words, guide my thoughts and feelings. In unforeseen events, let me not forget that all are sent by You. Teach me to act firmly and wisely, without embittering and embarrassing others.
>
> Give me strength to bear the fatigue of the coming day with patience. In any hour of the day, reveal Your will to me. Bless my dealings with all who surround me. Teach me to treat any test that I face throughout the day with peace of soul, clarity of mind and with the firm conviction that you are a God of love who is in charge with His children. In all my deeds and words, guide my thoughts, feelings, and actions. In unforeseen events, let me not forget that all are sent by You. Teach me to act firmly and wisely, without embittering and embarrassing others. Give me strength to bear the fatigue of the coming day with all that it shall bring. Direct my will; teach me to pray, pray Yourself in me, Lord Jesus. Amen.

To become true Christians often requires us to move out of our comfort zones and into the unknown. The testing or trials we undergo come in various ways. Yet perseverance results in spiritual maturity and completeness. As we noted earlier,

St. James wrote, "Consider it pure joy, my brothers and sisters, whenever you face trials of many kinds" (Jas 1:2).

When we experience the storms of life, we should be like the tree that digs its roots ever more deeply for a greater grip on the earth. We must "dig our roots" more deeply into God's grace and cling to his promises so we can weather whatever storms come. Most comforting of all is that we know that God will never allow us to be tested beyond what we are able to handle. His grace is sufficient for us, and his power is made perfect in our weakness. "For whenever I am weak, then I am strong" (2 Cor 12:9–10).

PART III
HARVESTING

50

THE BREAKUP

In 1973, I made a serious decision that was to shake the very foundation of my life and my family. As you probably know, priests are not immune from dysfunctional marriages, and after twenty-one years together I decided to end my marriage to Mary. Divorce is simply not an option for Greek Orthodox clergy. A divorce is a huge ordeal for anyone, but for a Greek Orthodox priest, it means even more. Divorcing my wife meant walking away from my entire career as a priest, from my ministry to the many people whom I had loved and served diligently.

This decision was not made lightly having reflected on its potential consequences including the emotional strain and hurdles that we would both face during the divorce process. Mindful of my journey this far, I was totally aware that no one's life is devoid of mistakes, pain, and regrets. No one lives a perfect life, regardless of a good background or family reputation. No one is immune to struggle, whether it is mental, emotional, physical, marital, financial or professional. It was a reality I had to endure, sometimes in doubt or fear; at other times, through periods of loneliness. My next steps required careful planning and purpose.

When my then-wife heard of my final decision, she was in terrible shock. "You are a priest, your colleagues admire you, many people respect you, and you are talking about divorcing me? Why?" That was the question that I could not answer. She fell on her knees, pleaded with me, and cried, "I don't want a divorce!" Her reaction evoked deep feelings of guilt. *What is this woman going to do with what I'm leaving behind—her life, maintaining a house, and raising three children?* I had no serious, convincing answers that could justify my decision; and following my decision, repairing the relationship no longer seemed possible.

Occasionally, rational thinking would overpower my guilt, and I would realize that, in time, Mary would understand that we were both responsible for our emotional breakup. Hopefully, we would eventually acknowledge our own individual failings and even learn something about ourselves and rediscover our human potential through this painful process.

Our expectations of each other had caused anger and frustration. Most likely, we had unrealistic expectations of each other and our relationship. My vocation called me to mingle with people, clergy colleagues, for example, to discuss church-related and personal issues. This excluded my wife but not intentionally. Art was her gift, and she met daily with another friend and attended a school of arts.

Of course, somebody had to shop for food and household items, somebody had to cook and attend to the cleaning and maintenance of the home. Someone had to balance the checkbook and pay the bills. Mary took over these tasks, and we never discussed or talked about my participation to facilitate life and living. I took it for granted that this was my wife's part of married life that she enjoyed.

Seeing eye to eye with one another on everything that came our way became difficult. We were two different people with different values and habits, we could not possibly agree on life's unfolding experiences. She enjoyed walking in the park. I preferred to go swimming at the YMCA. Mary was gregarious and loved to dance and socialize. I was an introvert and preferred solitude, reading, meditating, and writing. She expressed her anger and sometimes rage openly. I managed to repress my feelings of anger, keep silent, and withdraw. Eventually, I got an ulcer. My therapist suggested that I bring my wife to our next session. When I told my wife that it might be of some benefit to go to therapy together, she said, "You need therapy! I don't. I'm okay."

Of course, such differences create confusion and discomfort, but do they have to cause a conflict or war? Neither of us considered the possibility of accepting each other's differences. It would be ideal if our love *could* change all the undesirable qualities that we saw in the other. Jealousy was another issue that became evident. When I was writing a novel, she could not hear of it. "You are a priest, not a writer," she kept saying. So, to continue feeding my passion for writing, I would tell her that I was preparing Sunday school material for the following week. Admittedly, while this was a lie, it would avoid an argument.

Certainly, leaving a woman with a broken heart was painful, but the reality for me was that my heart had already been broken long before I decided to divorce. I was hurt and disillusioned, plagued by low self-esteem and feelings of failure clouding my mind and pushing me toward depression. Yet, one truth remained: I felt loved by God. I didn't reason it out intellectually; I knew it; felt it from a place deep within me. Despite my decision to leave my marriage, I was a son of a loving Creator. He cared and continued to love me with unfathomable love.

Divorce ended my marriage but not my relationship with my three children and their mother. From my pastoral experience, I knew that memories continue to haunt the survivors, who would likely seek some resolution that would not come easily. After I came to a definite decision, I spent agonizing weeks trying to find perhaps the best way to approach my children and tell them that I would no longer be living at home with them and their mother.

In my subsequent practice as a therapist, I had learned that no child of any age or gender can really understand the full implications of a divorce. Children want love, security, and care. Naturally, they want their parents to remain together to offer such a climate of comfort and support until they embark on their own journeys through life. *Could my children ever believe my promise that I would not disappear from their lives and that I would be around to attend to their needs?* I did not think so.

My decision caused emotional pain, ambivalence, and confusion, all of which had serious consequences. While the emotional impact of the divorce had taken place long before my final decision, the legal navigation was still quite difficult and needed serious consideration. It seemed that I had entered a new country without a passport, directions, or maps. And I had entered it absolutely alone. It was a strange land, and I had to pave my own roads as I walked and chose my own land-marks. Insanity and hopelessness seemed the natural byprod-ucts of my journey.

At this crossroad in my life, I needed to make new choices that involved challenges, risks, and courage. Facing the world and public opinion were not priorities. I had made my deci-sion, and it was now time for responsible action. Loss of secu-rity was a major concern; all the family income came from my church ministry. I needed to provide financial and emotional support for my family.

One day I isolated myself in a small room and, as ridicu-lous as it may sound, I chanted a brief funeral service and gave myself a eulogy. Mainly I spoke the truth about myself as I per-ceived it: the wrongs I had done, the sins and unwitting errors

The Breakup

I had committed. I asked God's forgiveness. That eulogy was one of the few transformative actions of my life.

Facing the truth about myself was necessary but not sufficient. My own perception of what precipitated the divorce was determined by personal disenchantment with the life I was living and by my vision of a future life. *If you do not want to consider yourself a failure,* I told myself, *you need to do some self-repair work, face the truth about who you are, chisel off the rough edges, review your potential, and become a better person.*

I thought of a caterpillar. Its life begins as a tiny worm, which moves slowly on plants or trees, eating tender leaves in order to grow. A full-sized caterpillar encloses itself in a tiny cocoon and dies, confined in darkness. In time, a colorful butterfly emerges from the cocoon and gives flight, dancing from flower to flower. It is hard to imagine this miraculous transformation; from a caterpillar to a butterfly. Like the caterpillar, my life started slowly, and went through variations and multiple experiences.

The process of growth into a new life was troublesome. My vision became blurred, and I could hardly see where I was going. My physical appearance remained intact, yet an invisible transformation had taken place. Out of my darkness, like the butterfly, I jumped from flower to flower, seeking the most colorful and fragrant one—*a newness of life* that promised purpose and meaning. The painful transition and self-transformation that I was going through affected each member of my family. I knew the road ahead would be steep and thorny. I prayed for direction and for God's mercy not to condone or approve my decision, but to give each member of my family the strength to endure the transition.

Abandoning the familiar for the unknown was risky. It was unsafe, and I felt acute anxiety fueling my fear around the final dissolution of my family. Disturbing nightmares woke me in the night. Early morning dreams terrorized me. The word *rectify* echoed in my brain. *Rectify what? The ruins of my marriage or the uncertainty of my future? Did I have the desire, stamina, or skills to repair anything? Can a cracked pane of glass be repaired? At best, the glass can be replaced. I simply reacted to what was happening in my psyche. Confusion, guilt, and worries about the future!* Slowly, I learned to live with the insecurity of the unknown and tolerate the events of life as they occurred.

Epictetus, a Greek philosopher once said, "Humans are influenced and disturbed not by the events of their lives but by the way they view or interpret the events." In thinking about this, I considered my divorce and the likely departure from the security that the Church had provided. The breakup was a long period of anxiety, emotionally painful, and scarring for the entire family. I had to provide reasonable financial support and stability for my children and their mother. In order to accomplish that, I needed to take charge of my life and get a job. I had to deal with my fragmented self so I could regain composure. I sensed an inner impasse and felt deep grief, fear, despair, and loneliness. I prayed to God for help. I cried. I knew that I was crying about my losses: people I loved, the love of my family, and the security of my priestly role in society, my Church. Despite the exhaustion of combatting critical issues every day, a deeper yearning was lingering in my heart. It was real and, as crazy as it may sound, this yearning provided moments of comfort. I wanted someone special and kind-hearted to reach out for me, who would take my hand, squeeze it gently, look into my eyes and say, "Here I am. I care for you. I love you."

51

RECOVERY

After two of the major events in my life, the divorce of my wife and my withdrawal from church ministry, there was emotional pain, confusion, regret, despair, and a fathomless sadness. I was a priest, who had performed hundreds of marriages and had praised the virtues and blessings of married and family life. I was now seen to have abandoned both my family and church ministry that had served the spiritual needs of people for over twenty-one years. I felt like Judas, a traitor.

I felt conflicted, seeking solutions that I could not easily provide. At my age, my character had already been shaped and would not radically change, but my inner self needed transformation. Having explored life's challenges through early childhood and priestly formation, especially the obstacles to a healthier lifestyle, I concluded that it was my responsibility to identify the obstacles and resolve them.

Resolution implied discipline, a gradual process of identifying and rooting out destructive patterns of behavior and negative thinking, and carefully replacing them with constructive thoughts. With this new approach, I questioned what it is that I want out of my life. What steps were needed to attain a satisfying existence? Where did I fall short? Why was I so unhappy? What else could I do? I had tried psychotherapy for years and had been medicated by two different psychiatrists, yet still I felt unhappy and sometimes depressed.

Hearing my questions, my spiritual mentor commented that whatever healing means are available to you, if they do not seem to be helping, at least be grateful that you are alive and can still take charge of your life.

So I started from where I was in terms of my own personal religious orientation and belief system. Different religions serve the spiritual needs of different people. According to my cultural and religious background, I considered a new spiritual path that was best suited to my present state of mind and natural inclination.

Granted that most religions contribute to the benefit and spiritual stability of humanity, I explored and examined the fundamental, positive human qualities, such as the acceptance of self and of others, and showing care, compassion, forgiveness, goodness, generosity, kindness, and love. These are the qualities of the Holy Spirit, God's gift to all people. As human beings, we are subjected to similar conditions of life and need these basic spiritual qualities. They facilitate our daily life and create a more pleasant world.

While, in my case, it was Papavasile, the priest of our small town in Greece, who instilled these Christian virtues in our innocent teenage hearts; it is never too late, even as an adult, to reconsider these values. Consequently, I decided to cultivate these values and integrate them into my daily actions.

Involvement in a spiritual group can create belonging, community, and a caring connection with others. Furthermore, a meaningful spiritual framework, where people feel supported, provides a sense of acceptance and enables a person to face life's adversities with courage and understanding and to discover a sense of purpose—the foundation of a happier lifestyle.

Faith has sustained countless people through difficult times. God did not create the universe nor our specific planet, Earth, to be in a state of perpetual happiness. Nor did God create us to be spiritually and socially couch potatoes, oblivious to the opportunities that need help around us. We are created with an intense, built-in desire to live life to its fullest—to operate at peak performance. There has been a great deal of joy using what was available to me for my well-being and for the good of others, but there has also been pain and frustration.

Affluence and financial security are two alluring attractions that many people pursue but few attain them. Once attained, they appear to provide endless material possession and external happiness. However, do they provide a sense of inner peace and joy?

A number of years ago, on her program *20/20*, Barbara Walters asked the multimillionaire Ted Turner, "What is it like to be so wealthy and powerful?"

"It is an empty bag," Turner replied. In five words, the comment is a poignant reminder that regardless of how much we attain, it can never be enough. The wealthy man could not fill his bag. He was not as happy as one would think. Joyful living is not a station in life—it is a condition of the heart. It does not come from living up to some socially designed expectations and measure of performance. It is not defined by what others expect of you. It is defined by what you realistically expect of yourself and of others.

You and I cannot find inner joy by comparing our own accomplishments to what others have done or intend to do. Instead, it is found in living with the knowledge that we are operating at our own peak of performance, using gratefully the gifts, talents, and ability that God gave us to their full extent.

Believing that God is the giver of all good things brings me comfort and inner joy. It also brings me peace, strength, and purpose. Each time I have asked the question, "Is this all there is?" I have heard the gentle response, "*That's not all there is. There's more.*" In view of my frustrations, disappointments, and struggles, there is always much more that our loving Creator wants me to experience and to accomplish in fulfilling my earthly destiny.

52

A FATEFUL DAY

"History repeats itself." I had heard this saying several times as a young person but was not aware of its meaning. By the age of seventy-five, I had finally and painfully realized its true meaning.

On *Tuesday*, May 29, 1453, the city of Constantinople, the capital of the Byzantine Empire was invaded by the Ottoman Turks. The tragic fall of the city was followed by the conquest of the entire Byzantine Empire that brought to an end a glorious thousand years of civilization. As a result, the Greek nation had to succumb to Ottoman Turkish subjugation for four hundred years.

On *Tuesday*, September 11, 2001, came another fateful day, when the great nation of the United States was viciously attacked by terrorists, threatening an end to our cherished ideals of freedom, safety, and peace. Until then, America had enjoyed unprecedented peace and prosperity and had then become subjugated by fear.

I remember vividly being woken up early in the morning by a phone call from my son, Basil, who lived in Florida. Disturbed and crying, he cried out, "Dad, are you aware of what has happened?"

"No, I'm not aware. What's going on?" I asked. "I arrived home from Greece late last night, but tell me, what's the matter? You sound upset."

"Well, turn on your television, and you will see," he said.

"I turned the TV on and a sense of utter fear filled my heart as I watched the broadcast of crashing airplanes, crumbling buildings, and massive loss of life.

For a while, it seemed as though fear dictated my every move. When all this happened, perhaps you were one of those who asked, "Where is God?" Honestly, I asked such a question myself.

As our fears continued in the days following this terrible catastrophe, we witnessed something amazing. Amid the tragedy, people of all races, nationalities, and economic backgrounds pulled together and worked in unity. Lives were saved, families were comforted, and thousands of tons of rubble were cleared. A comforting message rang out: *Terror cannot overcome us if we do not allow it. Evil may triumph for a while, but in the end, it will be defeated.* My faith had to meet the challenge. Seeing the collapsing walls, the thick smoke from the raging infernos, I banked on my faith and felt a tinge of relief, as I said, "Peter, man of little faith." It is with confidence that St. Paul tells us, "For here we have no lasting city, but we are looking for the city that is to come" (Heb 13:14). In other words, at times in our life we may experience pain, like Jesus on the cross, but only in passing. Through the resurrection, all pain and sorrow fade away. The Lord calls us to have courage because he has defeated the Devil and destroyed death.

Over the years, the United States has experienced sporadic outbursts of violence in the form of serial killings, kidnappings, rapes, and high school massacres. What was it about the destruction of the Twin Towers and the attack on the Pentagon that so traumatized America?

A Fateful Day

The attack struck the very nerve center of American identity. The World Trade Center and the Pentagon were not simply large buildings previously deemed impervious to attack; they were the preeminent symbols of Western civilization and capitalism.

There is never any justification for acts of terror against innocent people. It is understandable why most of us, while grieving and consoling the mourners, feel anger and seek retaliation. War against terrorism is a new phrase, a new kind of war. It is not fought against nations or armies but against networks and ideologies that disregard all boundaries that used to be defensible. Now the enemy is closer. It is no longer on the other side of a border but in the daily fabric of our lives. This type of warfare seems new to us, and yet it is actually very old. It is an interior war that has raged since the beginning of time. We are consumed by the pursuit of happiness and the accumulation of material things at any price. The focus of many has been on the pursuit of health, wealth, entertainment, and pleasures. This war sees no end. It is a war against the human soul. We are at war against our own being.

In our effort to prove that we are free people, we become oblivious to some major realities of life. "The earth is the Lord's and the fullness thereof," claims the Bible. Nothing is ours, including our lives. Everything is a gift from God. Yet we have ignored and insulted God. Under this cloud of ignorance, we include those parts of the world where people live in poverty—homeless and hungry, diseased and without medication and proper care.

We've learned to close our ears when we hear that one out of every three people on this planet does not have enough food, and that one billion are literally starving. We have narrowed our attention to *getting through* or *doing well* in our own personal lives, and don't have time to focus on what happens to those in the rest of the world. Such complacency leads people to ask, "Why should we care about others?"

To move beyond this complacency, we need to see the spirit of God within each person, and we must try to respect the sanctity of every human being. If our civilization is to survive, we need to invite God back into our lives, not merely through words but with acts of love, compassion, and generosity toward others.

Of course, this yearning for God becomes more pronounced in difficult times. When things do not go well—when we fall ill and feel pain; when we are in dire need and have exhausted all known resources—we lift up our eyes toward something invisible. Like on that fateful day in 2001, we cry out in pain, "Oh, God, where are you? Please help me!" We expect God to be available when we need him. We expect God to be in the ambulance on our way to the emergency room. When we prosper, however, and the wind is in our sails, we ignore God, or we pay him little more than lip service. That is not loving God; that is using God, like a spare tire. You and I are free to choose how to respond, but God is always present in our lives, despite ourselves.

53

ANGELS APPEAR

God does not have human hands to embrace us and to show us that he loves us even when we fail him. But he sends angels, loving and caring people, to bring his love into our life. When colleagues—priests who knew me for many years—heard about my situation, they offered help, but they were in a quandary. One of my classmates in the school of psychology was Rabbi Joseph Goldman. He and his wife, Sally, offered their home if I needed a place to reside. Vicky and Norman Brosniak, friends of the Rabbi, offered a room in their house where I could stay as long as I wanted. I'll never forget their kindness. They became lifetime true friends.

Another caring angel stood out in his generosity. He was my church neighbor, the late Monsignor Charles Murphy, who went out of his way to provide immeasurable comfort. Obviously he knew the heartaches that lie ahead of a man who leaves the church. He put his gracious arm around me and whispered, "You are one of our brothers, and we'll do anything in our power to help you." When he heard my story, he offered me substantial help. He provided me with a room in his rectory and three meals a day for six months. This unexpected offer left me in tears. Rarely had I seen such generosity. I was a member of the Greek Orthodox Church, and here was a Roman Catholic priest who called me his brother.

Monsignor Murphy knew human suffering. He did not indulge in judgments or theological abstractions. On the contrary, he was available to me when I needed someone to talk to, although I was already in intense psychotherapy. His presence emanated warmth and love. When he sensed guilt in my voice, he comforted me with genuine compassion. Although celibate, he knew enough about children's reactions when their parents divorced. He said, "It's inevitable that your children are going to be angry with you. They may find it hard to forgive you; they may even refuse to see you or talk to you. It is a normal reaction. Be patient, and don't let that be an obstacle. Talk with them gently, be emotionally available, and let them know where you live and how they can contact you. Our rectory is your home now. Give them our phone number that they may call whenever they need you. Avoid blaming or deriding their mother or defending your decision."

When I assured Monsignor Murphy of my appreciation of his hospitality, he said graciously, "You are a middle-aged man, and most likely, you will marry again someday, I know the Orthodox Church permits a second marriage. It often happens. Should you decide to marry again, don't expect your children to be happy about it. In the years to come, they may be able to accommodate, even accept, your new life. Leave that part in the hands of God. He always provides solutions."

As the years flew by, faster than I could ever have imagined, my children came to accept my new direction in life. I am grateful to God and to them, and our relationship is even better than before. Truly, all of us live under the grace of a loving God. Our past, sometimes ugly and painful, serves no purpose except to remind us of our human vulnerability. We can accept the past as past, without denying it or discarding it. At times we may reminisce about it, but we must try not to live in it.

Angels Appear

In thinking of God's continued blessings, Monsignor Murphy's friendship and hospitality is forever present in my life. He was a godly man and profoundly spiritual, well respected by his many fellow priests. While he was not a prophet, his thoughtful suggestions seemed prophetic.

54

ABANDONMENT

At the age of forty-eight, I dived into deep waters, not quite knowing their depth nor my ability to swim. My intended priestly mission had to remain unfinished. I was unemployed. The Church, my symbolic mother that I had loved all my life and had served diligently and creatively as a priest, was no place for a man who had broken his marriage vows. The splendor of Byzantine iconography, the melodic chants, and the fragrant incense that enveloped the altar every Sunday, were to become memories of a past life.

In a Greek Orthodox parish, a divorced priest is persona non grata. While members of the church hierarchy struggle to accept the idea of divorce for a priest, they themselves, who by canon law are celibate, have limited knowledge of the realities of married life. They don't realize that sometimes even clergy marriages can be dysfunctional. Ordination to the priesthood doesn't make a man infallible. Shouldn't the Church, as a loving and compassionate institution, be concerned and caring about the condition of its priests? Would an army officer ever ignore a wounded soldier?

On the parish level, some parishioners, even those whose lives I had touched and helped through troublesome times, spread vicious gossip, lies, and slander. People, whom I had served for years as their priest—whose children I had baptized and taught and whose joy and sorrow I had shared—distanced themselves. Certain people who had been faithful members of the church community had now become the source of mean-spirited tattling. I did not defend myself against such taunting tongues that claimed moral authority over my life. In such a hostile climate, defending myself would serve no purpose. Nevertheless, it was sad to see the Christian spirit evaporate from those devout members who had become my judges.

I have a habit of opening the Bible periodically and reading a random page. One morning, my eyes fell on the familiar gospel story of the rich man and a poor beggar named Lazarus (see Luke 16:19–31). Although I knew the story, I read it twice and kept asking myself, "How does this story apply to me today?

Briefly, the story is about a rich man who dressed in purple and fine linen and feasted sumptuously every day. One day, he died and was buried, but he found himself tormented by flames. The selfish and insensitive use of his material prosperity had caused his downfall from temporary happiness to eternal misery. The beggar, however, who was satisfied each day to eat a few crumbs that fell from the rich man's table also died, but he found himself in the arms of Abraham, a symbol of joy and lasting happiness.

At that moment, I closed my eyes and visualized myself sitting among the crowd in Jerusalem, listening to the words of Jesus. His words seemed applicable to my life. Here I was, a parish priest clothed in colorful vestments every Sunday standing before the altar, endowed with a wealth of talents, and prominent among the clergy and laity, yet like the rich man, I ignored my priestly commitment. Self-absorbed, I had succumbed to a grave error in judgment; in Greek, the word is *hamartia* which means a "tragic flaw." My life had gone from the position of the highest calling—in the service of God—to being satisfied with the leftover crumbs from the rich man's table, like the poor man, Lazarus.

In my own eyes, I had fallen from grace. I had broken the promise I had made at my ordination: to preserve and carry out the mission of Christ until the end of my life. What did Christ think of me? I now had no congregation, no pulpit, no family, and almost no respect from others. Was I in the company of the rich man in Hades? Tormented by guilt and regret, I wished that someone would rescue me from this place of torment. But this was not eternity. Perhaps I was also the poor man. There was some relief in thinking of myself also as the poor man of the parable, currently eating the crumbs that fell from the rich man's table. Now I was promised a new life in the arms of Abraham, a foreshadowing of happiness.

I felt like a soldier, perhaps a wounded one, but I could still find a proper way to serve Christ who would continue to guide me. I believed that in his eyes I was still a priest, and he would never abandon me.

A verse from the Letter of James gave me additional strength and courage: "Draw near to God, and he will draw near to you" (4:8). Christ, who approached people regardless of their sinful condition, had already set the example. He entered their hearts with unconditional love. His nonjudgmental approach motivated them to live a new life, devoid of sin. I had to come closer to Christ that he might enter my heart and give me strength in my difficult situation.

Dwelling on my transgression would serve no other purpose than becoming a relentless source of punishment and self-induced suffering. I chose to let go of what had happened and visualized Christ extending a compassionate arm, embracing and accepting me as the loving father had accepted his prodigal son. Who was I to deny his gift of love and forgiveness? If I were to regain peace, healing, and personal growth, I had to let go and forgive myself. Through God's grace, I began to see a new future unfolding.

Thankfully, those in the Department of Religious Education were supportive and continued to use the books I had authored and the visual aids I had produced. Nevertheless, I recall the archbishop standing resolutely behind his desk saying, "I am aware of your present situation. I want to know what plans you have for your future."

"I'm not sure. I have no definite plans yet," I said, thinking that he might be concerned.

"Ambivalence is unacceptable, Father," he said sternly. "You realize that I still call you *Father* despite the fact that you have abandoned the Church." Clenching the jeweled pectoral cross on his chest, he said: "You are causing a great scandal in ecclesiastical circles."

While believing that nothing he might say could dampen God's love for me, I said, "I love our Church, Your Eminence."

"Show it in action. Repent and return to our church. Otherwise, write me a letter requesting your defrocking. In so doing, you will not be deprived of God's grace."

I had no wish to be a victim of this powerful man's attitude. I had problems to solve: I had no income at hand, and I had a family to support. Instead, I chose to align my thoughts, emotions, and actions with the highest part of myself—my soul. I had to get to know myself better—mentally, emotionally, physically, and spiritually—and fill my heart with enthusiasm, purpose, meaning, and a large dose of humility.

Lowering my eyes and my tone of voice, I said, "Your Eminence, I need to make a living."

"That is not a concern of the Church. You have made a bad choice. What do you expect the Church to do for you now?"

"I have done extensive work for the educational department of the archdiocese. I could work in that area, anonymously."

A reasonable income from the church might carry me through to the end of my studies in psychology, I thought. I had one more year of training, and then a new career as a psychologist lay ahead of me.

"The Church is compassionate; that door shall remain open to you," he said.

"Thank you," I said, gratefully reaching to shake his hand. He pulled back and dialed a phone number; our dialogue was over.

I left his office, envisioning possibilities. "That door shall remain open to you" were encouraging words. The following day, I called Father George, the head of the Department of Religious Education, and asked him in what areas I could be of help. Father George knew of my gift for producing educational materials and, in the past, had assigned me some major Sunday school projects. Working in his department would provide a small income. But never count the chickens before they've hatched! That previous evening, Father George confided, the archbishop had informed him by phone that he didn't want the department to have any contact with a divorced priest. Soon after, all the publications and visual aids I had produced were removed from the department and were no longer available to parishes.

When I heard the archbishop's order, my world came crashing down, and it seemed as though all the previous losses of my life had returned to haunt me. I completely lost my bearings, as well as my sense of personal integration in the Church and the larger community. It's hard to describe my difficulty in finding inner joy amid the profound loneliness and anguish that had descended upon me. However, from my training as a psychologist, I realized that the Church was no longer able to provide the support I needed.

In this state of desperation, I received an unexpected phone call that gave me incredible relief.

55

TRANSITION

It was a cold February evening in 1974 when I went to visit my children at their home. Outside the front door, I found three large garbage bags each with my name on them and containing most of my belongings—clothes, shoes, and books. A sudden flare of anger rose within me, stifling my desire to see my children. The inside of the house was in darkness, and the large front window was open.

As I picked up my bags, I heard loud music of an old Greek song: *I'm waiting for the pawn broker tonight to pick up whatever remains from a love that was hit hard by a cruel divorce. Rag and bone man take whatever you want from a relationship that no longer exists. Fill your sack with memories, good and bad as they are, for I have no longer any strength to look at them, they remind me of what I lost.*

Angrily, I grabbed the bags, threw them in the backseat of my car, and drove off. That unsettling evening and the days that followed were dark, yet I sensed some energy, some life force that exists within survivors, an unleashing of vitality that motivates action. I did not feel sorry for myself, although during difficult times and especially lonely nights, I prayed, "Lord, if there is a time to take me away, this would be a good time." Apparently, God had other plans.

Thinking about the injustices of life, wallowing in self-pity, or commiserating with others would have been a waste of energy. Rather, I accepted three real facts: first, life is not fair; second, it did not have to be; and third, it was my responsibility to do something about it. I had some knowledge and the strength to deal with difficult decisions. My first task was to find a job. It was not easy. I was continually met with the same responses that I was either overqualified or underqualified.

Those potential employers were correct. What work could they offer a person approaching his fifties who was trained only to be a priest? The fear of not finding employment began to surface, causing excruciating headaches and sleepless nights. Despite my fears for the future, I was in a period of transition with one hope—that tomorrow would be a better day. I entertained the hope that there *was* a new life ahead, one that I could face and responsibly design.

God has a plan for each one of us. How we adjust to that plan and design our life is up to us. We may have to go through the desert experience, but faith in a loving God will eventually bring us out of darkness. He invites us to "come closer" to him, where we can find his light and love—even if we are not lovable. Where we can find forgiveness—even when we feel unforgivable. Can we accept his compassionate and unconditional invitation?

Regardless of how my own family, my culture, and the church viewed my decision, I had to make a new beginning. The Horatian axiom that "whoever makes a new beginning has half of the job done" was of little comfort. In my current state of limbo, how would I know which path before me represented a genuine beginning? I needed to start somewhere, somehow, but I needed a viable way.

While writing this chapter I was inspired by Henri Nouwen's book *Here and Now*, where he writes,

Transition

We must learn to live each day, each hour, each minute as a new beginning, as a unique opportunity to make everything new. The "oughts," the "shoulds," and the "what ifs" fill our minds. The past and the future keep harassing us. The past with regrets and guilt, the future with worries.

Like the saying "Gradual wisdom of today, if I only had you yesterday," I wish I had known of such wisdom during my times of tribulation. It could have helped enormously with my bouts of ambivalence, uneasiness, frustration, insecurity, and confusion. My feelings, interwoven with guilt, needed to be reevaluated and put in perspective. How long could anyone swing between guilt and innocence, action and passivity? Where was my faith in a caring, loving, and forgiving God who is always present in our lives? Did I place God on a throne too high above me, so my weak prayers could not reach him? What was really happening to me—the olive picker, the former priest? What purpose would be served by distancing my life from God?

Struggling against my own self-doubts and insecurities, I had to understand and combat the furies within myself that subtly undermined my plans, casting doubt on my capabilities. Having spent seventeen years of my life in Greece, I still carried fragments of an immigrant mentality, one that was scared to death and hesitant about anything new and unfamiliar. Although I had made many external changes, I still lived by the safety code that I was taught in my youth: I'll take any job available; I don't mind washing dishes again. Work never scared me as long as I could have a decent meal, a roof above my head, clothes to wear, and I was able to support the family I had left behind.

As the clouds of confusion crossed my mind, a sudden ray of sunshine broke through bringing light into my life. It was an unexpected intervention that provided new hope. Wendell

Shackelford, the director of Instructional Systems at Harcourt Brace Jovanovich Publishing Company, had interviewed me five months earlier. He called and offered me a position as editor of the curriculum for a training program for minorities seeking employment. In addition to paying me fairly for my services, Wendell offered me personal support and the gift of his friendship, both of which touched my heart. It was his genuine emotional support and encouragement that allowed me to continue my courses and complete my education in the field of clinical psychology.

Faithful friends are lifesaving medicine, a sturdy shelter. Whoever finds a friend has found a treasure. It was not a matter of chance that Wendell reached out to me, eager to help. It was divine intervention, a spiritual experience. Through Wendell's offer, I could see the hand of God, and in time, I found myself growing in grace and wisdom. Over the years, Wendell and I shared many experiences, mostly joyful ones. Benjamin Franklin once said, "A brother may not be a friend, but a friend will always be a brother." Wendell proved to be a good brother. I hope I have been a good brother for him as well.

It was then that I began to realize that true friendship is a divine gift; God makes his presence known when two people are able to be together and share thoughts, feelings, experiences, ideas without evaluation, criticism, judgment, or the risk of becoming vulnerable.

True friendship does not seek personal advantage. It is neither mutually exploitative nor mutually possessive. There are no controls or manipulations; each person is free to be their true self. Between real friends, there is no power play or competition, and consequently, there is no ground for feeling hurt.

Through this time of emotional suffering, when both of us had gone through a divorce, our friendship provided comfort and healing. We shared common issues and did what we needed to maintain the bond of friendship. There was no need to impress each other with drama or success. We only allowed our inner selves, our souls, to connect and then enjoyed the results.

For years, I knew that certain people, instead of running to a psychotherapist's office for guidance, sought out the company of a good friend who they could trust, to solicit help and advice. This has led me to define for myself what is "friendship." To do this I considered the concept of the ancient philosophers who thought of friendship as the highest good and the power that friendship provides. Then I examined the spiritual aspects of friendship. Through my inner journey, I learned to appreciate the friendship that Jesus offers in calming our restless soul. Accordingly, choosing the right friend becomes paramount to shaping one's character and finding happiness.

The quest for happiness is a serious matter. It is not a destination. It is a journey that each person begins by being happy with every step. One evening, Wendell invited me to dinner. I met him at a restaurant that we had once enjoyed. This particular evening, as we sat and glanced at the menus, I noticed an exceptional smile in Wendell's face. "You look so happy," I said.

"I am...I am very happy...and remember," he said, "I'm treating you tonight."

I was glad to see my friend in such a joyful mood. "I think there is something you want to tell me," I inquired, eager to hear the source of his happiness.

"Good news," he said "About a month ago, I met this young woman, an artist and very attractive. Well, Peter, my friend, this coming Saturday, I have a date with her and I am excited."

I was happy to hear Wendell's good news. That night back in my apartment, when I was reflecting on his excitement, I pondered on our lives, trying to figure out the special things that make us humans happy. I had some idea what might make me happy. But skeptical about the idea of happiness that is momentary, I prayed for an experience of long-lasting joy. What a fantasy!

56

AN ENVELOPE OF LOVE

One particular Saturday morning, I received an unexpected phone call. It was a gentle voice that I heard: "Father, this is Pat, a member of the choir," she said. "Would you be in your church office in the next hour?"

"Yes, I'll be here until noon," I said.

"I need to see you for a few minutes, thank you."

"You sound a bit anxious. Are you okay?"

"Oh, I'm just excited. I'll be there in fifteen minutes."

Once Pat arrived, I recognized her as one of the beautiful young women who sang in the newly found choir every Sunday. She hardly said "good morning" as she handed me a large envelope.

"Father, take this. It is a round-trip ticket to Greece and some cash for Nick, one of the younger cantors in our church."

"Whose idea was this?" I asked and invited her to sit for a few moments and tell me about this generous gift.

"Two weeks ago, after choir rehearsal one Thursday evening, a few choir members met for coffee, as we often do. Nick had joined us that evening and told us how he missed Greece, his birthplace, and that he wanted to visit his parents, particularly his mother who is not well."

An Envelope of Love

One of my choir friends suggested that he go to Greece and visit his parents, and that his mother would feel better when she sees him.

He replied sadly, "It's an expensive trip, and at this time I don't make much money as a busboy. I'm looking for a better job."

Silence prevailed, but our eyes kept turning compassionately toward Nick.

"Later that night, our silence resulted in action. I called two of my friends who truly admired Nick's chanting and asked them if they had any idea how to help this member of our choir. They responded favorably, and they kept calling their friends asking them to help them in buying a ticket to Greece so that Nick could visit his sick mother. Within twelve days, we collected enough money for the round-trip ticket. Some cash is also enclosed in that envelop for his parents."

Still holding the envelope, I shook Pat's hand and said, "I can see that you represent God's right hand in doing his work for those in need."

Fully aware of the female power in the ministry of the church, I thought of my friend, Andy McCabe, who had recently written the book *How Women Will Change the World*.

"How should I handle this wonderful gift?" I asked.

"Father, members of the choir, respectfully request that you give this envelope to Nick without mentioning any names."

"What shall I say when he asks me?"

"This is a gift from the church in appreciation for your chanting."

I knew that Pat had been very helpful in harmonizing people's contributions and promoting philanthropic endeavors for the church. She often volunteered to help with any church project in which I was involved. For example, she helped considerably when I was coordinating the Heart Mission to

Greece. She was then working at the C. R. BARD pharmaceutical company. She spoke to her boss about the American doctors who were going to Greece to do open-heart surgery for the indigenous heart victims. The president of the pharmaceutical company and his associates responded favorably. Within a week, eight hundred pounds of medicine and surgical tools were delivered at our Holy Trinity Church in Westfield, New Jersey. The doctors were grateful for such a needed contribution, and I thanked Pat, still in admiration of her helpful initiatives. Young and full of vitality, her beautiful eyes glittered when she looked at me and said, "Father, is there anything else I could do for you?" She paused for a few seconds and asked emphatically, "Anything?"

"Anything?" I responded loudly, attempting to suppress my spontaneous thoughts *she might be* the answer to my heart's yearning for a good friend. Instantly, I disguised my thought with a smile and silently kept thinking, *Dearest Pat, you're beautiful and have a loving heart, but you're too young to be my intimate friend or even my mate. And I'm too old to meet your youthful needs.* But passion overshadowed logic, and I immediately began to declutter my desk. I did not want her to withdraw from the ministry of our Church. Her vitality and eagerness to help appeared to be an anchor of hope and a source of true comfort. Though I kept wondering, *Could she be simply a friend?*

But who was I kidding? Logic and priestly dignity dictated that I could not use this younger woman—or any other possible excuse—to diffuse my recurring loneliness and/or escape my responsibilities. I had to accept that the emotional mess of my divorce was my fault, and it was time for me to do something about it. I needed time away from my immediate environment to explore my deeper thoughts.

Compulsively, I returned to Lesvos, Greece, the place where I had spent the first seventeen years of my life, and considered plans about sharing my life with Pat. Soon after my arrival, I visited remote shrines and little chapels where, as a younger person, I used to light candles and pray for guidance and protection. What I had felt then—in my teens—I felt once again as a middle-aged man: relief, comfort, and joy, along with unprecedented confidence.

As I prayed, I imagined Pat to be not simply a friend but my lifetime companion. By the time I had to return to the United States, I had reached a decision. I needed to find a day when I could muster enough courage to propose to Pat. However, I had no idea if she would accept such a proposal. It was my honest desire, but I left it in God's hands. I decided to stay over in Athens for ten more days. I wanted to spend time with my loving cousins and share with them my thoughts and plans.

In my mind, in Pat's presence, questions about my commitments to my family and church, and the havoc I had caused, demanded answers that I could not provide. I needed time to discern whether my thoughts and feelings were realistic. Above all, I wanted and prayed that what I desired was in agreement with God's will.

After returning to the United States, a whole month passed and I took no action. I visited a couple of friends and spent time with my cousin, Margie, in Media, Pennsylvania. She was a good and supportive listener.

Eventually, I called Pat, and we met in a park near the church. Excitedly, I described my recent experiences on the island of Lesvos. Her eyes told me that it was now time to tell her about my thoughts of her and my hopeful plans for us. Pat was in utter shock. "You mean, you really want to make me your life companion?" Tears began to fill her eyes, but she controlled them with a sweet smile.

"I have made a decision and I want to marry you, but I'm not forcing you to accept my proposal. If you don't want to be my soulmate, I will not ask you why. I will understand."

"Father," as she used to call me, when I was still a priest, "this is a serious decision," she said. "We both need to think about it seriously. Can we take some time out and not see each other for while? You were away for more than a month. I also see the need to take some time out and think seriously about your proposal. It's a lifetime commitment."

"Good idea," I said. "I realize you need to think about what I have said. I know what I want, but you can take as much time as you need to be absolutely sure what you want and then decide."

"I'll need at least four to five weeks...," she said hesitantly.

"Fine," I said, "take six weeks. I can wait," hoping she would come back with a positive response.

Despite the clouds of confusion that left me with no viable direction for employment, I was prepared to wait for Pat's decision. Suddenly, a ray of sunshine broke through. Pat returned in four weeks having reflected on my plans and offer. Glowing and smiling sweetly, she said, "Four weeks in silence and deep thought were enough for me to make up my mind. I did not need another week. My heart and my mind know that I can love you. If you still wish to marry me, that's my wish also. I can and want to be your lifelong companion."

Having not seen or spoken to Pat for those four weeks, her definitive yes—*I want to be your lifelong companion*—caused instant relief and ecstasy. My heart's long-time yearning to find someone who could say, "I love you," was realized.

With pounding hearts and warm hugs I felt blessed, enveloped in God's grace. Ecstatic with joy, we gazed at each other in silence and with moist eyes, unable to verbalize the serious thoughts that kept surfacing in our minds. We knew there was a steep mountain ahead that we both needed to climb; a great deal of work would be required to implement this decision.

57

NEW LIFE

It was some years later, on June 25, 1978, when I married Pat. She was young—twenty-three years younger than me—and her presence and loving company made me feel younger and happier. Besides being young and beautiful, Pat had a loving heart and a most exciting spirit. Internally, I felt that, like a mirror, she would reflect both my best self and my worst self—a mirror that would not change or distort my image but one that would reflect the truth about whom she really married. Once Pat and I committed to a life together, the seed of self-realization and personal fulfillment was planted and we both anticipated seeing what would grow and blossom.

Although I know that only God can love us truly unconditionally, in Pat, I felt drawn to such unconditional love. I was sensitive to her needs, wanting to be both loving and lovable. Initially, I visualized a simple and meaningful life together, but I also had doubts about my ability to make her happy. It was my dream and desire to make this woman happy, and my hope and wish that she would make me happy through her love of me.

During our engagement, we had long, loving and deep dialogues, yet not without the anguish of ambivalence: Am I doing the right thing? Is Pat really happy being married to me? With each conversation, our need for further communication increased. I delighted in the inflection of her voice, her laughter, her maturity, despite the fact that she was so many years younger. My whole being was afire with joy, and I wanted to talk to her and be with her forever. Eventually, I felt more confidence in myself and devoted my life to bringing joy into our relationship. My relatives and well-intentioned friends were skeptical: "She's too young," "It's not going to work," "As you get older the romance will end, and then...?"

Most of Pat's relatives did not approve of her relationship with me and totally disagreed with the idea that she and I could have a successful marriage. Regardless, being self-reliant and unaffected by their opinions, Pat followed the dictates of her heart. The fact that I was older was not an obstacle for her. She genuinely loved me, and she wanted to be my wife and lifetime companion.

Some of my priest colleagues had warned me that I would miss the glory of the Church and the excitement of being a spiritual leader. There was meaning and value in their comments, but I chose to follow my heart, and I took responsibility for the consequences. While I still feel occasional sadness of leaving behind the important role of being a spiritual leader and its glamorous church ritual, I've never been happier. Being married to Pat was a better choice for me.

Once we were married, Pat was busy with her work and making a home for us. My new career was rewarding and involved helping people find peace, emotional health, and purpose in life. But as we traveled together—locally and overseas—enjoying the spirit of togetherness, Pat began to desire children. "Are we ever going to have a child?" she asked me, with evident yearning in her eyes.

For a long while I thought seriously about the idea of having a child with Pat. I was already the father of three; my parental destiny had been fulfilled. How would my existing three children feel about having another sibling? In essence, I did not want to raise another child, but wouldn't it be selfish to deprive the woman whom I genuinely loved the experience of motherhood? It didn't seem fair. How could I do that to Pat?

Pat was not just a pretty face; she also had a beautiful soul and her nurturing care refreshed my soul as we grew spiritually together. Consequently, I discovered within me untapped resources of love and creativity.

Sometimes, we talked into the night, and at other times, we sat silently in each other's company, drinking a cup of herbal tea or sipping a glass of homemade wine. Through this human experience of being loved and showing love, how could one ever doubt God's unconditional love? We both wished to stretch out the honeymoon forever, but there were realities in life we both needed to face.

In my therapy practice, many married couples have come to my office for counseling. Obviously, they were not as happy as they had hoped they would be when they got married. After the initial romance and the first years of married life, they discover areas of dissatisfaction. I listened to the many problems that each couple has faced. After seeing a couple a few times and offering different options, I would ask them if they want to save their marriage. If they did, then I would be honest and share with them my experience of being a marriage and family therapist and also of being married myself for longer.

Sometimes, we are disappointed because as months and years go by, we realize that we did not marry an angel. We married a human being with strengths and weaknesses. To a degree, we are all limited, inadequate, blemished, and sometimes boring. No matter how rich our personalities or attractive our bodies, none of us can indefinitely excite and generate novelty, sexual attraction, and psychological pleasure within a marriage or even in an intimate relationship. Any relationship or a marriage is like a long journey and there is bound to be some long dull stretches. An alternative is not to travel with someone who expects you to be exciting all the time. And to recognize that forgiveness, kindness, and respect allows us to remain in marriage and continue nurturing each other.

58

THE BONDING RITUAL

On May 26, 1980, I drove Pat to the hospital, and in the delivery room, after a few agonizing hours, I witnessed the mystery of birth. With awe and happiness, I reached out to hold the tiny new being, a seven-pound, four-ounce girl, wailing her lungs out. The nurse in charge said, "You may touch your little girl." As I did, our daughter wrapped her thread-thin fingers around my index finger—and I melted. Whatever psychic button she had pushed at that moment turned my entire world upside down instantly. I fell incurably in love at first sight with this tiny girl. Carefully, I carried her to Pat and placed her gently in her arms.

Separated during the process of birth, mother and daughter were now reconnected, performing the unwritten ritual of bonding. The baby's wails ceased immediately, and Pat's sweet smile dismissed all thought of the ordeal of labor. Her eyes had a tearful glitter, a grateful smile. "This is my second harvest," I whispered, as I kissed her forehead, still wet with perspiration from her labor. "Thank you for making me a mommy," she replied, placing the baby next to her cheek.

"You did the hard work," I said, caressing her head. As I observed mother and child bonding, a sharp shiver of love went through me. How accurately the Bible describes human beings: "You have made them a little lower than God, and crowned them with glory and honor" (Ps 8:5).

So, at the age of fifty-four, I became the father of Katina—named in honor of my stepmother. The whole experience put me in contact with the more nurturing parts of myself. As I held, fed, and cared for this helpless infant, I felt my feminine side and regained some emotional contact with my mother, who had probably cared for me in a similar way.

Katina grew into a very attractive child with big brown eyes and long brunette hair that curled over her shoulders. When Pat returned to teaching, I spent the morning hours looking after our charming little Katina.

For school, she had a collection of adorable colorful dresses. I drove her there every morning and looked the perfect picture; I thought I must look like the perfect father. Noticing my excitement with Katina, some of the mothers, who also brought their children to school, asked, "This must be your granddaughter? She is so beautiful." I just nodded silently. I was nearing sixty then, and I was not about to explain details concerning Katina, my younger and second daughter. Do looks or years really matter? Aren't we more than our aging bodies? Does the heart ever get old? I looked at my Katina and kissed her rosy cheeks as we parted each morning. She would kiss me and say in Greek, "*S'agapo poly yiassou.*" And I would say, "I too, love you much. Goodbye." Her sweet voice would echo in my heart as I went on my way to work.

59

A SURPRISE

Life had taken a joyful turn, and I soared high, feeling an expanding love igniting my every move. As an adjunct professor at Seton Hall University, I was invited by different organizations to conduct seminars on contemporary issues such as parenting, family-living skills, self-esteem, parents and teenagers, combating conflicts, human sexuality, and other topics related to human development. Who would ever imagine that a barefoot village boy—an olive picker, who had grazed goats and survived the yoke of Nazis for four years on a Greek island—would journey to America, become a priest, and twenty-one years later, end up becoming an active psychotherapist as well as a professor teaching courses in psychology at the graduate school of a university? The story astounds even myself.

I began putting my psychological knowledge into writing. Once my books appeared on the market, people who read them began to seek me out for assistance in their personal or family difficulties. Some clients suffered more than others. I tried to discover meaning in the midst of their suffering and to help them to see that as every storm comes to an end, it leaves us with its lessons.

Gradually, as I became more immersed in my new career, I realized that the attention and respect that I got in my professional life was intoxicating and addictive. The details of my work—clients and their problems, conducting seminars and writing books—absorbed a good amount of time. I began to lose the ability to tune in to the people who loved me the most and whom I loved very much—my family. I did not hear them complaining, and I took for granted that they were okay. But how much of their lives did I know? Did I ask my wife or my daughter how they felt and what they were going through each day? I learned to make our bed every morning, since I was the last one to wake up. I took out the garbage, washed the dishes, folded the dried laundry, and spent time at home, getting involved in family life—being a regular person, just like anybody else.

My family knew who I really was. They knew the good, the bad, and how I would act a certain way to appear more perfect, more authoritative. They saw me when I was confused and unsure of myself, stressed, upset, angry, or depressed. But they loved me for who I was, not for what I did. If I had continued to undervalue my role in the family and not let go periodically of my professional persona, I would have caused irreparable emotional damage to my loved ones.

A loving experience from our growing daughter Katina opened my eyes to see the true meaning of how I was loved by my own child. She was about six years old when she saw me removing the crabgrass for our small garden.

"Daddy...Daddy, come! I have filled the bathtub with warm water and now it's full with soap bubbles. Come and have a bubble bath before dinner."

"A bubble bath for me?" I laughed.

"Yes Daddy, for you. Even Mommy said it will relax you."

Relaxing under hot water, after a while I was in a daze, and kept watching the soap bubbles as each one burst. What a metaphor, I thought: "Life consists of many bubbles which eventually break." But my thoughts were interrupted as the door opened. Katina rolled a cart into the bathroom and I saw a tray of hors d'oeuvres. The steam from the hot water in the tub accentuated the smell of tiny meatballs, cracked garlicky olives, and small cheese puffs.

"Daddy, Mommy made a drink of ouzo for you. Can I have some? Please Daddy."

"Ouzo? No. But when you become eighteen or older, we will decide if you can have ouzo....Now, please go and help your mother with dinner, and I'll be with you soon."

The family is the source of our deepest love, and we are happy when we are rewarded by such love. In turn, we nurture their love for us and contribute to their wellness. More often than not, the family can also be the source of our deepest hurts. A great deal has been said and written about dysfunctional families that cause pain and suffering. Those closest to us hurt us the most, whether deliberately or not. And if we are no longer members of a family, we experience an even deeper feeling, that of loneliness.

For physical illnesses, we have medical doctors who can help alleviate the suffering associated with most diseases. Where do we go when we suffer psychologically or spiritually? Psychology provides various therapies for different mental issues. As a seasoned therapist, I became aware that I could not provide a total cure for my clients who were hurting, but I could help pave their way to healing. It is the grace of God that provides the ultimate cure. At times, feeling my powerlessness to provide comfort to a suffering or depressed client, I would humbly pray asking the Physician of souls and bodies to restore the client to good health.

Occasionally, I encountered people who were severely depressed or suicidal. I had to refer them to a psychiatrist who, besides giving a diagnosis, could prescribe medication.

Most of us are aware that suffering and pain are inevitable. There is no escape from the realities of our fragile and vulnerable human condition. How each of us faces those realities is the challenge of maturity. There may be no easy solutions to our most difficult problems, yet we are aware that solutions exist. We need the courage and the patience to find them.

In 2012, after the publication of *Living in Difficult Relationships*, numerous people facing problems in their marriages or their intimate relationships called my office. While I welcomed their calls, I informed each person who sought an appointment that I am a marriage and family therapist and that marriage was not designed to make people happy. Joy, peace, and happiness come from the contribution and participation of each member in the relationship.

60

RECONCILIATION

One Friday afternoon, while in New York City, I passed by a theater and caught sight of a huge poster of Anthony Quinn who was starring in *Zorba the Greek*. I had seen the movie years ago and really enjoyed it. Suddenly, I had the urge to see it again and stopped at the box office to purchase a ticket. My train home to New Jersey was not until 4:05 p.m. which gave me enough time to see the movie and make my train.

Watching the movie rekindled a fire within me. I was impressed with how Zorba embraced his life creatively and undauntedly. Zorba was no saint. He was human, but he seemed to love life. He bounced back from adversities, helped other people, and got involved in all of life that came his way. Oh, how much I wanted to be like Zorba and for a few precious moments I felt that I was Zorba. I wanted to celebrate life as he did. His dance was like a wonderful dialogue with Jesus. I wanted to dance like that too—or at least feel free with Jesus and to understand how the newness of life that Jesus offered can be stronger than death.

Gradually, I was able to redefine myself and worked on what I wanted in life: more freedom, more energy, a decent way to make a living, and new goals. In 1978, I earned a doctorate degree in psychology to add to my master's in education.

This helped with my transition from the religious sphere to a related secular field. For me, psychology is the study of the soul, especially the troubled soul that yearns for relief.

In letting go of my former self, a different person began to emerge through my new career. But I still had to reconcile myself with lingering past hurts. How could I be an effective therapist and bring harmony and peace to the lives of others if my own life was still unsettled?

God is the great forgiver and reconciler. It was time to let go of how I felt about the unkind treatment of my successor, my colleague, who had taken over the church whose foundation I had worked so hard for seven years to establish. Seven years after leaving the priesthood and my ministry, I decided to return to that church as a layperson with my wife and my daughter Katina, who was now ready to attend Sunday school.

After the Sunday liturgy, I stopped by the church office to register as a member and pay my dues for the year. Six weeks later, my colleague sent me a letter with an emphatic statement saying, "You and your family should no longer come to *his* church. He also returned the dues that I had paid with an official personal check which he, himself, had signed.

I decided to visit him and found him sitting at what had been *my* desk in my former office. I asked him by what authority he had to stop my attendance at *his church*, as he called it. In an abrupt and arrogant voice, he said, "You have caused a scandal in this parish that took me seven years to restore."

"Is the scandal my divorce or my second marriage?" I asked.

"Both, and the whole parish was upset."

"Upset? How sad, and it took you seven years to restore harmony? You must have worked very hard," I said with a tinge of sarcasm, smiling and shaking my head.

"I did. I did," he said, ignoring my sarcasm.

"Father, you may not know this," I said, looking at him directly and feeling the anger in my own voice, "His Eminence, Archbishop Iakovos, and the Ecclesiastical Court have officially accepted my divorce and officially approved my second marriage, which took place at Holy Trinity, Greek Orthodox Church in New Rochelle, New York."

Hearing this, his face flushed, but his eyes were disbelieving. He cleared his throat, "Good for you, and I wish you good luck," he replied with a fake smile.

"Well, I thought my letter to you was rather clear. Sorry, but you can no longer attend my church."

"Your church?" I said, preparing to leave. "I always believed that the church is *God's* dominion. It is the place where people gather to worship God, a spiritual clinic, according to St. John Chrysostom, where the sick people and the sinners experience God's forgiveness and healing presence."

"Well, obviously you know what the church is all about," he said and proceeded to open the door for me.

Taking a peripheral glance at my former office, I bid it a sad and silent goodbye. Pity mingled with indignation at the priest, a former colleague, who did not want me to be a member of his parish.

In time, however, his rejection proved to be an unexpected benefit to my family as we joined another Greek Orthodox Church, St. Demetrios in Union, New Jersey, where we felt welcomed by their priest and many of his parishioners. Here, I was asked if I could teach our faith to a group of twenty-five teenagers, and to preach the Sunday sermon periodically. It was a relief and happy occasion for my family and myself. Involvement at St. Demetrios restored my self-image as a priest, but it also brought an end to my anger toward my colleague. I was able to let go of my feelings about his hostile treatment and to realize that God wanted me to work in another vineyard, where I also found personal fulfillment.

Seven years later, I had an opportunity to visit the archbishop. When he saw me in my layman's clothes, he smiled and said, "I welcome the psychologist." This time he was very receptive and invited me to stay for lunch. Cordially, he indicated that I should sit next to him. He introduced me to his personnel as Father Peter Kalellis and spontaneously said, "Have you noticed? I still call him 'Father' because the priesthood is irrevocable. Once a priest, always a priest! Once baptized a Christian, you are always baptized. Besides, Father Kalellis is also a wholesome and fulfilled man, doing a serious ministry so much needed in our times."

Hearing his kind words, I bowed with respect and said gratefully, "Thank you, Your Eminence."

The archbishop seemed to be a different man—humble and kind. He extended his warm hospitality to me and requested that I send him a copy of my latest books and visit him again. When I returned home, Pat said, "You look very happy; you're glowing. What has happened?"

"It was a special visit," I said. "Simple reconciliation; I feel good about it."

I recalled my prior encounter with the archbishop at that crucial time of my life, when I seriously needed his help and he had ignored me. But now that my life had taken a new direction, I was able to let go of my anger and disappointment.

The archbishop himself was a prolific writer, and I was pleased to know that he had read some of my writings. He sent me a generous handwritten letter:

> *I feel joy and pride about your new direction in life. Truly, your ministry, which now includes the "written word," continues to be on target, helping the people of God. I noticed in one of your books, you called St. Paul,*

the "Apostle of Reconciliation." You have named him well because he had made it his mission in life to bring peace and reconciliation among nations. I pray for your good health and continued progress in writing.

In recent years, when I wanted to write a book about how we can grow spiritually, I asked the archbishop for his opinion. He sent me another handwritten personal letter. He suggested that in writing such a book, it would be helpful to consider the five major steps of spiritual growth: *self-awareness, self-knowledge, self-acceptance, self-purification,* and *fervent prayer.* "I trust that you are going to develop these five steps carefully, as you pursue personal enlightenment from God, the Father of all lights."

His advice became the basis for my book, Five Steps to Spiritual Growth. Unfortunately, Archbishop Iakovos died while I was still writing this particular book, but he left a lasting lesson with me: I needed to be able to adapt to new experiences on an ongoing basis, to avoid judgments and criticisms, and to continually readjust my thoughts so that I may view other human beings positively. The next challenge was to find peace and reconciliation throughout the rest of my life.

61

ANGER AND PAIN

As my career as a therapist expanded, I became increasingly aware of the extent of human suffering. No person ever came to me to share how happy he or she was. Every client that sought therapy seemed to have a problem of some kind that caused emotional and sometimes physical pain. Throughout life, people encounter any number of difficult issues that may propel them to seek therapy. I had learned that I could not always be a rescuer, but a part of my heart always yearned to respond with hope. The complexity of serious problems could not pull me into despair and make me a victim. I wanted to offer help wherever help was needed.

Psychotherapy is not entertaining. My practice in psychotherapy or marriage counseling for more than forty years has required energy, time, and commitment to each client who sought my help. Treating all clients without judgment or criticism, I have provided sensitivity and honesty, mirroring the reality of who they are and hoping that they will gradually realize their own potential and make their own decisions to regain peace. There are times that some people get angry with their therapist, especially when confronted with their contribution to their problems. It is easier to blame somebody else or circumstances than acknowledge their participation in the problem.

When anger is evoked in the process of therapy, it is important to remain calm, be patient, and wait until the client is ready to see and reflect on his or her contribution to their problem. For example, David, who was twenty-nine years old, six feet and five inches tall, came to see me. Initially, he complained that he could not find a decent job, and then he finally admitted that he did not like to go for interviews. I had asked him to look at different newspapers to see what jobs might be available. By the fifth week, when he came to my office, he looked sad and angry.

"I don't think there are any jobs available," he said. "But I did get a call to go for an interview, but I didn't want to go."

"Why not?" I asked firmly.

"I hate interviews," he said, with frustration clearly in his face.

"Did you look at any newspapers lately?"

"I don't read newspapers."

"So, you hate interviews, and you don't read newspapers. Do you expect an employer to come to your home, knock at your door, and offer you a job?"

"You don't know what it's like out there. You sit in a comfortable chair in your fancy office, listen to people's problems, and collect their money."

"You are right, but before you come back next week, I want you to call back the person who called you for an interview and bring with you a couple of newspapers in which you have looked for a job. Otherwise, you do not need to come back and waste my time and your money."

Enraged, he got up and pillared himself in front of my face and said, "You know, you are a shrink that collects money and does nothing. You piss me off because you cannot do anything for me. I could beat the hell out of you right now and walk out."

"I'm sure, you can. You are strong enough." He paused, tied his fists to scare me, pulled back and dashed out of my office, mumbling curses on his way.

"David, I'll see you next week," I shouted as he made his way out.

The following week, David showed up with a rolled up wrinkled newspaper and threw it on my lap.

"What's this all about? Are you telling me something?"

"Just look at page 12. I have underlined three phone calls and one man asked me to go for an interview."

"Good," I said.

David eventually did get a good job in a large computer store, and he liked it. He continued his therapy faithfully for six more weeks and eventually life took a positive turn for him. Two years later, he got married to Jenny, a woman he had known for three years and invited me to his wedding. I could not go because of other commitments, but I felt most rewarded to see this young man move on with his life. Every Christmas, he sends me a card with greetings, wishing me well and updating me with his latest news.

62

PAINFUL ENDINGS

Most professionals in the healing arts will admit that the cases that patients bring to them do not always have a happy ending. By the end of July of the same year, Henry, a middle-aged grieving father came to see me. A terrible car accident ended the life of Johnny, his twenty-one-year-old son. He brought a number of pictures of his son dressed in a colorful athletic uniform. Showing me the pictures and thinking of his son's sudden death, Henry could not control his tears, as he asked, "Why did God not protect my son?"

Not knowing what to do and what to say, I reached out and held this grieving father's hand, aware of his pain. There is no greater pain than the loss of a child. Grieving often takes place at different times for both a mother and a father and both also experience recurring grief at varying times. Furthermore, the nature of the parental bond affects the level and duration of the grief, and the loss of a toddler, teenager, or older child will sometimes affect a father more than the death of an infant, but not always.

In many cultures, society says that men are not supposed to cry. Often, men are determined to portray strength that prevents grieving and leads to emotional stress, anger, and depression later. A grieving father could feel ignored, abandoned, isolated, or overwhelmed. In such cases, it is important to seek comfort from friends, family, and co-workers, or wherever he can find support. It is also beneficial emotionally for fathers to give themselves permission to grieve. Of course, Henry was also supporting his wife, Lois, the grieving mother, who, in turn, was comforting the surviving siblings and other family members.

As I said previously, in my earlier days as a therapist I had learned that I could not always be a rescuer, yet I refused to allow the complexity of serious problems to make me a victim of despair. Nevertheless, there were times that, despite my good intentions, I was confronted with a tragic situation that left me feeling inept and helpless. On one such occasion, Henry brought his wife, Lois, to see me. With this grieving couple, all I could offer was my comforting presence, and with their permission, we offered a prayer together:

O Lord, Henry and Lois are hurting at this time, and I do not know what to say or do to ease their pain. They are good people, kind and generous, a source of comfort and joy to all those whom you have already sent to them. They are faithful members of your church, and their son has been taken from them. At the age of twenty-one, Johnny died in a car accident on Sunday night. Henry and Lois stand here today, a broken-hearted father and mother, seemingly alone and in complete despair, and they feel that their son's death is just not fair.

At this moment, their hearts react with human emotions, unaware that you know their anguish, having personally experienced the death of your own beloved Son on the cross. There is purpose in all that happens even when we are unable to perceive your plans.

Painful Endings

Our tears, dear Lord, express the deepest feelings when words fail. Lord Jesus, at this most painful time, in all their words and actions, guide their thoughts and feelings. Enable them to act firmly and wisely, without embittering or embarrassing others. Give them strength to bear the fatigue and pain of the coming days. Send your angels, some good people, to comfort Lois and Henry at this most painful and troubling time. Console them and instill the peace and understanding that they need at this time, for you, Lord Jesus Christ, are their God, in human form, whom they adore and believe. Amen.

63

A TALE OF HOPE

Some clients come to me with good intentions, and the results are usually positive. Others have a challenging time taking charge of their life. It was rewarding to see David, who had uncontrolled and self-destructing anger, find therapy beneficial to his life. That is my wish for everyone who seeks therapy.

Recently, the guidance counselor of a New Jersey high school contacted me to see if I treated teenagers. The counselor explained that one of their seniors, who has had an excellent record in academics, had begun to show signs of failing, skipping classes, and acting strangely.

First, I requested that I would like to meet with his parents. The counselor doubted that this would be possible since the parents had separated earlier in the year and the student now lives with his mother. He is angry and hates his father who has moved to the Carolinas. So we arranged that I would meet the student, whom she called Derek, the following afternoon.

Derek entered my office with an air of bravado—his hair disheveled, his shirt unbuttoned and hanging out of his shorts, and his sneakers' laces untied. He plunged himself into the chair across from me and kept moving his index finger as if it were on the trigger of a gun.

I paid no attention to his pantomime, and asked, "I know your name is Derek, but why are you here today?"

"I don't know. The guidance counselor told me I need therapy."

"What do you think you need?" I asked.

"Nothing. I have my own plans and you may not like them," he responded with a giggle.

"Would you like to share your plans with me?"

"I don't know if I can trust you," he said with a flare of arrogance.

"My work is based on trust and honesty. If you don't trust me, you can leave my office now, and we can stop wasting each other's time," I said, already feeling annoyed.

"Don't play shrink with me, Doc," he said, raising his voice. "If I tell you my plans, you may be scared."

"Try me. I have been scared many times in my life, but that didn't stop me from working and moving in my practice and on with my life."

Derek stretched his arms and legs and embraced himself, and said, "Doc, I don't know how to tell you what my plans are."

"I'm listening. Start anywhere you want."

"I have saved enough money to buy a gun and I know what to do with it," he said with assumed confidence.

"Use it, of course," I said.

"You guessed right! Use it! But before I use it on myself, a few others have got to go...you know—my father, if he ever comes back to Westfield, and some supposed friends. Last would be the scum in my school. Now his trigger finger was pointed at me.

"Am I one of the 'few others'?" I asked, concealing my concern and subtle fear.

"Oh no, Doc, not you!" he confirmed, shaking his head.

"Why not?"

"You're a good man—a silly old shrink—but at least you listen to what I say, and you want to help people. But I don't know if you can help me."

"I'll try, if you let me," I said, and kept processing my thoughts as I looked at this tormented youth who was threatening to end his life and possibly cause some larger tragedy. Already under stress, I was not quite sure how exactly to deal with Derek. I needed a strategy, some sort of uncommon therapy.

Derek, who was only seventeen years old, was caught in the dilemma of his parents' explosive divorce and felt abandoned. He had recently lost his girlfriend, his first love, to a popular classmate that he hated, was failing in most subjects, and had totally lost motivation. He spent his free time watching television and was late for school every morning. He repressed his feelings about such a life and became destructive of his personal possessions—stereo, computer, cameras, wall posters. Although I perceived some interest in his posture and interaction with me, his unexpected statement burst my bubble of optimism. There I was with a seventeen-year-old guy who threatened suicide. What kind of therapy could I use? I kept asking myself.

The following week, Derek walked into my office with an air of grandiosity. He held a violin case, which he rested by his feet as he sat across from me. It appeared to be heavy.

"Are you taking violin lessons?"

"Sure." He laughed as he lifted the case and laid it open on his lap. My eyes caught a gun, complete with silencer, and I managed to force a casual smile. "That's quite an unusual kind of violin. Can I see it?" I was hoping my voice did not reveal my anxiety and concern.

"Sure." He placed the case on my lap.

"What do you plan to do with this baby?" I asked, sensing my heart pounding. "I know a lot about these babies," I said, with a great show of confidence. Carefully, I lifted up the gun, and as I examined it, I instantly recalled that day when Alexis, the tavern keeper in my hometown on the Greek island of Lesvos, took me and my friends to a hiding place, where stacks of guns, like the one I was holding, were stored. It was during the Nazi occupation of Greece. American marines had smuggled the guns into the island, and Alexis was one of the few people who knew about the episode, for he had helped the marines in the operation.

"How did you get this gun?" I asked.

"I told you last week I can lay my hands on anything I want."

"I see you're a man of your word."

"You bet."

I replaced the gun and snapped the case closed. "Derek, for safety," I said, pointing to the storage closet under my bookcase, "Why don't you leave the gun with me. Nobody can touch it here. This is not the day to use it. We need to figure things out."

"I have my own plans," he said, thinking, *can I really trust this old shrink?*

"I know that, but it would be a good idea to leave the gun here until you have thought things through."

"How do I know I can trust you?"

"Derek, if you didn't trust me, would you have shown me the gun in the first place?"

"I suppose not." He exhaled with a sigh of relief. He began talking emotionally of his disappointment of the adults in his life. He had repressed a whole segment of feelings: the unexplained divorce of his parents, demanding, unreasonable teachers, and the losses he experienced.

If he felt there was at least one person he could trust, I thought, life might seem different. I took a key from my pocket and gave it to him. It was a risky, *uncommon therapy.*

"What's this for?" He asked curiously.

I handed over the violin case that contained the gun. "You can lock this baby in my closet, and anytime you need it, you are free to come in and get it."

"And how do I get into your office if you're not here?"

"I didn't think about that. Here's the spare door key," I said, as I retrieved it from the drawer of my desk.

"I can't believe you trust me with the key to your office!"

"Derek, you trusted me with serious secrets," I said.

He locked up the gun, and on his way out that day, he tested the door key.

"You're a good guy, Doc. A crazy old shrink, but good."

During the fifth session, Derek checked the closet. Satisfied that the gun was exactly where he had left it, he was now ready to reveal more information about his life. He belonged to a secret organization, the NNC, Neo-Nazi Club, whose purpose was to clean up the scum of the town, certain teachers, some parents, and a number of spoiled brats. He took the list out of an envelope and showed it to me.

The possession of a weapon and his membership in the Neo-Nazi Club enabled Derek to display an air of superiority, but beneath the display was an enraged abandoned young man who hurt deeply. I wanted him to learn that he was not the only seventeen-year-old who had suffered at the hands of adults.

At the next weekly session, I said, "When you handed your gun to me, you took me back fifty years or more to the time when I was sixteen. A Nazi soldier pointed his gun at me and scared the pants off me."

"What was a Nazi soldier doing in Greece?"

Derek suddenly realized that I had not always been a silly shrink and that years ago at one time I was also a young boy.

"It's a long story. Like the rest of Europe, Greece was invaded by thousands of Hitler's soldiers."

"Did you fight back?" Now I could see curiosity in his eyes.

"Indirectly," I replied.

"Did they hurt you?"

"The first day they landed on the island, they ransacked my home, took away my bike, and burned the little American flag I had fastened to the handlebars. They killed my father's best friend, Lefteri, and three months later, they killed seven high school students, classmates of mine who tried to escape across the island to Asia Minor."

"How terrible!" he said in a low voice of sadness. "Weren't you afraid they'd kill you?"

"All the time," I said. "Christmas time! One evening, three boys were singing Christmas carols to their neighbors. Singing alone, one boy played his drum." Tears escaped my eyes.

"Doc, are you crying?"

"Yes, Derek. I don't want to upset you. A Nazi jeep went by the carolers and for no reason, a soldier with a machine gun killed all three boys. It was a Bloody Christmas."

In shock and with sudden feelings of sadness, Derek said, "Doc, you were there. I cannot imagine how you must have felt as a teenager. But tell me, how long did the Nazis stay in your hometown?"

"Almost four years," I said. "Gruesome years of famine, fear, illness, and death. I saw people dying of starvation; hundreds of others were executed."

"How did you manage to survive?"

"It was not easy. I always had hoped that I would live to see my country free."

"Just hoping....that's what kept you going?"

"Yes, hoping, hiding, and praying."

"You should write a book about this." His eyes brightened with sincere interest.

"If I do, will you read it?" I smiled.

"You bet I will. I do some writing myself. I'm writing a story at this time."

Here, I thought, I had the eye of the needle to his soul. I had read two excellent poems on death that he had written and a maudlin story about Diane, a girl in prison. Indeed, I wondered if Diane were not a symbol of Derek's imprisoned psyche.

"I like your poems. You have a flair for imagery."

"I'm better with prose," he responded.

"When do you think you will finish Diane's story?"

"I don't know." He thought for a few seconds. "I don't know how to finish it."

"Well, will you leave Diane in prison?" I was pretty sure that Derek really was writing about himself—feeling completely trapped.

"I don't know how to get her out," he said.

"Maybe if I tell you how I survived the Nazi occupation, you may get some ideas."

The urge to tell Derek what had happened to me kept me awake that night. On each of the next five weekly visits that followed, I sent Derek home with a chapter describing what had happened to me and my three childhood friends on the island of Lesvos. He brought each chapter back, and we discussed various incidents. It was evident that my experiences evoked feelings in him about his own life.

"I don't know how you lived through such horrors," he said.

"I don't know either. Would you have survived?"

"If a Nazi soldier slapped me like he did to you, I'd have attacked him and choked the life out of him."

"That's how I felt—but he had a gun!"

"Why didn't you get yourself a gun?"

"If the Nazis discovered anyone with a gun, they not only killed the owner but his whole family."

Derek was stunned. His face was a mixture of empathy and confusion. He looked at me almost in disbelief. Perhaps it was curiosity, but his look created some doubt in the way I was treating Derek. In my training, I had learned, on the one hand, that patients pay the psychologist to listen to their stories; and on the other hand, that in relating my experiences to my patient, I was inviting him or her to come out of their own neurotic cocoon and see that other people have similar or even worse experiences.

By the end of the tenth week he brought me a rough draft of a revised version of his story of Diane. It is fascinating what symbolic material the unconscious can produce. Derek's Diane finds herself prisoner in a concentration camp, tortured by Gestapo soldiers, raped by Hitler himself, and pregnant. Again and again, she throws a thick burlap bag over the barbed wire fence and attempts to escape, but she is dragged back. Her father visits her unexpectedly, but he is not her father—he's Hitler. Her mother becomes a whore, dresses in sleazy clothes, and is patronized by Nazi soldiers. Both parents blame Diane for her imprisonment: "It's your own fault; you disobeyed us." Their treatment leads her to believe that being in prison is preferable to living at home.

"It seems that Diane prefers the security of misery in the prison," I said.

"She has no choice," Derek blurted out.

"From what you have read of my story so far, did I have any choice?"

"You had friends."

"Right! In your story, could Diane have any friends?"

"I guess she could be a friend to some of the prisoners in the camp."

"Suffering shared may not be as painful as suffering in isolation," I suggested.

"Did having friends help you?" he asked.

"You'll see when you read the next chapter."

Over the following weeks, I saw new vitality in Derek's face. He kept returning, and we shared our stories. His story of Diane contained self-discovery, and by the following spring, Derek had survived the descent of the furies upon his psyche. He no longer mentioned the gun. He was healing slowly.

In one of our sessions, Derek said, "Now I know all about you. Besides being a damn good shrink, you really survived hunger, fear, and the Nazi cruelty. Man! You had guts and courage."

"And hope," I added.

Several sessions went by without Derek mentioning anything more about his original plans that he had bravely told me when he originally came to see me. In one of his last sessions, he said, "Doc, do me a favor. Get rid of the gun and the execution list I had left with you."

He handed me the keys to my office and to the cabinet where I had kept his gun. I looked straight into his eyes and saw a different young man. Somehow, uncommon therapy worked well for Derek.

Before he left my office that day, he told me details about his involvement in his school's drama class, and he was particularly excited about a scholarship award he had received to study Shakespearean theater in England.

In view of the risk to accept and be Derek's therapist, I learned more about another approach to therapy and felt rewarded with the results. As we get older, we become more mature and we are willing to learn more about the practice of the healing arts.

64

LIFE AFTER LIFE

For everything there is a season, and a time for every matter under heaven: a time to be born, and a time to die.

—Ecclesiastes 3:1–2

As you have read, my journey thus far has been an adventure of different, uncommon, and even at times, some risky unexpected events that have taught me many bittersweet and rewarding lessons. This leads me, though, to wonder what will happen after my earthly life. Does anyone really know what happens after death? Even theologians, scripture scholars, and philosophers, who have sometimes devoted their lives to the subject of death, take a step back. No human mind or knowledge can answer what happens after our earthly life.

On one occasion, I commented to my wife that, someday, we must all die. My wife's response was short and firm, "For you, Peter, death is not an option." Such a response demonstrated her genuine love and desire that she does not want me to die. Nor do I want to die, but do I have a choice? By accepting the fact that someday we will die, we can embrace whatever time God gives us and continue living with inner contentment and gratitude.

By changing our mindset from "death is not an option" to understanding that, in loving someone, we are really saying to that person, "You will never die because, in this life and in the next, you will never be separated from God's family," we are opening ourselves to God's love. In other words, we believe that the person will never die and that there is nothing to fear after death because we are bound to Christ, and we will be with him.

My next door neighbor periodically challenges my faith. As a man of science himself, he finds it difficult to believe in a life after this one. As a fellow Christian, however, I have suggested that he enjoy and cultivate his faith in Jesus—noting that while still on earth he has experienced love, joy, peace, forgiveness, kindness—and to leave the issue of *life after life* in God's hands.

For peace of mind, I have occasionally examined my beliefs and feelings about death. I can accept the truth about death and have trained myself to acknowledge the feelings when they emerge. But am I less afraid? Not really. Still, negative thoughts surface: *What will my death be like? Will there be prolonged pain and suffering? Will I leave things unfinished? What about my loved ones that I will leave behind?* I really have no convincing answers and some anxiety is normal.

In truth, death can be an important ally in our appreciation of life. We do not need to be morbidly worried or preoccupied with death. It is far better to acknowledge our finitude as physical beings, realizing that our earthly existence is short and the time to love and be loveable is limited. Indeed, such realization can detach us from the madness of our socially constructed existence—our clinging to material accumulations, social status, and superficial desires as sources of ultimate security. Because of the brevity and uncertainty of life,

I know well that any day at any time I will abandon this body and continue to move with my spiritual self into a new life in God's presence.

Regarding any unfinished business, my loving wife offered me a simple answer: *Live life fully until you die. It is important to appreciate life, live it in its fullness, and be grateful.*

So, I have stopped worrying about death, and I try to love others more and be more grateful to God for giving me another day. We can join the Psalmist in proclaiming, "This is the day that the LORD has made [*for me*]; let us rejoice and be glad in it" (Ps 118:24).

God came to us in human form. Consequently, he is not hidden nor hard to contact; forgiveness, grace, and salvation are not the prerogative of the lucky few; we don't have to save ourselves; we don't have to get our lives perfectly in order to be saved; we don't have to make amends for our sins; human flesh and this world are not obstacles, but vehicles to heaven. We can help each other on the journey of life; love, truly human love is stronger than death; and to love someone is indeed to say: *You at least will never die!*

65

A TALE OF RECONCILIATION

God is Love, and God being eternal, so is His love eternal. As a result love is eternal, ever alive and active. In her limited human way Pat feels and believes that I will not die because she loves me. I'm happy to know that when my physical self dies, I'll be present in my wife's loving heart.

For the last seventy years, I've been seeking an unfathomable love. Often my mind leads me to the priest, Papavasile. As a young priest, I went to him with my personal issues. I remember how he counseled me with compassion and kindness. While his theological education was limited, his dedication and love for Jesus Christ and his church had no limits.

When I decided to return to the island of Lesvos, I attended Sunday services at the church where Papavasile had served all his life. I was sad that he was no longer there. After the Sunday services, I stayed in that church totally alone for a long time. At the right side of the altar was the cantor's podium. I recall singing alongside him as a teenager. Suddenly, I felt drawn to the podium where, in some dusty corner among church books, I

came across a book with the title, *My Story, Papavasile*. I began
to read his story and could hear his voice:

> In the early forties, the Nazis had caused havoc in
> the land of Greece. Hundreds of big and small towns
> were destroyed, and many devastated people were
> taken to Haidari, a concentration camp near Athens,
> Greece. Thousands died of starvation, terrorism,
> rape, and cruel executions during the four years of
> the Nazi invasion.
>
> I was at the altar preparing for the Sunday lit-
> urgy. When I turned to look at the main part of the
> church, I saw a young man, unknown to me, lighting
> a candle, making the sign of the cross and praying.
> I approached him silently and introduced myself.
> "I'm Papavasile, the priest of this parish. What is
> your name?"
>
> He bowed and kissed my hand and said, "My
> name is Dimitri, and I'm twenty-three years old, still
> looking for a job."
>
> "Where are you coming from?"
>
> "From Afalon, a neighboring town that has
> been burned to ashes." The pain and sadness he felt
> were evident in his voice as he said, "My poor par-
> ents died in the fire, but I was able to escape along
> with a neighbor. Now, for seven months, I have been
> walking to different villages, looking for a job and a
> place to live."
>
> In full empathy I said, "Dimitri, I'm truly very
> sad to hear about the death of your parents. Truly,
> I'm sorry. May they rest in peace! The burning of
> your town and the death of its people is another
> painful tragedy. Very sad! What you have told me

today has resurrected within me a personal, most painful loss that occurred in my life. I do not wish to talk about it now, but believe me, I feel your pain and I want to help you. I hope you find me willing to help you so you can sense some relief."

"Papavasile, thank you."

"Well, I do have a place for you to stay. It's small and clean next to this church building. And I've been looking for someone to take care of the church, and clean the inside. If you think you can do that, then you can have a job."

"Father, of course I can," he exclaimed. "How can I ever thank you? And I must tell you, I'm a good cantor. Since I was thirteen years old, I learned the Byzantine music and have been singing in our town church. If you want, I can help assist your cantor by singing along with him."

For a whole week, Dimitri's unexpected visit kept causing me an emotional earthquake which for a few days resulted in an unresolved conflict. I prayed to our Lord Jesus. Dimitri's story brought back the sad memory of Christos, my son that some-one killed during the Nazi Occupation. "Lord Jesus," I said, "Did you send me Dimitri to comfort me in my loss?"

Thinking that Jesus in his wisdom, had sent Dimitri to me for a reason, I felt some relief for a few days, until one morning I woke up with a dream. My son had just come home from college.

In view of Dimitri's appearance at my church and me liking him and wanting to help him, my thoughts of that fatal day of my son's death, once again became my present reality.

A Tale of Reconciliation

Feeling the sadness, I stopped reading and began to wonder how anyone or anything could comfort parents who suffer the pain of the loss of their child. The priest and his wife were profoundly wounded and not even a skillful counselor could provide healing and comfort. Endless prayers and memorial services were attended by many of Papavasile's parishioners, who offered heartfelt sympathy to him and his wife. But could any human being reach and erase their grief? The only source of comfort was their faith and prayer to the Healer of all wounds, the Lord Jesus Christ.

I returned to this priest's story:

It was one cloudy Friday morning during Lent that I heard a strong pounding at the front door of my rectory. My wife had taken my daughter to visit her sister for a couple of days, and I was alone. Curiously, I rushed to see who could be visiting us this early. As I opened the door I saw a woman, her head covered with a black mantel, sobbing and crying uncontrollably. I recognized her. She was known as an errand woman and also a carrier of the latest news of our little town.

"Stratya, what's the matter? Why are you crying?" I asked.

With sobs and more tears, she said, "I wish I were the dead one."

"What are you trying to tell me? Who died?"

"You have been a good man and our respected priest for many years," she said, "and I have a hard time to tell you."

"Stop crying and tell me," I said firmly.

"At dawn this morning, I found your son cold and unconscious at our town's fountain. And thinking he might be asleep, I kept shaking him to wake him up, to see if he was okay, but he did not respond."

"Stratya, who and why would someone kill my son?"

"I don't know. But one day that killer will be discovered and he should be punished for his crime."

Christos was my only son, a simple and innocent young man, hardly twenty-one years old. He was a very active church member and often sang along with the psalti of our church. I was hoping that someday he may become a priest and continue my ministry.

Vitally interested to read more of Papavasile's story, I turned another page and read,

Our daughter was of great comfort to my wife and myself. Seeing her as excited, growing fast and gradually talking about marriage, our grief slowly subsided, and we turned our attention toward her. Married life began to knock on her loving heart. There was a glow of joy in her face when she told her mother how the church interior looked spotless since Dimitri became the caretaker. My wife shared our daughter's excitement with me and added: "People who attend church regularly, they like him very much and enjoy hearing Dimitri's chanting." Obviously, both my wife and daughter were also impressed by his youthful voice.

Noticing their enthusiasm, I said, "This coming Sunday, after vesper services, I will invite Dimitri for dinner."

"I think it's a good idea," my wife said, and my daughter smiled and raised her eyebrows. At dinner time, I noticed how both my women were praising our guest. At times, I glanced at my daughter's face, her interest was evident. Besides a heartfelt "thank you," Dimitri remained silent and periodically sighed.

The following Wednesday morning, as caring parents we took time to discuss how we felt about Dimitri becoming our son-in-law. Then we talked to our daughter about him. She blushed, her eyes filled with tears and she said, "Over the last two years, I have grown to like Dimitri very much. I hope he likes me."

With sudden enthusiasm, we both embraced our daughter and in a firm tone of voice, we said, "He would be a lucky man marrying you." On Friday, before he started cleaning the church, I invited Dimitri to come into my office and briefly told him about our family discussion.

Being the beginning of Lent, a spiritual season, my parishioners and a few friends had a small Lenten party and dinner in our rectory. When I announced the engagement of my daughter to Dimitri, a spontaneous applause filled our home with joy and screams of congratulations for the newly engaged couple. Andy and Paul, my two closer friends asked, "What's the date of the wedding?"

"After Easter...after Easter," I shouted.

During Lent, my wife and daughter were excited in preparing all the details about the wedding.

I kept very busy with my church responsibilities —serving at the altar, seeing parishioners who came to see me for their annual confession, visiting people at the hospital, and bringing Holy Communion to the sick.

It was a Good Friday evening, known as the Lamentation Service for Christ. After the end of this dramatic service, there was a line of people waiting for me to hear their confessions. Dimitri, who had been chanting through the entire service, was the last person in line. Respectfully, he approached me and said, "Father, would you be able to hear my confession this evening?"

Still wearing my vestments I said, "Of course, come near the altar."

"Thank you," he said. "It's time for me to confess my sins and receive Holy Communion for Easter. It's something good to do before marriage, isn't it?"

"Of course, and I'm glad to hear your plans," I said, feeling proud to have Dimitri as my son-in-law. "I need to go inside the altar and change the color of my vestments." I said, "I'll meet you in front of the altar."

Dimitri waited for me; he probably did not understand why I had to change the color of my vestments that was purple during Lent. But when he saw me approaching him in a bright snow-white-stole, he smiled.

"It's a color of joy for both of us Dimitri to be in our Lord's house and in his service. Now I'm ready to hear your confession."

"Papavasile, I have mentioned to you," Dimitri said, as more tears made him pause, letting him tell me what his tears could not verbalize, "how I had hardly escaped, but I felt revengeful and sought ways to fight against the invaders. Walking randomly one dark night, I kept looking for a possible safe place. Yet vengeful thoughts boiled through my mind. The first Nazi soldier that I meet tonight,

A Tale of Reconciliation

I'll kill him, I said, grinding my teeth threateningly. Suddenly, I heard water pouring into a stone basin. I realized it was the familiar fountain about a ten-minute walk from my town. I was thirsty, but I stopped the moment I saw someone bending under the pouring water and quickly tiptoed toward the fountain. Suddenly, my vision blurred as I smelled a strange perspiration odor. It dawned on me that this young man must be one of the invaders of our homeland. Then, like a predator, forcefully I jumped from behind, grabbed who I thought was my enemy by the neck, ignoring his screaming protest. Tightly I squeezed his throat with all my strength and left him hanging breathless on the basin of the fountain. But, as if my crime was not enough, I yanked a chain with a cross from his neck. Look. Here it is."

As I looked at the cross, I realized it was my son's. I had given him this cross as a present for his graduation from high school. Now I was totally aware that this was the man who killed my son. Guilt-ridden for his crime, Dimitri cried and sobbed for a long time. I turned and looked at the cross of Jesus Christ that stood in the center of our Church altar. My whole body felt electrified as new thoughts cried in my brain: "Papavasile, Jesus Christ the Son of God died on the cross for this penitent young man. Why are you waiting?" I shook my head and in silence I whispered words that I did not want Dimitri, this penitent man to hear: "Lord Jesus, forgive me and help me to forgive this young cantor who plans to marry my daughter." I struggled to place my hand on his forehead to pronounce forgiveness, but I could not. I felt nothing, not the slightest spark of warmth or kindness. And so again I breathed a silent prayer. "Jesus, I have prayed, I cannot forgive him. He killed my son, how can I allow him to marry my daughter? Please forgive me."

Then pulling my hand back, I took his right hand and as I held it, the most incredible thing happened. From my shoulder along my arm and through my hand a current seemed to pass from me to him, while into my heart sprang a love for Dimitri that almost overwhelmed me.

It was a moment that I discovered and believed that it is not on our forgiveness any more or our goodness that the world's healing hinges, but on God's. When Jesus tells us to love our enemies, he gives, along with the command, his love itself.

Closing the pages of the book, I took the handwritten story of Papavasile to the local archdiocese to be placed in the ecclesiastical archives. The archivist, Father Fotios, took a look at the title and made the sign of the cross. "May he rest in peace," he whispered, "Papavasile was a priest of priests. In the years to come, may be fifty years or more from today, the Official Church will canonize Papavasile and his name will be commemorated among the saints."

66

THE LESSONS OF AFRICA

Sometimes we can be surprised how different events can bring us equilibrium; how something enjoyable and uplifting can follow a painful event. In my case, I happened to hear of the wonderful missionary work that Father Alexander Veronis, a priest from Lancaster, Pennsylvania, had initiated in Africa. He and his wife, Pearl, had devoted their lives to missionary work, being available both materially and spiritually to the indigenous populations of Kenya and Uganda in Africa.

Motivated by the idea of the mission, I called Father Veronis to commend him on his work in Africa and to ask if I could offer any assistance. He thanked me and said, "Peter, the great land of Africa attracts people for different reasons: Enterprising company executives want the wealth that can come from exploitation; politicians pursue their own personal interests; adventurers go on exploration journeys; holiday makers go on safaris; and others go as missionaries. Africa is considered a poor, underdeveloped continent, harassed by hunger, haunted and stifled by domestic politics. Its future is an enigma."

His brief description spoke of his deep emotional involvement in his work in Africa. "Father Veronis, your contribution must be phenomenal and much appreciated," I said.

"It's a drop in the ocean," he said. "God's vineyard in Africa is large and fertile, but we need more workers."

"I wish I could be of some help," I said, not knowing exactly what kind of help I could offer.

"Peter, I have been there with my wife several times," he said. "At this time, twenty-five young Greek-American boys and girls, including my son Luke, are already there helping to build homes, schools, and worship centers. It's time for you and your wife to participate. It's an experience of a lifetime," he said.

Astonished at his boldness, I said, "What do you think I could contribute?"

"Anything! Those people need any help they can get. As a therapist, you can help troubled individuals and troubled families. You can teach family-living skills. Just being there, even for a while, you can touch many souls and give people hope."

"Give me a couple of days," I said. "I need to think about such a commitment."

Inspired and moved by the superior achievements and zeal of this priest, I felt unable to respond to such a challenge. On the one hand, I questioned whether, as a self-employed man, I could leave my practice and domestic responsibilities and go to Kenya as a missionary. On the other hand, I wanted to accept this challenge unconditionally. If I don't do something like this now, when would I do it?

That night, I lay awake giving more thought to the invitation and the disparity between the lives of those in Africa and my own comfortable life in America. Throughout it all was the ever-present question: Why am I so privileged while others are so deprived?

The following day, my wife and I discussed what we could possibly offer the people in Africa. Pat responded with enthusiasm, "Let's all go as a family. I'm sure we can help as a family." When she told our young daughter, Katina, our decision, they both were excited and motivated by the possibility of being of service.

Father Jonas, a native African priest, and Father Emmanuel, a Greek-American resident missionary, received us at the airport in Kenya. Their warm welcome embraced our souls. Along with eight other missionaries, they took us to a simple yet sacred chapel where Byzantine icons, simple sketches of the divine, underscored thoughts of eternity. The sweet fragrance of incense blended with the smell of the flowers surrounding the altar. A melodious a cappella choir sang a doxology.

Father Jonas emerged from the altar wearing colorful vestments and holding in his hands the mysteries of heaven in the form of a lit candle. "Everything is dark here in Africa, but the light of Christ shines upon all," he proclaimed gently. As the pastor and spiritual leader of thousands, he welcomed our group and wished us a pleasant stay. Briefly, he pointed out the conditions and needs of his people. Then, lifting the candle high, he said, "Beloved brothers and sisters, thank you for keeping our candle burning brightly."

We were named the "Teaching Group" and it was suggested that we visit the smaller communities around Nairobi, before moving on to other parts of Kenya and Uganda. We were greeted by native Africans with glowing faces, joyful clapping, drum banging, dancing, singing, bodies swaying back and forth in unison—all of which served as a joyful prelude to our program.

We asked what their songs meant. A young man who spoke English reasonably well volunteered a translation: One song spoke of the hardships created by social evils in their homeland, and how the comforting teachings of Christ offered hope and a new way of life; another song spoke of the generosity of virtuous souls who were eager to alleviate the needs of the poor; and other songs were hymns of praise to a God of love and compassion. The lyrics, composed mostly by young people, were sung with enthusiasm and served the purpose of teaching a lesson about God; inspiring everyone to live a godly life. As I listened to the interpreter, I felt admiration for the initiative of the leaders of the youth and the receptivity of their followers.

The populations of Kenya and Uganda experience widespread poverty and deprivation. In each region we visited, I witnessed a lack of food, drinking water, and clothing, and an absence of medical care and medicine. In a remote region of West Kenya, there was a line of women, all carrying infants, followed by two or three additional children, headed in my direction. I was told that they had brought their children to see me, the doctor. I didn't know whether to laugh or cry. These poor people had heard the word *doctor* and came for medical help. With regret, I had to explain that I was not a medical doctor. In America, people who pursue higher education, I said, are given the title of doctor. I watched the crowd retreating, their faces revealing their disappointment that I was not a *real* doctor.

Higher education was nonexistent in that area. Even elementary education was limited; each class containing about eighty students. School conditions were primitive: the buildings were old with tin roofs, large rooms with bare walls, and uncomfortable wooden desks where three or four students sat squeezed together. Yet, each class was peaceful and well-behaved.

In one of the classrooms, our daughter Katina, then eleven years old, remarked, "You guys are very quiet. In America, there are only sixteen kids in my class, and you wouldn't believe how much noise we make." She taught African kids American songs, and she showed them how to blow bubbles with gum that we had brought from the United States. She served as a nurse distributing Band-Aids to the barefoot kids who hurt themselves when working in the fields.

In West Kenya, we visited a school of seven hundred students. All of them were barefoot, although it was winter. When it rained, the classes had to pause due to its deafening noise on the tin roofs. During recess, the students were required to plow the field for half an hour and then come back to class. For lunch they were served a dish of corn boiled in milk and a banana, and after lunch, they would invite Katina to join in their games.

Katina was the main attraction one afternoon when she showed the children how to inflate a balloon. We had brought with us several hundred colorful balloons, and we gave one to each student. I will never forget their excitement. It was the first time they had seen a balloon; they thought it was a fantastic gift.

That particular evening, as the stars studded the dark-blue African sky, four boys arrived at the tent where we were staying, prepared to entertain us. Benjamin, a nine-year-old boy, held a homemade violin with one string attached to a hollow bamboo cane. The bow consisted of a bent stick whose ends were connected by a string. Paradoxically, this instrument made a sweet sound, as the boys sang, "Twinkle, Twinkle, Little Star" in full harmony. The singing continued in the Swahili language while the boys danced for us. It was a blessing to watch and observe their spirit of togetherness and contentment.

We visited several regions where people lived harsh and difficult lives, lacking in the basic needs and comforts that we Americans so easily take for granted. Despite these hardships, there was love and a desire to offer hospitality and share their faith in Christ. Unlike our church participation in the United States, their worship was full of enthusiasm and energy as they sang, shouted joyfully, clapped, and danced, showing spirited participation in the services where God's presence was abundantly clear.

Three hours from Nairobi, in a village named Nyeri, we found a small convent occupied by five nuns; three were from Finland and two from Greece. Their mission was to care for forty young children from the surrounding villages. Leonidas, a priest in his late sixties with a gracious disposition was the spiritual director of this convent. He looked like a prophet with his striking bluish eyes and long white beard. Impressed by his dedicated service to these children, I asked how many years he had been a priest. "One year," he answered joyfully.

"I used to be a judge in Athens, Greece. When I retired, I decided to do something worthwhile with what was left of my life. I studied three years for the ministry and became a priest."

"What brought you to Africa?"

"I wanted to erase some of my sins," he said in a contrite voice. I remained silent, not knowing what to say. He continued, "I was gifted with the ability to manipulate and control others through words. I thought I could influence others to see things my way. I had the power to evaluate, judge, and condemn people. I devoured them with words. Arrogantly, I did many wrong things."

As a man who had held such a prestigious position, a judge in Athens for many years, he had abandoned what was probably a luxurious retirement, to come and help the indigenous of Africa! Sitting with him over a modest meal consisting of boiled greens, a few black olives, and a piece of dry bread was a humbling experience. I believed I was in the presence of a holy man. I felt lighter and content. What this priest had discovered was a life of simplicity, a service to the less fortunate that gave him inner joy.

He said, "I thank God who pointed a new direction for me. Here, I don't have to win friends. Here, I have learned how to love God by caring for the needy. These people genuinely believe that God is the owner and giver of all good things. Free in spirit, they never complain, are content with the little they have, and know that tomorrow is in God's hands. A simple meal a day, and something simple to wear, makes them happy. I have decided to spend the remainder of my life in this place."

Perhaps the former judge, now a priest, had grasped the exuberant spirit of simple caring and sharing. Escaping conformity with the world of affluence, he stood among the indigenous of Africa in all humility and kindness, making himself available as their spiritual father. One morning during breakfast hour, a young couple dressed in black joined us. Father Leonidas introduced them as Mr. Costa and Mrs. Maria, who came from Salonika to serve as missionaries. As they sat for some herbal tea, they both looked very sad. In private, Father Leonidas told us that they had lost their young daughter and had decided to come and be of service to the poor of the poorest in Africa. Here, this grieving couple, he said, finds relief as they process their grief.

In Uganda, we met Theodore Nakiama, an old black bishop and devout spiritual leader of a very large congregation. His hospitality was simple: He welcomed us with genuine gratitude for our presence and told us stories about his work and the needs that he was trying to meet. "Somebody gave us a gift of a thousand dollars," he said and smiled. "I did not know what to do with such an amount. I decided to drill a well. Water is a major issue in this part of the world. Now, many people walk three or four kilometers to the well to fill their containers. They are overjoyed, pumping water into their plastic buckets. We need to have many more wells drilled, and that's a major expense," he added, with an imploring sigh.

When we returned to the United States, Pat and I spoke to several people about the water situation in Kenya and Uganda. A few benevolent souls offered help immediately, and within two years, seven more drinking wells were drilled. One wonders how many hundreds of wells could still be drilled in that vast land that is blessed with fertile soil and natural beauty.

A day before our departure, Father Paul Mavisi approached me and said, Dr. Kalellis, may I speak with you in private?"

"Of course," I replied.

"I need a big favor from you."

"What can I do for you?" I asked, wondering what that big favor could be.

"When you go back to the United States, stretch out your arms," he demonstrated the motion. "Give a huge hug of thanks to our American friends. Tell them how grateful we are for their help. Tell them that we love them and shall pray for their good health and prosperity."

My family and I felt blessed for having had such a rich experience. We went to Africa as teachers, but we came back as students. We learned a great deal from those people. In their simplicity, there was wisdom; in their humility, there was gratitude, and we gained more than we were able to give. If there was material poverty, it was concealed by their wealth of spiritual joy.

67

GRACE IN ACTION

No sooner had we returned from Africa, when I received a phone call from Papagiorge (Father George), a priest from Samos, a Greek island that I had visited three years earlier. Father George had recently read a Greek translation of my book *Five Steps to Spiritual Growth*. With a warm and excited tone, he said, "You have written a great book, much needed in our times. I purchased one hundred copies and distributed them to different members of my congregation. It is my hope that you can visit our island again this year and speak to some of the people who read your book. You could also have fun visiting the beautiful sights of our island."

Pat and I arrived at this picturesque island in the first week of August, 1993. At the airport we were welcomed by Father George, who drove us in his small car to Kalidon, a most wonderful hotel surrounded by olive and pine trees on the top of a hill overlooking the Aegean Sea. During the days that followed, he took us around the island and extended generous hospitality, proudly describing the little villages along the way.

Pat and I were impressed with this priest whose faith and humility accompanied his inspiring personality. By the second week on the island, the seeds of friendship blossomed and, like lifetime friends, we enjoyed each other's presence immensely. One evening sitting by the sea and savoring a glass of the local wine, Pat asked, "Father George, what made you decide to become a priest?"

"Do you really want to know that?" he responded with a smile.

"Yes, of course," Pat and I replied in unison.

He took another sip of wine, cleared his throat and said, "It's a long story, I don't want to tire you."

"No, no....We would like to know, we are friends."

"I was a professional soccer player on one of the prominent teams in Athens," he began looking attentively at us, wishing to see our response to his story. "I was gifted in the art of running fast and in the skill of tricking and tripping my opponents, and then unfailingly, scoring. I was offered a contract and hefty salary by Atromitos (Intrepid), the Athens Football Club," he said with evident pride.

"And you did not accept it?' I asked.

"I could have been a very wealthy man in a short period of time," he said with a twinkle of joy in his eyes. "But I chose to be in the ministry of our Lord."

I was touched that he turned down the contract—leaving behind fame and wealth, the glamor and promises of Athenian life—and returned to his small village on the island of Samos to serve God's people as a priest.

"Any regrets?" I asked. "You could have been rich and famous."

"No regrets. I'm wealthy, working for a loving and generous boss, my Lord Jesus, and serving the needs of his people."

It is Father George's daily priority to serve. Beside Sunday and Holy Days services, he gently enters the lives of his people and helps wherever help is needed: visiting the sick, counseling those who are emotionally troubled, pointing a Christian direction to the young people, and rendering a supportive hand to the poor.

One of his parishioners told me that part of Father George's salary sometimes goes to those who need financial help. While he doesn't publicize his charity work, it sometimes becomes evident when the telephone company turns off his service for not paying the bill. Frequently, the car rental company takes away the car he uses to attend to the needs of his people because he hasn't paid the last two month's rent.

Understandably, with his salary of nearly $1,200 a month, and a wife and four children, he would be behind in his payments. But Father George never complains about not having enough. "God always provides," he says. He has learned to embrace his people with love and kindness. "The supporting power of God's love is present and reverberates in all human activities," he claims. "No, not at first sight, nor at first sound, but in hidden ways this love sings a song in every human heart and plays a role in the history of the world. This love is a driving force that can be confessed in faith and experienced in prayer. Proper prayer brings us closer to God's love."

Sometimes, during serious discussion, he would insert a funny anecdote that can have his audience in stitches. "Humor helps the healing of our suffering souls," he says with conviction, while laughing heartily.

He then told us the following story:

A poor peasant in a small village had a pig. That's all he owned. The pig spent its day in mud, not unusual for a pig. One day, as the pig dug deeper into the mud, it pushed out a big steel box. The peasant curiously picked up this heavy box, brought it indoors, and opened it. He nearly fainted at the sight of what that box contained. It was full of shiny gold coins. Unexpectedly, the peasant became wealthy and instantly began to treat the pig as a person and called her "my lady." He hoped that someday his pig would have piglets that could be a good income for his older years. One day, as he entered the pig's sty, he burst into tears. His lady had died. At once he called the local priest and said, "My blessed lady has died! I would like you to come to my house and offer a prayer for her."

"Of course," the priest said. "I'll be there as soon as I can." When the priest realized that the "blessed lady" was a pig, he felt insulted and upset. "It is a sin to have a prayer service for a pig. Shame! Asking me to pray for your pig. I'll report this to our bishop."

The bishop summoned the peasant to his office and with evident anger he said, "You have asked a priest to perform a funeral service for a pig. It is a major blasphemy. It is a sin against God and his church."

The peasant bowed his head to show respect and said, "Your Holiness, my blessed lady, this extraordinary pig, was a most generous benefactress."

Annoyance mingled with curiosity, the bishop noticed that the peasant was pulling something from under his coat: three small bags.

"Your Holiness, this pig that I call 'my lady' was thoughtful and generous. She left a will. The first small bag filled with gold coins, she left for the orphanage; the second one, she left for the church school, and the third bag, which is a bit heavier than the other two, she left for your Holiness."

With a big smile the bishop said, "How sweet! You mean she even remembered me? May her memory be blessed and eternal! Let's plan to have a special memorial service for her next Sunday."

In one of our conversations, I asked, "Papagiorge, where do you derive your faith and commitment to carry out God's work?"

"Before I answer, let me tell you another story that got me in trouble with my bishop. I risked being suspended for six months, but it did strengthen my faith:

Five years ago, while still a young priest, I was assigned to be a chaplain in a colony of lepers on a Greek island, known as Leros. Being limited in theological dogmas, I felt compensated by a strong faith in God and my commitment to serve the afflicted. The first year as chaplain, during Holy Week, on Good Friday, in my eagerness to explain the Passion story to a large number of lepers, I nailed onto a large cross, a colorful and graphic effigy of the body of Christ afflicted with leprosy. When my bishop heard about this, he called me to his office and, in front of four other priests, he reprimanded me, "How dare you defile the body of our Lord Jesus, making him appear as a leper! That's a major blasphemy."

Hearing his angry voice, I closed my eyes, and at that moment I could see a large number of lepers waiting for their death. I sighed deeply and said, "Your Eminence, how else could I make these lepers understand that God really loves them, except by making Christ one of them?"

The bishop shook his head and pulled himself back on his cushioned chair. The message was clear. God becomes one of us in Jesus Christ, regardless of our emotional and physical condition, to reassure us of his love. Do we want to feel God's presence in our life? If the answer is *yes*, then we have to think about him, studying his teachings, gleaning his wisdom and visualizing him closer to our hearts.

When we leave God out of our daily life or turn to him only in dire need, God does not abandon us. He loves us and wants us to know who he really is in our life. Every hour of each day, he continues to care as a father cares for his children. God loves the just and shows mercy upon the sinners. He wants to be part of our lives, helping us to refine our thoughts, cleansing our minds and delivering us from life's adversities, evil and stressful situations."

"I do admire your faith, Papagiorge," I said, feeling deeply moved by his words.

"For many years," he said, "I've tried to get a glimpse of God by looking carefully at the varieties of human experience: loneliness and love, sorrow and joy, resentment and gratitude, war and peace. I sought to understand the ups and downs of the human soul, to discern their hunger and thirst that only a God whose name is Love can satisfy. I tried to understand the purpose of the present life beyond the eternal, the perfect love of God beyond our paralyzing fears, and the divine compassion beyond the desolation of human anguish and agony."

"Profound thoughts, dear brother in Christ," I said, feeling a tinge of guilt. I looked him straight in his eyes and said, "I was a priest also and initially I had similar thoughts and convictions. Church and priesthood were the best choice that I had made. I had all the means to succeed in my mission. What had happened to my enthusiasm and destination? I'm still wondering about Christ's work that I left behind."

In a spirit of gentleness, Father George reached out, took my hand, held it between his two hands and said, "Peter, you are still a priest in God's eyes. You may think that you have abandoned God and his Church, but that's wrong thinking.

God has never abandoned you. He pointed your life toward a new direction."

Then he said, "Now you are a better priest than me. As a psychotherapist, your priesthood continues to be more focused and serious. You pay attention to each person's specific problem and pave the way for healing."

This priest restored our faith and carved a sharp image of friendship and love in my mind. As our day of departure approached, Pat and I wanted to stay longer, but we had already made other plans. As Father George was taking us to the airport, I said, "When we first met almost three years ago, you shared a dream with me: Someone had given you a piece of land located midway up the mountain. And you told me that you wanted to build a chapel, a simple but sacred place of worship to draw your people away from the city noise and their busy lives, close to nature and closer to God."

"And you still remember my dream?" He said in wonder.

"I do, and I remember how excited you were about the idea."

"I pray to our Lord to help me realize my dream," he said.

"Is this chapel to be named after a saint?" I asked.

"It is to honor St. Fanourios, the miracle worker, revealer of lost items and direction for people's lives. I have strong faith in this saint and feel grateful to him, for he always points the way in my ministry."

We had arrived at the airport. Silently, he looked at me, but I could see in those sparkling eyes the sincerity of this vessel of God and sensed a subtle request. This man wants a chapel, not for self-aggrandizement, but for the spiritual welfare of his people, I thought.

"My wife, Pat, believes in the graces of St. Fanourios," I said. "I know she wants to help in your project. Papagiorge, we'll do our best to help."

Upon our return to the United States, my wife and I discussed this priest's dream. She was not simply impressed with the idea but she responded with enthusiasm, "We must try to help in any possible way," she said.

At that time, I wrote an article about Father George's dream for the *Hellenic Chronicle*, a newspaper that originated in Boston. Then the miracle happened. Many people responded generously to Papagiorge in Samos, and on September 20, 1999, he celebrated the first Divine Liturgy for the continuous health of the donors.

St. Fanourios is one the most loved and honored saints by most Greek Orthodox Christians, yet to many people he is still the unknown saint. For the past five centuries, his memory has been celebrated every year on August 27. This less familiar saint, beyond any doubt, could be characterized as a gift from God, and his presence as a man of God reflects miraculous power. God's grace and miraculous power have come to us through this chosen saint. Small and large chapels and churches are erected in his name. Countless Christians find St. Fanourios an intimate companion during the difficulties of everyday life. He reveals lost items, points to a true direction in our plans, supports our noble efforts, and brings us closer to Christ.

A few years later, my friend, Andy McCabe, and I visited the island of Samos, Greece. I had been there before, but this was Andy's first visit. One of the highlights of our trip was visiting the glorious chapel of St. Fanourios. We both entered this sacred chapel, lighted candles, and sat quietly for a few moments of prayer and meditation. Alone and in silence, we turned and looked at each other, relaxed, smiled, and absorbed the ambiance of this holy place.

I thought of my wife and felt intimately close to her. How I had wished that she were sitting next to me at this moment.

Having now been married for four decades, we still love each other and are grateful to God for our life and the blessings we have cherished together.

Silently, my mind began to reflect on my life: the village boy, the olive picker, the seminarian, the priest, and now the psychotherapist. There were feelings of anxiety, anger, fear, insecurity, guilt, and resentment.

As I reassured myself of God's presence, I found in my back pocket a list of faults that I had written during a recent retreat in Norfolk, Virginia. It was a long list, from the age of five to the present. After a final review of my sins, I held the sheet of paper over a candle and watched as the flame turned it into ashes. No longer carrying that list in my pocket, I felt lighter and more content. This ritual of surrendering my life to God's love and mercy was soothing for my soul.

My candle burned slowly and became shorter, but its glowing flame danced gracefully in the dark, still giving light to its surrounding, and inspiring my soul. The lighted candle became a symbol that represented the light that I could bring to our world—not unlike my ministry of connecting with many people through my writing.

68

THE HOLY MOUNTAIN

During my ministry, I knew many people who had visited Mount Athos, also called the Holy Mountain. It consists of an array of monasteries built on the highest peaks on a peninsula in Northern Greece. In the recent years, two thousand monks, devoted in prayer and the attainment of a spiritual life, occupy the different units. In speaking with some friends who had spent time on Mount Athos, I was impressed and inspired by their experience. Seeing their enthusiasm, I wanted to visit this Holy Mountain someday, possibly with another person who had already been there.

While in church one Sunday, Sharon, a priest's wife, shared with my wife, Pat, that her husband, Father Greg, was going to Mount Athos with Bishop Elias. Pat informed her instantly of my desire to go there someday. Before noon the next day, Father Greg called and told me that Bishop Elias knows me through my writing and was delighted to hear that I wanted to go to Mount Athos. A week later, all three of us arrived at Mount Athos.

Soon after our arrival, we were warmly welcomed by two young monks who gently informed us that Mount Athos is truly a sacred place, not designed for tourists. It is a place of prayer, worship, and meditation. They took us to our cells—

small austere rooms, with small narrow cots where we would be spending the nights. They informed us that dinner will be served at 4:00 p.m. followed by a vesper service. "Our mornings start at 4:00 a.m.," they said. They wished us a pleasant and inspiring stay, and with a bow and a warm handshake they left.

What an amazing view from on the top of the highest mountain. In 1784, with the arrival of Hieromonk Paisios from Kavsokalyvia and his brotherhood, the community's number had increased in its spiritual life. As the number of monks increased, a new wing was built in 1815. The monastery's old *Katholikon* (church) is a monument of the highest artistic importance, but moreover, it is the ultimate liturgical space for divine worship and contemplation.

The life of a monk is ordered by his worship and love of God. His commitment is to be mindful and keep God's holy commandments. He practices an ascetic life, applies the holy virtues by loving his neighbors, his monastic brothers and praying continually for the many guests who visit the monasteries. As a rule, monks support the Orthodox faith through prayer and maintaining the tradition of the Fathers of the early Church.

I was mistakenly under the impression that the monks of the Holy Mountain were mostly older men who were seeking to have a painless, shameless, and peaceful ending to the last years of their life. However, the majority of the two thousand monks residing there were young and highly educated— doctors, lawyers, scholars and teachers, who had sought solitude in a monastic calling.

Following the monastic daily calendar was a challenge. I managed to arrive by 5:00 a.m. to attend morning services that ended at 7:00 a.m. Breakfast consisted of herbal hot tea, a slice of homemade bread and cured olives. (Meat and dairies had never been available and fish was offered only once a week.)

The next and last meal of the day was dinner at 4:00 p.m. to be followed by Vesper services. Snacks were never offered through the day. Following the monastic diet, I lost five pounds over the six days I was there, yet I never felt hungry. No wonder the monks looked rather slim, yet they were healthy and always interacted with us in the spirit of gentleness.

The ministry of the monks is characterized by their spirit and obedience. For example, the ecclesiarch, the guest master, the gardener and orchard keeper, the cook and keeper of the refectory, the baker, and the physician, as well as many others, worship God with dedicated service and by caring for the life of their brotherhood. The ascetic spirit of Mount Athos is truly motivated by the Holy Spirit, which conveys the grace of God beyond the boundaries of the monasteries to the world, becoming a lighthouse on our path to God.

69

THE HOLY LAND

Pat and I had hoped that someday we would have the opportunity to visit the Holy Land, the place where Jesus Christ walked. Reading the gospel stories of his life, death, resurrection, and ascension to heaven, only increased my desire and enthusiasm for such a personal spiritual encounter. So, when I heard that a local church group was preparing their annual visit to Jerusalem, I called the person in charge of the group and asked if my wife and I could join them. Fortunately, they still had two seats available for our trip, so we needed to move quickly and get our passports ready.

We arrived in the Holy Land in the early hours of the morning. Our guide greeted us at the airport and took us to our hotel where we left our carry-on luggage. An hour later we began our tour. Although we had had little sleep on the flight, we were motivated and keen to start our tour of where Jesus had walked, preached, performed miracles, forgave sinners, healed the sick, and brought people back to life. It didn't take us long to visualize Jesus as the good shepherd, stretching his arms, embracing his people, and with unconditional love, inviting everyone to follow him and his example. As we passed through the narrow streets of old Jerusalem, we envisioned him being surrounded by crowds, comforting the afflicted, breaking bread, and eating with the poor and the rich alike. He emphasized that people should not live by bread alone, but should be nourished with spiritual food, the words of God. In his three years of ministry, Jesus showed us, through his example and teaching, how to live and to love.

Pat and I experienced an additional blessing when we visited the actual place where our Lord had been crucified. Simultaneously, we fell on our knees as tears of gratitude filled our eyes. The Lord's crucifixion—his sacrifice—tells us that God loves the world, loves each one of us, and accepts us unconditionally. Jesus demonstrated God's love through his compassion and mercy, and by calling all to salvation through the promise of blessings to come. Inspired and moved deeply by the sacredness of the area, Pat and I sat silently to pray and meditate.

I visualized myself being present and witnessing the cruelty to and mockery of Jesus. My body shivered and shook as I thought of Christ's tragic death. Seeing his agonizing face, I imagined his voice uttering those seven short sentences and recalled our priest, Papavasile, reading on Good Friday in Moria those same last words of Jesus:

> "Father, forgive them (*afes aftis*) for they know not
> what they are doing."
> To the penitent thief, "Today you shall be with me
> in Paradise."
> Then, looking down at the terrified, grief-stricken
> young man—John, the beloved Apostle—he
> said, "Behold your mother." Then turning his
> head and looking at Mary, his mother, he said,
> "Woman behold your son."
> I could hear his painful cry, "My God, my God, why
> have you forsaken me?"
> Markedly dehydrated, Jesus gasped another cry, "I
> thirst."

The Holy Land

A sponge soaked in vinegar, mixed with bile was
lifted to his lips. Apparently he didn't take it.
In little more than a tortured whisper he said,
"It is finished." His mission of redeeming the
world from its sins and corruption had been
completed.

Before he allowed his body to die, he uttered his
last cry, "Father! Into your hands I commit my
spirit."

Pat and I left the place of crucifixion and walked silently through the narrow streets of Jerusalem.

Later that same day, we found ourselves in front of a large church where the actual tomb of our Lord has been preserved. Inside were numerous candles burning, lit by people of faith reassuring themselves that they will continue to carry the light that Christ has brought into their life. I saw a glow in Pat's face as she lit her candle. "Take heart," I whispered. "Christ did not remain in the tomb. He showed that he had power over death by rising on the third day after he was buried."

As Christians, we are grateful that we have the great sequel in the infinite mercy of God—Jesus arose from the dead and the miracle of his resurrection was witnessed by his followers. The suffering of Jesus offers us a lasting lesson: God is not apart from the trials of humanity. God is not aloof. God is not a mere spectator. God is participating in our lives. God is not merely tolerating human suffering or healing suffering. God is participating with us *in it.* That is what gives us meaning, purpose, and hope.

On that same day, as noon was approaching, we met a group of four men and heard them speaking in Greek. They were from Salonika, Greece. When we introduced ourselves, the leader of that group, Makarios, who was a monk, told us that they were on their way to Gethsemane. With interest, I asked if Pat and I could join them. All four answered in unison,

"Of course." It was another of the holy places that we wanted to go.

It was a hot day, but when we arrived at the Garden of Gethsemane, we found a place of shade and sat on a marble bench to rest. Pat had brought two sandwiches for our lunch. It seemed strange for only us to be eating, while Makarios and the three other men, who were seated across from us, were not. Hesitantly, Pat offered one sandwich to Makarios, who took it gratefully and began to cut it into four pieces. The sandwich seemed to expand as he cut it. In silence and disbelief, Pat and I looked at each other. We were positive the sandwich she gave to the monk had grown to feed the four men.

After visiting the shrines in Gethsemane, it was time to return to our hotel. In wishing us well and a safe return to the United States, Makarios shook our hands firmly and said, "It is my hope and prayer that someday we will meet again in this Holy Place. If not here, we will definitely meet in the upper Jerusalem, heaven." Pat and I thanked him and his three followers and wished them a safe journey back to their home in Greece.

Two weeks later, we received a note reminiscing about our wonderful time together. Makarios included photos of our small group sitting on the marble bench. On the back of one photo, he wrote, "We all ate and were satisfied by the grace of Mrs. Pat Kalellis." He had seen it too. We all knew we were fed by the grace of the Holy Spirit.

Infused by joy and grace, we climbed to the top of the hill where Jesus delivered the Sermon on the Mount, the Beatitudes, a summary of Christian discipleship. Each of the beatitudes represents an *attitude* for living and begins with the Greek word, *makarios* which means "a person who has found absolute happiness and serenity within." Our understanding of the word *blessed*, *makarioi* in plural form, denotes a state of contentment, inner and lasting joy, exuberance, which a person experiences living a godly life. This was especially meaningful to me for I had recently devoted much thought to these "attitudes" in writing my book *God's Power within You*. Momentarily, I could visualize Jesus sitting on the peak of the hill, nature's amphitheater, surrounded by hundreds of people listening to his words:

> Blessed are the poor in spirit, for theirs is the kingdom of heaven.
>
> Blessed are those who mourn for they will be comforted.
>
> Blessed are the meek, for they will inherit the earth.
>
> Blessed are those who hunger and thirst for righteousness, for they will be filled.
>
> Blessed are the merciful, for they will receive mercy.
>
> Blessed are the pure in heart, for they will see God.
>
> Blessed are the peacemakers, for they will be called children of God.
>
> Blessed are those who are persecuted for righteousness's sake, for theirs is the kingdom of heaven.
>
> Blessed are you when people revile you and persecute you and utter all kinds of evil against you falsely.
>
> Rejoice and be glad, for your reward is great in heaven.

With faith in Jesus as our life's companion, I have discovered meaning and purpose in my life. Personally, this faith instilled motivation and strength in my work and in my life with my family. Far from being perfect or better Christians than anyone else, Pat and I share our faith and feel empowered to move forward to do God's will as best as we can.

Despite life's adversities, every human heart seeks inner joy. In my younger years, I often searched for joy in the wrong places—celebrations, dances, theaters, travels—mainly in what the world was offering, but the following words of St. Paul helped me to become more grounded in where to find my joy:

> Rejoice in the Lord always; again I will say, Rejoice. Let your gentleness be known to everyone. The Lord is near. Do not worry about anything, but in everything by prayer and supplication with thanksgiving let your requests be made known to God. And the peace of God, which surpasses all understanding, will guard your hearts and your minds in Christ Jesus. (Phil 4:4–7)

As our plane took off on our return flight to the United States, I made the sign of the cross and in gratitude for the experience of visiting the Holy Land, I penned the following prayer:

> *Lord Jesus Christ, each time my heart and lips offer a prayer and my hand moves spontaneously to make the sign of the cross, I realize the intimacy of the cross in my life.*
>
> *It was with the sign of the cross that my Church received me on the fortieth day of my life. It was the sign of the cross that blessed the water in which I was baptized and became a Christian. And it is the cross that will seal my grave when I die. When the triumph of the resurrection of the dead takes place, it will be*

your cross that proclaims the message of joy among the silent graves.

Lord Jesus Christ, the miracle began when the cross, the tool of death and dishonor, a symbol of our salvation, revealed the ultimate expression of divine love. The tree of death was transformed to a tree of life because it was quenched and sanctified by your precious blood. When you carried your cross to Golgotha, you, the sinless God in human form carried the sins of the world. Your crucifiers witnessed the death of the God-man, who came back to life as God.

Your cross represents grace and blessing. Your crucifixion and resurrection demonstrates divine power and support. It confirms your gift of joy, illustrating the divine plan of your heavenly Father, to bring salvation into the world.

Regardless of our adversities, we sense your agony as we hear your reassuring message of love, and that we cannot love only those who love us but should strive to love also those who do not love us, exactly as you loved and let go of your crucifiers.

Lord Jesus, you have shown us the value of patience in that we can endure the difficulties, trials, and tribulations in life, just as you endured the pain of the cross. You have shown us the value of repentance in that, as we repent for our sins, we are forgiven, just as you welcomed the crucified thief into Paradise the moment he repented for his crimes.

Lord Jesus, as we face daily problems, trials, and opposing forces, strengthen our faith that we may come closer to your loving presence and be part of your eternal kingdom. Amen.

Part IV
THANKSGIVING

70

GRATITUDE

If you have followed this personal journey and seek joy, you will know that it is essential to be grateful especially for the small things that we often take for granted. In fact, I have found that a good way to begin each day is to say, "Thank you, God, for another day." Not only does this bring me joy, but it also starts my day with a positive attitude.

Realizing what is important in our life—our priorities—is closely linked with gratitude. We always have a conscious choice to choose certain things in our life, including better health, our friends, and even our personal pursuits that bring us happiness. They are blessings.

Today, bars and taverns often advertise that they have a "Happy Hour." It is a period of the day when drinks are sold at reduced prices in a bar or restaurant. Anyone of age is invited. In recent years, I came to know a small group of friends who, in their search for happiness, resorted to a tavern every single day. So my friend, Paul, who knew them, related the following story:

In a basement tavern amid smoke and swearing a group of four men, huddled together, were drinking last night, like any other night, to wash down the poisons of life. As they placed their arms upon each other's shoulder, the middle-aged man named Steve spat on the floor and cursed, "Oh what a great torment this terrible life has been! No matter how hard my mind has tried, it cannot recall a bright day!" For ten years, Steve's father was bedridden, paralytic, a specter-like; Wally's wife was slowly dying from cancer, she had wasted away to a scary skeleton. Mike's son was unjustly rotting for years in a prison for a crime that one of his friends had committed, and John's daughter had become a prostitute.

As they were moaning and groaning, they kept asking, "Who can we blame for our blundering fate. Can we blame God who probably hates us or can we blame our deranged minds? Maybe we should blame the wine that we have been drinking every night. But still we don't know who to blame. So here we are cringing in this dingy tavern where we always drink, allowing others to step on us as if we were worms. Like cowards, doomed and undecided, maybe we are waiting for a miracle that never comes."

Obviously these four characters did not want to make different and new choices to pursue healthier changes in their life. Self-pity and lack of motivation shucked their energy, leaving them in despair. They were tormented by their condition when their lives were too small for them, and they lived in such a way that they were waiting, waiting for something or somebody to come along and change things so that their real lives, as they imagined them, might begin. What each of them needed was some gratitude for what they already had in their life—eyes to see, feet to walk, hands to work, and above all, the freedom to make a better choice.

Before calling for a national day of fasting, President Abraham Lincoln stated, "We have been the recipients of the choicest blessings of heaven. We have been preserved, these many years, in peace and prosperity. We have grown in numbers, wealth and power as no other nation ever has grown; but we have forgotten God! We have forgotten the gracious Hand which preserved us in peace, and multiplied and enriched and strengthened us; and we have vainly imagined, in the deceitfulness of our hearts, that all these blessings were produced by some superior wisdom and virtue of our own."

This is a tremendously powerful statement! Since the time President Lincoln gave this speech, the wealth, prosperity and peace experienced by the United States is far greater— along with the attitude of pride, selfishness, and ingratitude.

Recently, a client came to me for therapy. His main issues were depression and unhappiness. In his early thirties, he had a good job, was married to a caring and successful woman; he loved his wife and they owned a beautiful home. He began,

"Doc, I have everything I need in my life, but I'm not happy."

"What is missing?" I asked.

"I don't know," he said.

"In my work as a therapist, 'I don't know' usually means that you do know."

"No, I don't," he said.

"Ted, you may lack gratitude," I suggested.

"Gratitude for what?" he asked rather annoyed. "I have worked very hard to attain what I have; nobody has given me anything."

"What about the things that you take for granted?" I asked.

He paused, and after a brief silence he asked, "What things?"

"Ted, in today's fast-paced world, many people do not seem to have time to say even a mere 'thank you' to God. Work, traffic, family, soccer practice for their kids, medical appointments, social events, and countless other things are their main priorities. One wonders why we have so many unhappy people in a country that enjoys plentiful food, shelter, electricity, running water, wealth, air conditioning, heating systems, transportation, sanitation, and many other blessings." I looked at him directly, and with a semi-smile, said, "Ted, you have eyes that can see, ears that can hear, a brain that can think, hands that can work, feet that can walk. You are alive and healthy. Aren't these givens worthy of some gratitude?"

"But everybody has these," he said, lifting his shoulder to let me know that he was not impressed with my response.

It seemed that I could not do much or say anything to bring this client into another reality of his life, to help him see who he really is, as well as his expectations of others and of himself. So I shook his hand and said, "Well, if you want to be happy, start your day by being grateful for the things that you take for granted."

Ted called a week later and cancelled his next appointment. Perhaps, he was not ready to see and experience the reality of living with an attitude of gratitude that makes most people happy.

71

THE MIRACLE

There is no joy or happiness or any celebration of life that is not somehow interrupted with a tinge of sadness or an obstacle to bring clouds of disruption to our daily life. A crisis can drain our energy and delay some motivation for some important work, especially when we feel uncertain how to confront it. Yet, deep down, we know that our belief in a caring and loving God can sustain us through the storm and bring some relief.

In 2012, my loving wife, Pat, was diagnosed with a non-Hodgkin's lymphoma that was rare, aggressive, and already in stage four. Tumors in her bone marrow prevented the production of healthy marrow to be created and therefore caused tremendous havoc to her immune system, as well as extraordinary fatigue. She was treated effectively with chemotherapy over six months, and in the Spring of 2013, her oncologist happily informed us that the cancer was gone. Pat and I were elated. Joyfully, we celebrated her recovery, which coincided with our birthdays and our thirty-sixth wedding anniversary.

By the following summer, Pat's blood counts started to decrease and fatigue set back in. A biopsy indicated that the cancer had returned. *Cancer* is a word that nobody likes to hear. From a technical standpoint, cancer is a change in the normal growth of cells, causing them to spread and destroy healthy tissues and organs. From an emotional perspective, cancer is one of the most devastating experiences a person and his or her family may have to endure. While it is not exactly a death sentence, "death" is often the fear that first comes to mind when someone receives such a diagnosis.

Thanks to advances in research and development, many types of cancer that were virtually incurable not too long ago are now treatable. While there is always reason for hope, cancer can be devastating to the individual and the family. If you or a member of your family or a close friend has suffered from cancer, you will understand the emotional and physical impact of this illness.

When we were told that the lymphoma had returned, the recommendation was to treat Pat with a more aggressive form of chemo and for her to undergo an allogenetic stem cell transplant.

We thank God for sending us a twenty-nine-year-old man, who was identified as a perfect match for Pat, and who was willing and able to be her donor. It was a tremendous sacrifice on his part, and we continue to be very grateful to him.

Pat's treatment, accompanied by the fervent prayers of many people who cared for her, brought promising results. Pat and I have both felt God's presence throughout her illness, as several of our dear friends gracefully volunteered to help. Our daughter, Katina, and her husband, Peter, were amazing in their consistent support and in their swift availability to assist with any possible emergency.

Pat's situation emotionally affected our family, and we continue to be grateful to many people for their prayers, as she continues to rebuild and strengthen her immune system. Believing that God is in charge, we derive great comfort as we pray and read verses from the Bible. Faith in God's love and mercy helps us to rise above any potential crisis.

Although on the surface we have tried to appear brave, we have both had to confront the fear of the dreaded disease and of our mortality. Over the years, we have watched several members in our community, some relatives and other close friends, battle cancer. We have found hope in St. Paul's words: "So we do not lose heart. Even though our outer nature is wasting away, our inner nature is being renewed day by day. For this slight momentary affliction is preparing us for an eternal weight of glory beyond all measure" (2 Cor 4:16–17).

Toward the end of 2014 Pat started experiencing complications from the transplant and after months of trying to manage care from home, the doctors at Memorial Sloan Kettering Cancer Center decided that Pat needed to be hospitalized for stronger treatment.

During this stay she got noticeably weaker while the complications became greater. On her third month in the hospital, things started to take a turn for the worse. The doctors discovered a perforation in Pat's intestine and said emphatically that if they did not operate immediately, she would die. There was no time for a second opinion and we had no idea if she was strong enough to survive this operation.

Under the careful guidance of her surgeon, Dr. Garrett Nash, the two-hour operation in the middle of the night was successful. He was able remove the damage and reconnect her intestines and there was no need for a colostomy bag. It took two days for Pat to recover from the post-surgical medications and communicate with us. She told us that she was "done," and we didn't blame her.

We pushed for a meeting with her medical team to assess her condition. We were told there were very few options to consider; we could start hospice or go the experimental route with a treatment which only had a success rate of 30 percent. While the doctors pushed to begin hospice and eventually to make arrangements for my wife to be in the comfort of her home, my daughter and I agreed that stopping treatment would need to be Pat's choice.

Despite all this devastating news, we were grateful she survived the surgery and on a positive note we found out the virus that was leading this life-threatening complication had decreased in levels, following the surgery. My daughter was adamant that if Dr. Nash had removed two feet of virus infiltrated intestine, there was less virus for her to fight. The doctors did not agree and suggested we consider starting hospice.

Returning home in utter despair that evening, I could hear the word *hospice* as an option. When I opened the door to our house I momentarily considered a world where my Pat would no longer be present. I went into our bedroom where we have our home sanctuary and fell on my knees before the icon of Christ and began to cry, saying, "Lord Jesus, let me die and let my Pat live. I'm approaching my ninetieth birthday, I have lived long enough and I'm grateful for all your blessings over the years. Please, take me away, and let my wife live. She's younger by twenty-three years, give her a longer life and let her enjoy our three grandchildren."

Twice a week, during the several months that Pat was hospitalized, I used to take a taxi from Penn Station to visit her at the hospital. On one particular Thursday in July, all the taxis were occupied and quickly passed by. Finally, one taxi driver from the right lane made a quick left turn and stopped to give me a ride.

"Where do you want to go?" he asked gently.

"To Memorial Sloan Kettering Cancer Center at 1275 York Avenue," I said.

"Why are you going there?" he asked.

"For my wife."

"How is she doing?" he asked again with a softer voice, giving me the impression that he cared to know my wife's condition.

"She's been struggling to fight a life-threatening virus for the last few months, and still we have no results," I said. "But I pray to God for a miracle."

The Miracle

"God will make your wife well," he said; and pointing his finger to me, he added, accentuating every word, "and-you-do-not-worry!"

Sitting in the back seat in deep thought and concern: *Will my wife be able to survive her condition?* Several times before we arrived at the hospital, the taxi driver repeated in a stronger tone, "God will make your wife well...and you do not worry."

"Thank you for your good thoughts," I said, and gradually, as we approached Memorial Sloan Kettering Cancer Center, he made a sharp, risky turn in his effort to put me right in front of the main door.

I took out my wallet to pay him. He let go of his wheel and, from his driving position, reached out to the back seat, grabbed my hand, squeezed it firmly and said, "No, no, money; I do not want you to pay me."

"No! No!" I said. "It's not right, I would not feel good if I don't pay you." I saw the number on the meter, $22.00, and added $3.00 more to give him a tip. Still firmly holding on to my hand and shaking it, he said, "You don't have to pay me. Your wife will get well, and *you*, try not to worry."

With tears in my eyes and a smile, I said, "Thank you. But I would like to have your name and your address."

"No name and no address just go and see your wife and do not worry."

I wanted to send him a thank you note, but he prepared to leave; and while his gentle voice still echoed in my ears, I thought, "Was this man a taxi driver or an angel?" *Clearly, God uses certain good people to do his work!*

Not long after meeting the taxi driver, Pat's situation took a miraculous turn. As she continued to tread water, I tried to keep my head well above water. Fervently, I prayed and asked our Lord to guide Pat's doctors to make the right decisions so that she would make a full recovery. I kept asking God to strengthen all the members of our family that we may endure whatever came our way.

By the second week of August we were working toward the idea of rehab, not hospice. Pat started to eat and was working with her physical therapist daily, starting with little things, like standing up and washing her face. Eventually, she was standing up and walking around the hospital floor with a walker and assistance from the nurses. Eventually she was eligible for the clinical trial.

Within eighteen months of her experimental T-cell therapy, her body had almost totally accepted the donor's cells and rebuilt her immune system. Pat had been brave through this journey. She had a positive attitude toward life. Her oncologist called her recovery a *miracle.*

Regardless of the outcome, each of our family members and many friends showed us a glimpse of God's presence. Through the ordeal, God has confirmed for us with these words:

> I love you. You are precious in your fragility and in your current critical condition. Your life is my gift to you and I keep you close in my presence as something most precious. Be at Peace!

By the fall, Pat left the rehabilitation center and was able to come home to rehabilitate. Throughout that time, she was concerned about how I was managing. She wanted me to eat well, rest, and keep a balanced routine. She wanted me to continue my counseling practice and creative writing. I continue to be grateful for Pat, my ever-loving wife, and for all my friends, who read my published books and continue to inspire me.

72

INTO YOUR HANDS

Very truly, I tell you, when you were younger, you used to fasten your own belt and to go wherever you wished. But when you grow old, you will stretch out your hands, and someone else will fasten a belt around you and take you where you do not wish to go.

—John 21:18

This text has become a major theme for me in recent years as I gain the courage to relinquish my control on life and allow others close to me to lead my life into the future.

Throughout my life there have been seven times when, without my consent and against my will, I have been led to other pastures. At the age of three, I was taken from my birthplace in Philadelphia, Pennsylvania, to Lesvos, the Greek island of my father's origins. When I was twenty years old, I was taken back to the United States, "the promised land." The following year, the pastor of my church suggested that I should become a priest and apply to the Greek Orthodox seminary in Brookline, Massachusetts. Three years later, I returned to

Philadelphia for graduate studies and attended the Philadelphia Divinity School.

I enjoyed my studies and life at the Philadelphia Divinity School. It felt familiar and comfortable, and was also fun. With that being said, I was ready to move somewhere new and to challenge myself to create a new home for myself that wasn't already mapped out for me. Three year later, as an ordained twenty-six-year-old priest, I was assigned to a parish in Jersey City, New Jersey. After two years, I was asked to serve the Saint Sophia Cathedral in Los Angeles, California. Then, after ten years, Archbishop Iakovos assigned me to a new community in Westfield, New Jersey.

In 1972, when I was already in training to become a psychotherapist, I recall one of our professors, Dr. Dick Johnson, spoke to the graduates about the major stressors in life. He outlined certain events that cause stress, but two of these stressors, *divorce* and *relocation*, resonated with me, as each one had a serious impact on my life.

Now in my nineties, and after more than fifty-four years of creative life in New Jersey, I'm experiencing depression and stress, as I try to embrace the thought of leaving the familiar and moving to an unfamiliar environment. Part of me resists moving. In fact, most people feel the stress from the moment the decision is made and often the move becomes a terrible experience for everyone involved, including the people assisting in the move. The thought of moving necessarily brings with it an expectation of relinquishing control of my life and my future plans, but it is also an opportunity to surrender to my love for my family that knows no limits.

Of course, my initial reaction to all these moves was resentment; I had no control of my life. Moving beyond resentment required being more positive and not drawing negative hypothetical conclusions. I recalled those words that Jesus spoke to Peter that appear at the opening of this chapter.

While the world suggests that we are dependent on others in our youth and that, as older adults we can go our own way and become independent, the Lord suggests a *new* way, in fact, the opposite of this approach: when we grow older and more spiritually mature, we must allow those around us, our loved ones who truly care for us, to gird us and lead us where we would rather not go!

And so, being interdependent and obedient to the voice of unconditional love, I decided, along with my loving wife, Pat, to let go of our familiar life in New Jersey and embrace the challenge of making a *new* life in Virginia Beach, Virginia. Here, we join our daughter, Katina, and her husband, Peter, and their three children, our grandchildren, Stacy, Peter, and Victoria.

Feelings of guilt that I might depend largely on my daughter for help causes me overwhelming sadness. This is something that I may have to struggle with for whatever years of life I have ahead. However, Pat and I are grateful for this opportunity of building an intimate solidarity with our family and making new friends.

Stella and Jack, two good and generous friends over the years, have extended exceptional hospitality, in helping both Pat and me to adjust in our new environment. As their kindness continues, we are grateful to them, for they continue to be available to us whenever there is a need.

I feel unsurpassed enjoyment when attending St. Nicholas Greek Orthodox Church with the family where I can once again experience the melodic chant of the Divine Liturgy and a peaceful and spiritual environment for prayer. I admit this is one of few times that I've felt the spirit of Jesus Christ present among hundreds of worshiping believers. Seeing Pat and I for the first time and realizing that we were new participants at the Sunday Liturgy, Father John approached us, shook our hands, and extended a heartfelt welcome.

At this point in my life, I'm grateful to spend time with my family and friends, who are humble, content with their lives, and face their struggles with courage, and yet they are also willing to help others—a blessing worthy of great thanksgiving!

Be Thankful

Be thankful that you don't already have everything
    you desire,
  If you did, what would there be to look
    forward to?
Be thankful when you don't know something,
  for it gives you the opportunity to learn.
Be thankful for the difficult times.
  During those times you grow.
Be thankful for your limitations,
  because they give you opportunities for
    improvement.
Be thankful for each new challenge,
  because it will build your strength and character.
Be thankful for your mistakes.
  They will teach you valuable lessons.
Be thankful when you're tired and weary,
  because it means you've made a difference.
It's easy to be thankful for the good things.
  A life of rich fulfillment comes to those who
  are also thankful for the setbacks.
Gratitude can turn a negative into a positive.
  Find a way to be thankful for your troubles,
  and they can become your blessings. (*author
    unknown*)

Epilogue

Seeing no end to my journey, but another beginning ahead.

As I evaluate my journey, I often wonder what effect my presence, interaction, and behavior has had on others—my loving wife, four children, five grandchildren, two great-grandchildren, and friends. Have I been accepted and understood without being judged? Are they aware of how much I love them and care for their wellness? Their love creates a nurturing environment, which has allowed me to mature, reflect, respond, and make life's transitions responsibly.

My own personal therapy and practicing psychotherapy professionally has been fulfilling. Certainly, I have become a better person—more able to accept, to forgive, to understand, and to love myself and others.

A variety of themes emerge throughout this journey. The overall theme has been the cycle of growth that I learned in my early years as an olive picker and relates to the stages which form the main parts of this book: planting, growing, harvesting, and thanksgiving.

The first stage of life—*planting*—is often spent struggling with problems of identity and survival—becoming educated, earning a living, and relating to others to enhance our survival. At times, we may become preoccupied with these goals that sap all our energy, and view life as nothing more than coping, scratching for a living, struggling to make ends meet, and yearning for a secure job and lifestyle. This outlook presents life as one great problem that needs solving. Certainly, life presents many problems, but I prefer to see life as *an exciting journey*. With this different perspective, I realized that adversities, conflicts, and suffering do not disappear without a change in who I am and how I live, think, feel, and respond.

Furthermore, with this new outlook, we enter our second stage—*growing*—where we mature by realizing that, if we want to change "*who I am*," we must be aware of "*what I do*." For many, this reality can be a huge challenge. It requires genuine awareness of our circumstances, a willingness to take risks, and *a leap of faith.*

As a therapist, I have seen derelicts, neurotics, substance abusers, addicts, and depressed clients making extraordinary adjustments in life because of their decision to seek a healthier direction and lifestyle.

For myself, in addition to my successes, I have also faced obstacles and difficulties, through which I discovered the most lasting lessons: patience, persistence, and a strong and consistent relationship with God through prayer. When things looked impossible, the support and comfort of friends also helped me to regain the necessary perspective and courage to pursue my goals.

In recognizing the lessons of our past, we begin to reap the rewards or fruits of our life—*harvesting*. If you have read this far, then you can probably agree with Father George, who once told me, "You are still a priest in God's eyes." In fact, it is from this foundation that my desire to be a therapist surfaced and enabled my ministry to become more practical. My studies and the experiences of people who sought my services, interwoven with personal events and experiences, have taught me many lessons. In sharing these with you, I hope they will benefit your own personal journey.

Epilogue

As with all my writing, my intention is to offer readers hope and self-confidence to face the future with courage, optimism, positivity, persistence, and excitement, knowing that we can take charge of our own lives. Through our struggle to maintain a peaceful existence and foster integrity, we rediscover our potential to accomplish the goals that bring us inner joy.

In North America, we celebrate the wonderful tradition of *Thanksgiving* that comes after the harvest—our fourth and final stage. In this book, I have recounted the many struggles through the different stages of my life that have taught me that good things are only accomplished through hard work, prayer, patience, perseverance and persistence. Even small, seemingly insignificant episodes can shape our character. Despite the obstacles, embrace life without fear or expectations but with *gratitude*.

Most of us are the architects of our own lives. Consequently, we can have a say in the plans, otherwise, our life will be planned by others. This is especially true, of course, when we become confused and life seems dark and chaotic—with no direction, no purpose, and no goal. This emotional condition can cause fatigue and passivity, resulting in frustration and even anger at ourselves and the world. We cannot change the world, but we can make the necessary changes to live creatively and rewardingly. As a result, we make our world a better place to live.

It is my hope that the voice that came to me from within and helped me through the difficult times in my life, may also come to you. Above all, remember that you are surrounded by the presence of a loving God who communicates with you through each breath that you take and with every pulse of your heart. Regardless of your age or status, when you come to know who you really are—in all your strange complexity—the unexpected miracle will appear in your life. Give thanks for this miracle and embrace it. *You are that miracle!*